SECRET
ROME

Ginevra Lovatelli, Adriano Morabito and Marco Gradozzi

JONGLEZ PUBLISHING

travel guides

Ginevra Lovatelli is the author of the first version of this guide. She organises original private tours to discover Rome.
Website: www.secretrome.com

Adriano Morabito, a Rome native who is still passionate about his city and its less well-known sites, began focusing his attention on urban speleology in 1999. He is one of the founders of "Roma Sotterranea", an association active in the exploration and study of underground tombs of historical and archaeological interest: www.romasotterranea.it

Marco Gradozzi
A Rome native who still lives in the Campo Marzio district, Marco Gradozzi has a passion for archaeology, photography, music and folk traditions. He has been an active participant in the "Roma Sotterranea" association since 2005.
Website: www.romasurvey.it

Other contributors: **Jacopo Barbarigo**, **Marylène Malbert**, **Hélène Vuillermet**, **Ariane Varela Braga** and **Viviana Cortes**.

We have taken great pleasure in drawing up
Secret Rome and hope that through its guidance
you will, like us, continue to discover unusual,
hidden or little-known aspects of the city.
Descriptions of certain places are accompanied
by thematic sections highlighting historical details
or anecdotes as an aid to understanding the city in
all its complexity.
Secret Rome also draws attention to the multitude
of details found in places that we may pass every
day without noticing. These are an invitation to
look more closely at the urban landscape and,
more generally, a means of seeing our own city
with the curiosity and attention that we often
display while travelling elsewhere …

Comments on this guidebook and its contents,
as well as information on places we may not have
mentioned, are more than welcome and will enrich
future editions.
Don't hesitate to contact us:
• Jonglez Publishing, 25 rue du Maréchal Foch,
78000 Versailles, France
• E-mail: info@jonglezpublishing.com

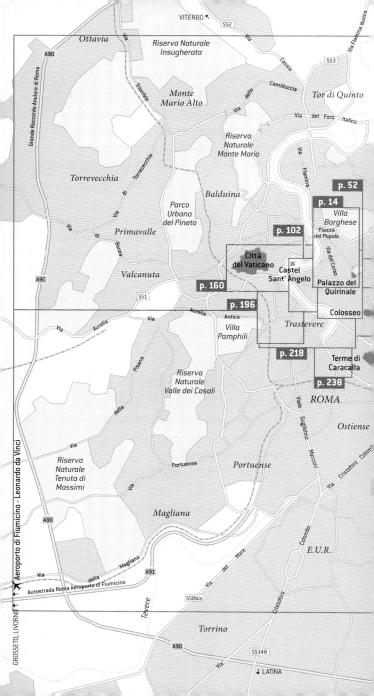

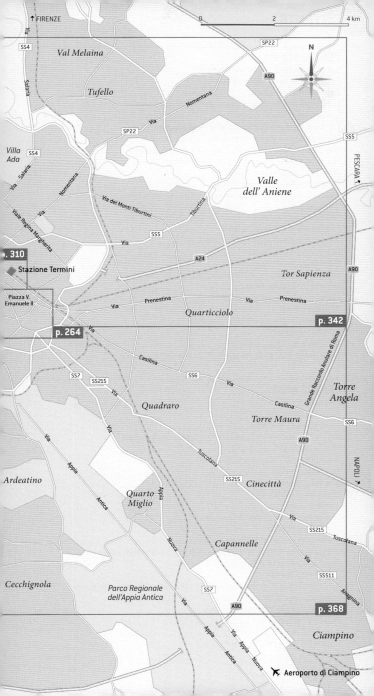

CONTENTS

CENTRE SOUTH

CONTENTS

CONTENTS

OUTSIDE THE CENTRE

INDEX

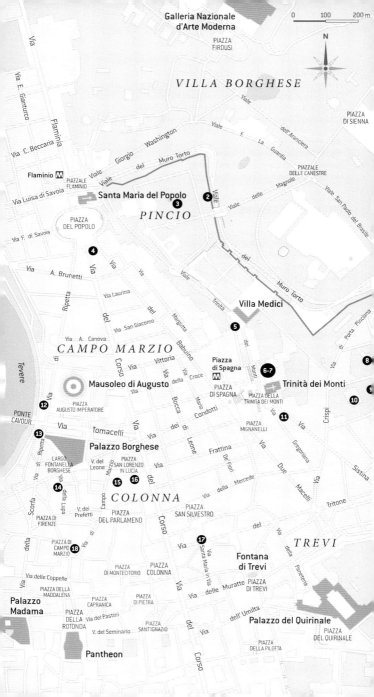

CENTRE NORTH

HENDRIK CHRISTIAN ANDERSEN MUSEUM

Villa Helene, 20 Via Pasquale Stanislao Mancini
• Tel: 06 3219089, 06 3234000, 06 3241000
• Fax: 06 3221579
• Open Tuesday to Sunday, 9am-8pm
• Opening times for the museum's cafe on the first floor: 10:30am-6pm
• Admission: Free
• Tram: 2, 19 • Metro: A – Flaminio

> **The artist's residence as a museum**

V illa Helene is an elegant building just a stone's throw from the Tiber. It was built in 1922 by the Norwegian sculptor and painter Hendrik Christian Andersen, who moved to Rome in 1897. The villa is an extremely interesting example of a studio-residence transformed into a museum, and it was reopened to the public after restoration work in 1999. The ground floor is composed of the studio, where Andersen planned and created his works, which he then exhibited to the public in the other room, the gallery. There are about forty large plaster and bronze sculptures exhibited in both areas. The first floor, once the artist's residence, has drawings, paintings and smaller sculptures.

Over two hundred sculptures, as many paintings and about three hundred pieces of graphic art including drawings and plans make up a collection that is not only surprising in terms of its size, but also and especially because everything, except the paintings, is dedicated to the artist's sole great plan, the creation of a "world city". To disseminate his idea of a utopian modern city that would be an experimental centre of new ideas for art, philosophy, religion and science, Andersen and the architect Ernest Hebrard published an illustrated book in 1913 entitled *Creation of a World Center of Communication*.

A visit in spring is particularly pleasant as you can sit and have something to drink in the Caffè del Museo and take a break in the sun on the lovely first-floor terrace.

PERIOD ELEVATOR ON THE PINCIO ❷

Viale dell'Orologio
• Metro: A – Flaminio or Spagna

Rome's first public elevator

Along the north side of the Pincio gardens, the Aurelian Wall overlooks Viale del Muro Torto. Opposite the water clock (see opposite), a small building in 16th-century Tuscan style rises above the wall. A still-legible inscription behind a grille dispels any doubt: ATAC – ASCENSORI.

This inscription refers to a device installed in 1926 by the former tram company of the Government of Rome, ATG (Azienda Tramviaria del Governatorato di Roma), as it was having a tramline laid in the street below. Here there was a stop for lines 45 and 46, which connected Piazza Verbano and Piazza Indipendenza respectively to the Trionfale district. In this way, passengers had a direct link between the Pincio and the tram stops, allowing them to descend 15 metres in 20 seconds.

The device was powered by an electric battery and had two cabins (numbered 1 and 2) whose generous dimensions – 3 x 1.9 metres – had space for eighteen passengers. There were also service stairs to access the cabins in case of a breakdown.

Each elevator had an attendant to operate it and sell tickets; there was also a mechanic. The service ran from 7am to 11pm, with departures every 5 minutes to coincide with the arrival of the trams.

In 1959, when Viale del Muro Torto was upgraded for fast-moving traffic, the road was widened, the rails taken up and the trams replaced by a bus service, but its timetable did not match those of the elevators. They were

decommissioned and since then have only reopened for a short period during the 1960 Olympic Games.

The structure is not in very good condition: the building overlooking the Pincio, as well as the two doors on the Muro Torto, would need to be restored in order to perpetuate the memory of Rome's first public elevator.

THE PINCIO WATER CLOCK

❸

Pincio promenade
• Metro: A – Flaminio or Spagna

One of Rome's two water clocks

The remarkable water clock on the Pincio promenade, not far from the entrance near Piazza del Popolo, is the work of Dominican priest Giovan Battista Embriaco, who designed the Palazzo Berardi clock, and municipal architect Gioacchino Ersoch. The former designed the automatic clock and the latter was responsible for the landscaping and for fitting the clock mechanism inside a fountain.

When the city of Rome decided to revamp the Pincio promenade in 1871, the Dominican monk offered his services "to the capital of the kingdom". Ersoch, meanwhile, chose a rather complex installation: a transparent box meant to protect and at the same time show off the hydraulic mechanism fed by the Acqua Marcia that flowed through the gardens.

He mounted the clock in a small tower with pillars imitating tree trunks and set it on a rock in the middle of a lake – its rural surroundings were an allusion to the wild, primitive nature that was so fashionable in the late 19th century.

There is another water clock at Palazzo Berardi (see page 138).

THE DINNER AT EMMAÜS IN SANTA MARIA DI MONTESANTO ❹

Church of Santa Maria di Montesanto
198 Via del Babuino - Piazza del Popolo
• Mass of the Artists: Sundays at 12pm

> *An anachronistic painting*

I n the chapel of Souls in Purgatory, to the right in the church of Santa Maria di Montesanto, is a recent painting so anachronistic as to be an unexpected find in a Roman church.

Painted by Riccardo Tommasi Ferroni (1934-2000), *The Dinner at Emmaüs* takes up the well-known theme of the Emmaus pilgrims. Although the composition of the painting is classical, there are several striking details, such as the very contemporary trainers worn by one of the pilgrims who is nonchalantly leaning on the table chatting with Jesus, who himself is wearing a traditional light-coloured robe.

THE ARTISTS' CHURCH
Santa Maria di Montesanto is the artists' church. From late October to 29 June, music is played during the Sunday midday mass. An actor generally reads the texts and, at the end of the mass, a prayer for the artists is said. The Mass of the Artists tradition began on 7 April 1951, ten years after a group of artists had begun to hold meetings with Monsignor Ennio Francia, to celebrate a mass in their honour.

THE TRIDENT: THREE ROUTES FOR PILGRIMS TO ROME
Diverging from Piazza del Popolo, the three streets known as the Trident were planned in the 17th century to direct pilgrims towards their itineraries when entering the city by the north gate. By taking the former Via Leonina (now Via Ripetta, built by Pope Leo X in 1515) they rejoined the Tiber and the Sant'Angelo bridge and then went on to Saint Peter's.
The former Via Clemenza (now Via del Babuino, opened in 1525 by Clement VII) headed in the direction of Piazza di Spagna and then on to Santa Maria Maggiore. Finally, the former Via Lata (now Via del Corso) led to San Giovanni in Laterano.

THE FIRST KNOWN GROTESQUES OF THE RENAISSANCE
The church of Santa Maria del Popolo is home to a superb painting by Pinturicchio, in the first chapel to the right of the main entrance. The painted decorations to each side of it are the first representation of grotesques following the discovery of the Domus Aurea (see page 283).

THE CANNON BALL OF VIALE DELLA TRINITÀ DEI MONTI FOUNTAIN

⑤

Viale Trinità dei Monti, opposite Villa Medici
Metro: A – Spagna

A real cannon ball in the centre of a fountain

In line with the entrance to the Villa Medici is a majestic granite fountain that, with the panorama of Rome in the background, has inspired many artists, such as the painter Jean-Baptiste Camille Corot who immortalised the scene in 1826.

The basin of the fountain came from San Salvatore in Lauro; Cardinal Ferdinando de' Medici is thought to have acquired it from the monastery in 1587 for 200 ecus. The setting, however, came from a square close to San Pietro in Vincoli. It was probably constructed around 1589 by Annibale Lippi, one of the architects of the Villa Medici.

There is an incredible story about the provenance of the cannon ball from which the water flows in the centre of the fountain.

In 1655, Queen Christina of Sweden, a prominent figure in 17th-century Roman life, is said to have had the cannon fired from Castel Sant'Angelo in the direction of the Villa Medici in an attempt to wake up the master of the house to go hunting. Three traces of the impact on the heavy door of the Villa bear out this version of events, while one of the balls was recovered to be set into the fountain opposite …

At the time, however, the villa was no longer much used by its then owner, Cardinal Carlo de' Medici.

Another theory goes that Queen Christina (a bit of a loose cannon herself) had promised the painter Charles Errard, director of the Académie de France in Rome, to knock at his door at a certain time of day. At the appointed hour, she was still at Castel Sant'Angelo and found a way of keeping her word by having the cannon pointed at the door of Villa Medici … Note that this version is most certainly false: the Académie de France was established in 1666 with its headquarters at Sant'Onofrio (it only moved to the Villa Medici in 1803, having successively occupied several Roman palaces). What does seem sure, however, is that these legends grew up not only to justify the marks on the door, but also the impetuous character of Queen Christina of Sweden!

THE ANAMORPHIC FRESCOES OF TRINITÀ DEI MONTI CONVENT ❻

Trinità dei Monti convent
Monastic Fraternities of Jerusalem
3 Piazza Trinità dei Monti
• E-mail: maison.accueil.tdm@libero.it
• Open twice a week, Tuesday at 11am and Sunday at 09.15am, book
through visitesguidees.tdm@libero.it
• Note: the second anamorphic fresco is currently being restored

A quite astonishing optical illusion

On the upper floor of Trinità dei Monti convent, you can visit a corridor that runs right round the cloister and features two rare anamorphic paintings (see explanation opposite), the result of the residents' research on perspective. Until the 18th century, the convent housed French monks of the Order of Minims, some of whom were carrying out important scientific work, such as Father Emmanuel Maignan (1601-1676) and his disciple Father Jean-François Nicéron (1613-1646), both of whom held a special interest in optics and perspective. Their work in this field culminated in two anamorphic frescoes painted on the upper floor of the convent, on either side of the cloister, but there is some disagreement as to which monk they should be attributed.

Nicéron, who wrote a treaty on perspective, *Thaumaturgus opticus*, spent only ten months in Rome in 1642, but he probably assisted his master in executing one of the two frescoes, following the principles set out in his text.

The first anamorphosis, painted in grisaille, depicts Saint Francis of Paula at prayer, kneeling under a tree, an image that can be seen from the end of the corridor. But if you stand directly in front of the fresco, the figure of the saint disappears, recomposing as a marine landscape with a bay enclosed by hills. A port can be seen as well as towers, greenery and several figures. The scene is thought to be the region of Calabria in southern Italy where the saint lived, and shows episodes from his life. The two men in the water near a sailing boat, between two spits of land, recall the time when Saint Francis was refused passage by a boatman to cross the Strait of Messina, so he laid his cloak on the water and sailed across on it. Likewise, the figures lost in this desert landscape symbolise the hermit's way of life.

At the same level on the other side of the cloister is another anamorphic fresco, this time depicting Saint John the Baptist writing the Book of Revelation. A similar work can be found in Paris in the former convent of the Minims, which used to stand in what is now the Place des Vosges. The ideal vantage point to reveal the figure of the saint is on entering the room. But like the other painting, if you stand directly in front of the picture you see a landscape, that of the island of Patmos where Saint John received a vision of Christ.

WHAT IS ANAMORPHOSIS?

The basic principle of anamorphic perspective is to project the line of vision in order to present an image as it would appear to the observer at a given distance, and to transfer the drawing, or simply a grid, to the surface to be painted at an oblique angle.

The technique thus produces a deliberately distorted image that appears in its true shape if reflected in a certain kind of mirror (for curved anamorphoses for example) or viewed from a predetermined angle (most often oblique).

The most famous example of this technique is in Hans Holbein the Younger's painting *The Ambassadors* (1533), where the strange shape in the foreground is actually the distorted image of a human skull.

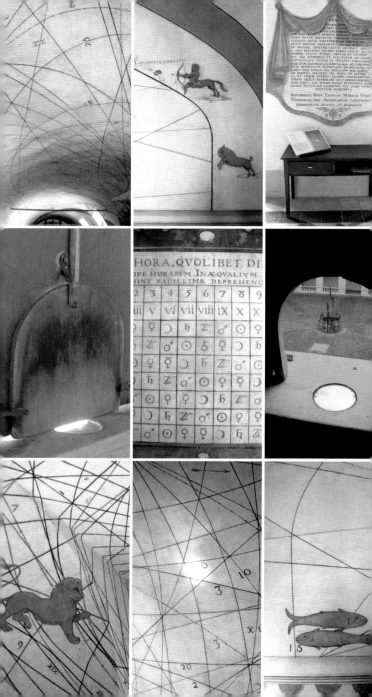

TRINITÀ DEI MONTI CONVENT SUNDIAL

Trinità dei Monti convent
Monastic Fraternities of Jerusalem
3 Piazza Trinità dei Monti
• E-mail: maison.accueil.tdm@libero.it
• Open twice a week, Tuesday at 11am and Sunday at 09.15am, book
through visitesguidees.tdm@libero.it

> *A rare
> catoptric
> sundial*

The two anamorphic frescoes at the convent (see preceding double page) are separated by a sundial that fills the entire vault of the corridor overlooking the cloister. This ingenious system is the work of Father Emmanuel Maignan, for whom gnomonics (the art of building sundials) was but a secondary interest — mathematics, optics, and especially philosophy and theology, being the subjects that interested him most.

This example is a catoptric sundial, which shows the hours by the reflection of sunlight rather than by the shadow of a stylus. A mirror placed on the sill of the central window reflects a beam of light along the angle of 'incidence' to indicate the solar hour on the vault. A dish filled with water and mercury can similarly be used to achieve the same reflective effect.

The uniqueness of this astrolabe lies in the mass of information that can be derived from the vault according to the position of the beam of light. Arabic numerals in black, along the length of the black line, show the hour on the former Rome meridian (one hour in advance of the Greenwich meridian); using the Roman numerals (small and green, with green lines) Italian time can be read off (i.e. how long since sunset and, by extension, the time remaining until the following sunset); and the red lines indicate the celestial coordinates.

Also featured on the vault are the twelve signs of the zodiac and the names of cities of every continent, from the Solomon Islands to Babylon, from Mexico to the region of Goa; their local time is shown by the reflected sunlight.

Painted on the wall itself are several framed instructions on the usage and history of this sundial, while a painting identifies the planet corresponding to a given moment in time.

Another catoptric sundial, also built by Emmanuel Maignan, can be seen on the main floor of Palazzo Spada (see page 97).

CASINO BONCOMPAGNI LUDOVISI (DELL'AURORA LUDOVISI)

8

46 Via Lombardia
• Tel: 06 483942 or 06 4883668
• Tours by prior appointment, cultural associations or groups

> *A Guercino masterpiece and Caravaggio's only fresco*

A few steps from Via Veneto, hidden behind high walls, is the Casino dell'Aurora (Dawn Pavilion). Along with the Casino Grande (now part of the US Embassy), it is the only building to have survived the destruction of the famous Villa Ludovisi, built on the site of the Horti Sallustiani (Gardens of Sallust) in the 17th century by Cardinal Ludovico Ludovisi, nephew of Pope Gregory XV. The property, which was much admired by Goethe, Stendhal and D'Annunzio, fell victim to real-estate speculation in the late 19th century, but is still a private residence of the Boncompagni Ludovisi family.

In the early 17th century, when Ludovico Ludovisi bought the property and vineyards from Cardinal Francesco Del Monte, he immediately commissioned the Bolognese Giovanni Francesco Barbieri (nicknamed Guercino, "the squinter") to paint the *Aurora* fresco on the ceiling vault of the Grand Hall (1621-1623). This had to compete with another work on the same theme by Guido Reni painted in 1613 at the Borghese family villa (now Palazzo Pallavicini-Rospigliosi, see page 313). Artistic and political rivalry merged and Guercino produced a masterpiece.

In the centre, Aurora drives her chariot drawn by two horses. She spreads flowers around her and the Hours stream out before her. To her left, her husband, old Tithonus, lifts a veil and watches her departure in astonishment. In the arch to the left is an allegory of Day, with the genie Lucifer ("light-bearer") holding a flaming torch, while to the right Night sleeps on, head in hand and an open book on her knee. The architectural setting is the work of Agostino Tassi, who was also responsible for the decoration of the room on the first floor, where Guercino painted an allegory of Fortune.

In the small alchemical laboratory upstairs is the pavilion's second treasure, Caravaggio's only fresco. Painted in oils around 1597 for Cardinal Del Monte, the artist's main patron in Rome, it depicts Jupiter, Neptune and Pluto with elements of the Universe and signs of the Zodiac. In this allegory of the alchemical triad, Jupiter (with eagle) symbolises Air and Sulphur, Neptune (with sea horse) Water and Mercury, Pluto (with the three-headed dog Cerberus) Earth and Salt. The artist has painted them in a bold style and the figure of Pluto (with clearly visible genitals) is thought to be a self-portrait.

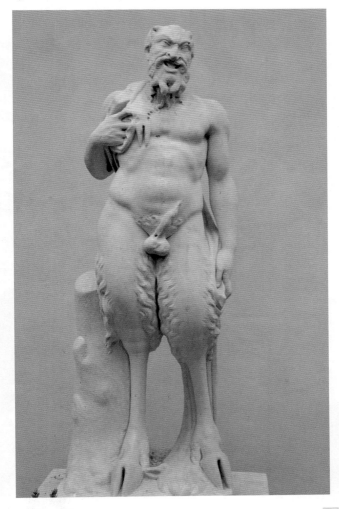

VILLA MARAINI

9

48 Via Ludovisi
• Guided tours: every Monday at 3pm and 4pm (in English, French and Italian), on request only, by writing to: visite@istitutosvizzero.it
• Admission € 5
• Metro: A – Barberini; Bus: 61, 63, 80, 83, 116

A superb panoramic view from an artificial hill

I n the heart of the Ludovisi district, close to Via Veneto, Villa Maraini offers one of the most spectacular views over the city: from the tower of the villa is a 360° panoramic viewpoint that is only 3 metres lower than the belvedere on the dome of Saint Peter's Basilica.

This luxurious and eclectic building combining Renaissance and Baroque influences was built between 1903 and 1905 by Emilio Maraini, a successful captain of industry born in Lugano, Switzerland, in 1853. He began to produce sugar from beets that he had grown in the countryside around Rieti and in a few years became the "sugar king". He then obtained Italian citizenship and even became a member of parliament, which is why he moved to Rome. A short distance from the church of Trinità dei Monti he bought some land where tonnes of stone, gravel and rubble had been piled up, partly for the construction of Via Ludovisi. Rather than just dispose of the rubbish, Maraini had the idea of building his house on top of this artificial hill.

The majestic three-storey villa, set in lush gardens, was designed by his architect brother Otto, who was also involved with the construction of the Excelsior Hotel on Via Veneto.

Inside, stucco, columns, frescoes, tapestries and marble figures grace the rooms, among which is the unmissable grand ballroom overlooking a loggia open to the garden. The monumental staircase with its three landings, flanked by two columns and graced with an incredible marble parapet, leading from the ground floor to the first floor, is very impressive. The villa's decorations are

the originals, embellished with copies of antique sculptures.

The owner's widow, Countess Carolina Maraini-Sommaruga, donated the villa to the Swiss Confederation in 1947. Since 1949, it has been home to the Swiss Institute, whose mission is to promote scientific and artistic exchanges between Switzerland and Italy.

THE BREASTS OF BERNINI'S "CHARITY" AND "TRUTH"

Cappella Da Sylva, church of Sant'Isidoro
41 Via degli Artisti
• Visits by appointment (tel: 06 4885359)

*Sensuality
censored*

Some works of art can inflame the spirit more than others. If the nudes of Michelangelo's *Last Judgment* provoked such a scandal that Pope Paul IV had their private parts covered up (a delicate task entrusted to Daniele da Volterra, who has gone down in history as the "*braghettone*" or breeches-maker), Bernini's sensual sculptures created for the Da Sylva chapel – although less well known – met a similar fate.

The chapel is in the church of Sant'Isidoro, near Piazza Barberini. Construction of the church for the Spanish Franciscan community began in 1622. It was dedicated to Isidore of Madrid, patron saint of agriculture. A few years later the unfinished building was handed over to a group of Irish Franciscans. They had assembled in Rome around Brother Luca Wadding, who had founded a college with a well-stocked library there.

In 1663, the small Cappella Da Sylva was added to the right of the high altar, to accommodate the funerary monuments of the family of Portuguese nobleman Rodrigo Lopez da Sylva, knight of the Order of Saint James and eminent member of the Iberian community in Rome. On the left is a bas-relief monument to Rodrigo and his wife Beatriz da Silveira, framed by the naked figures of Charity, who seems to be offering her breast to visitors, and Truth, with a radiant sun on her breast, both sculptures by Giulio Cartari. On the right is the monument to his son Francisco Nicolò da Sylva and his wife Juana, flanked by representations of Justice and Peace, the work of Paolo Naldini. All the bas-relief portraits were made at a later date, in the early 18th century. The wall paintings and the *Immaculate Conception* at the rear of the chapel are by Carlo Maratta.

In the second half of the 19th century, "Charity" and "Truth", with their generous, sensual breasts, were deemed indecent by the Irish priests, who covered up their Baroque nudity with heavy bronze "bras" fixed to the marble and painted so that they seemed part of the original.

The statues, which were restored in 2002, have now recaptured all their former evocative power.

THE FAÇADE OF PALAZZO ZUCCARI

Via Gregoriana
• Metro: A – Spagna

> **Monsters
> on the façade**

Palazzo Zuccari occupies an area comprising the last part of Via Sistina and that of Via Gregoriana and its façade is probably the most curious and unusual in the city. The cornices of the main door and of the windows are all formed by gaping monsters' mouths.

Federico Zuccari, the famous Baroque artist, bought the land in 1590, struck by its wonderful location, and he built the house and the studio for himself and his children, drawing inspiration for the palace's façade from the "monstrous" style of the famous monsters of Bomarzo, close to Viterbo. This architectural whimsy was both criticised and admired, but in any case soon became the ideal house for artists in the area. Through the Accademia di San Luca, Zuccari left the dwelling to foreign artists, but his wishes were not respected and when the artist died, the building was passed on to another owner.

The Queen of Poland lived there from 1702 and for decades the house was the centre of high society in the city. After several changes of ownership, Zuccari's wish finally came true and the building became an inn for foreign artists. Winckelmann and Reynolds stayed there, David and Nazareni painted famous works there, and it appears in *Il Piacere* (The Child of Pleasure) by Gabriele D'Annunzio. In 1900 Henrietta Hertz, the last owner, left her collection

of paintings to the Italian state and the palazzo and its library to Germany, allowing for the creation of the famous Biblioteca Hertziana (Hertzian Library), specialised in art history and still open today to scholars with special letters of recommendation.

The building, which is closed to the public for restoration, is full of important works, such as the frescoes of Giulio Romano.

In the basement the ruins of the villa of Lucullo, from the end of the Roman Republic, were found.

IDROMETRO
MDCCCXXXI

LARGO
S ROCCO
R.IV

THE MARBLE FLOOD GAUGE OF PORTO DI RIPETTA

⑫

Largo San Rocco
• Metro: A – Flaminio or Spagna; Bus: 70 – Lungotevere Marzio

> *The last of Porto di Ripetta's five flood gauges*

People crossing Largo San Rocco rarely notice this long strip of marble embedded in the wall of the church of the same name: it is, in fact, the last piece of the magnificent water-level gauge from the ancient port of Ripetta.

Apart from the metric scale along its length, the levels reached by the Tiber during its terrible centennial floods are also recorded. The highest mark refers to the inundation of December 1598, when the river reached the exceptional height of 19.56 meters above sea level: the force of the water was enough to destroy three arches of the ancient Ponte Emilio (now Ponte Rotto, meaning "broken bridge", near the Isola Tiberina), making it permanently unusable.

The first scientific measurement of the height of the Tiber at Ripetta dates back to 1744. Then, from 1781 to 1801, daily records were kept of the water level in relation to the seventh landing, which together with the port steps, thus served as a water-level gauge – so the height of the river could be checked at a glance without getting wet feet.

In 1818, with the establishment of a corps of roads and bridges engineers, a proper water-level gauge was designed for the Ripetta and installed in 1821. It consisted of five strips of marble set at different heights in various parts of the port complex. The first three were on the steps below the old customs house, the fourth on the edge of the riverside customs and the fifth on the façade of the customs in Via di Ripetta.

The 1870 flood marked the end of the port of Ripetta and the thousand-year link between Rome and its river: to contain the annual flooding, the *muraglioni* (high protective walls) were built in 1888. The old customs house was also demolished and the four strips of marble on the riverside disappeared along with it. In 1937, when construction work began on the Ara Pacis Museum, the fifth marble strip, which meanwhile had been fixed to an old house, was again removed and attached to a wall on Largo San Rocco – this time with a purely decorative role.

Other water-level gauges can be seen in Via dell'Arancio (Palazzo Baschenis), Via de' Prefetti (Palazzo Firenze), Via del Corso (convento degli Agostiniani Scalzi di Gesù e Maria), Via della Lungara (Palazzo Corsini), Ponte Cavour and Ponte Milvio, and near the Acqua Acetosa fountain.

THE COLUMNS OF RIPETTA

Piazza del Porto di Ripetta
• Metro: A – Flaminio or Spagna; Bus: 70 (Termini), Lungotevere Marzio

> **All that remains of the magnificent port of Ripetta**

As well as the fountain in the small Piazza del Porto di Ripetta, there are two marble columns which are often overlooked: they are all that remains of the ancient and magnificent port of Ripetta.

Although the shape of the columns is inspired by the milestones of antiquity, the "hands" carved on the surface, the dates and the popes' names leave little doubt that these are two water-level gauges. They preserve the "memory" of the Tiber's most disastrous floods, including those dating from before the columns were erected (1704).

Ever since antiquity, the Ripetta portuary zone had been a stopover for oil and wood merchants from Umbria, Sabina and Upper Lazio. In the Middle Ages the port was known as Porto della Posterula. In 1700, Pope Clement XI decided to make it a more practical port of call, refurbishing it with travertine taken from the Colosseum after the 1703 earthquake when part of the monument collapsed. The fallen stone was reused in the construction of the port, including the columns and the fountain.

In 1704, Clement XI opened the Port of Ripetta, designed by the architect Alessandro Specchi, who was also responsible for the Spanish Steps, which lead down to Piazza di Spagna from the church of Trinità dei Monti. In 1870, after yet another flood, the Italian government decided to build high walls to make life safer for the citizens. The port was filled in and the fountain and columns that stood opposite the church of San Girolamo degli Schiavoni were moved to what is now Piazza del Porto di Ripetta, built on the rubble of the church and the congregation of Masons, also demolished in the late 19th century.

The term *Ripetta* (small riverbank) was used to distinguish the port from the main anchorage, *Ripa Grande* (large riverbank), located on the right bank of the river under the monumental complex of San Michele, which was designed to take boats coming upriver from the Tyrrhenian Sea.

BLESSING OF THE THROATS

Church of the Madonna del Divino Amore in Campo Marzio
12 Vicolo del Divino Amore
• 3 February, after mass
• Masses at 7:30am, 8am, 9am, 10am, 11am, 12pm and 6:30pm

> *Protect your throat from the rigours of winter!*

nce a year, in the deep midwinter, an extraordinary blessing helps you protect your throat and get through the winter safely. On 3 February, the feast day of Saint Blaise, masses are held throughout the day at the church of the Madonna del Divino Amore in Campo Marzio. After each mass, the priest gives the blessing by holding two candles in the form of a cross and touching people on the throat with them, repeating: "Through the intercession of Saint Blaise, bishop and martyr, may God deliver you from ailments of the throat and from every other evil, in the name of the Father, the Son and the Holy Ghost." The source of this tradition is the life of the saint himself (see below).

WHY IS SAINT BLAISE INVOKED TO PROTECT THE THROAT?

Born in the 3rd century AD in Armenia, Blaise was elected bishop of Sebaste. When the Christians began to be persecuted under Diocletian, he retreated to a cave surrounded by wild beasts, where he carried out several miracles including saving a child who was choking on a fishbone stuck in his throat. Blaise laid his hands on the child and prayed that he and all those who asked in his name should be healed, thus saving the child's life. Shortly afterwards, at his command, a wolf gave back a pig that it had seized from a poor woman. She later killed the pig and brought him its head and feet, with a candle and some bread. He ate the meat and

told her that whoever lit a candle in a church dedicated to him would reap the benefit. These two incidents were the source of the tradition of blessing the throat with wax candles.

Tortured with an iron comb or rake, Blaise was finally beheaded in 287 or 316, according to different sources.

INNUMERABLE RELICS OF SAINT BLAISE

Blaise is probably the Roman Catholic saint with the greatest number of "official" relics. If all those who claim possession are to be believed, Saint Blaise would have had over a hundred arms. Although his body is said to be buried at Maratea, in southern Italy, another body lies at San Marcello in Rome. The church of Santi Biagio e Carlo ai Catinari (Biagio is Italian for Blaise) allegedly retains the saint's "throat bone".

Traditional saying: "If on Candlemas day it be shower and rain, winter's gone and will not come again."

THE RUINS OF AUGUSTUS' SUNDIAL

48 Via Campo Marzio
• Metro: A – Spagna
• Visits by appointment (tel: 336610144 or 06 33612607)

*The sundial
obelisk*

The spectacular Egyptian obelisk that is admired today in Piazza Montecitorio was once part of a giant sundial. The *Horologium Augusti* was in the centre of the gardens commissioned by the Emperor Augustus, which occupied all the Campo Marzio area at the time.

The clock was made up of a huge rectangular marble slab that measured 110 metres long and 60 metres wide according to some sources, and according to others it was even 150 metres by 70 metres. In the 9th century BC, the obelisk of the Pharaoh Psammetico II from the 6th century BC was brought to Rome by Augustus after the conquest of Egypt and was erected in the middle of the clock. It collapsed in the Middle Ages and remained buried for centuries. It was found in the middle of the 18th century and was erected in Piazza Montecitorio by Pope Pius VI, who tried to get the sundial working again. Bronze letters and rulers were set in the great marble face, and when the shadow of the obelisk would fall on it, it would indicate the time, the day and the month. The remains of the sundial, which had already been restored once before, towards the end of the 1st century AD, were discovered 5 metres underground about twenty years ago, in the basement of number 48, Via di Campo Marzio. Parts of the marble slab with the sundial line have been preserved, as have the transversal lines corresponding to two days, the inscriptions regarding the Leo, Taurus, Aries and Virgo signs of the Zodiac, and an indication of the winds that blew over the Aegean sea until the end of August.

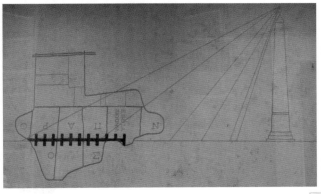

POUSSIN'S TOMB

Church of San Lorenzo in Lucina
16a Via in Lucina
• Open Monday to Saturday 9am-12pm and 4:30pm-7:30pm,
Sunday 9:30am-1pm and 5pm-8pm
• Guided underground tour the first Saturday of the month at 5pm
• Metro: A – Spagna

> *Men of genius often herald their end with a masterpiece: it is their soul taking flight*

Poussin's tomb, commissioned by the French writer Chateaubriand between 1828 and 1832, when he was ambassador to Rome, is a white marble structure with a niche containing a bust of the painter. Below the bust figures a relief representation of his famous painting, *The Arcadian Shepherds*. Strangely sited between two of the church's side chapels (tombs are usually in the side chapels), the tomb was sculpted by Léon Vaudoyer, Paul Lemoyne and Louis Desprez, three pupils of the Villa Medici, the headquarters of the Académie de France since 1803.

Below the bas-relief, a Latin epitaph reads:

"Hold back your pious tears, in this tomb Poussin lives / He has given his life without himself knowing how to die / He is quiet here but if you want to hear him speak / It is surprising how he lives and speaks in his paintings."

Although much ink has been spilled over the phrase "Et in Arcadia ego" (see page 48), the existence of this tomb is probably only a straightforward homage to an artistic genius. As Chateaubriand said in *La vie de Rancé*, "Admirable tremor of time! Men of genius often herald their end with a masterpiece: it is their soul taking flight".

MIRACULOUS WATERS
OF THE MADONNA DEL POZZO

Church of Santa Maria in Via
Cappella della Madonna del Pozzo
24 Via del Mortaro
• www.santamariainvia.it
• Closed for lunch (12:45pm-4pm; 1pm—4pm Sundays)

*In Rome
as in Lourdes*

Rome, like Lourdes, has its miraculous sources. You can, for example, visit the church of Santa Maria in Via in the heart of the city, behind the Alberto Sordi Gallery (located between Palazzo Chigi and the Trevi Fountain), and enter the Madonna del Pozzo chapel just to the left of the entrance. This is where, in 1256, the miracle took place that gave the church its popular epithet, "little Lourdes".

A well in Cardinal Capocci's stables began to overflow so copiously that the entire place was flooded. A painting on stone of the Virgin Mary, probably from the depths of the cistern, was floating on the water. The cardinal rescued it and built a small shrine at the site. The miraculous image has been venerated ever since as Our Lady of the Well.

The legend goes that those who had drunk water from the source soon experienced a miraculous recovery. The site attracted more and more pilgrims and the church was enlarged in the 16th century.

Even today, from behind the railings in the chapel, the faithful can drink water from the well or take away small quantities for the sick.

ET IN ARCADIA EGO

The phrase "Et in Arcadia ego" was probably used for the first time in a painting by Guercino, *The Shepherds of Arcadia* (1618), commissioned by the Barberini family and now in the museum of the Galleria Nazionale d'Arte Antica of the Palazzo Corsini, opposite the Farnesina.

The words are shown carved on a block of masonry, by way of comment on two shepherds leaning on their staffs contemplating a skull.

The phrase next appeared in Poussin's first version (1628-1630) of a painting by the same name (now in the collection of the Duke of Devonshire at Chatsworth House in the UK), before gaining fame in the second version of the picture, probably painted around 1638 and now in the Louvre in Paris.

Note that another, lesser-known painting kept at the Brive museum (France), entitled *Paysage aux bergers d'Arcadie* (anon., late 18th century), also bears the famous phrase and that a marble bas relief in the garden of the English property of Shugborough Hall also deals with the subject. The interpretation of these words carved in stone has been endlessly discussed.

If Goethe, Schiller and Nietzsche understood it to mean, "I too have lived in Arcadia [and I have been happy there]", the most commonly accepted interpretation (due in part to art historian Erwin Panofsky) is "And even in Arcadia there I am [death]".

In other words, even in an idyllic and paradisiacal place like Arcadia, death is waiting for us all one day; stay humble and try to discriminate between the essential and the pointless and futile.

Without going into all the more or less far-fetched interpretations, some have seen links between this phrase and the celebrated enigma of Rennes-le-Château, several aspects of which make reference to Poussin's paintings. In one of the coded manuscripts discovered at the site appear the names of Poussin and the Belgian painter Teniers; the inscription

"Et in Arcadia ego" was also said to have been found there. Finally, some commentators have noted that the tomb in Poussin's painting and the surrounding countryside apparently corresponded to a tomb that once actually existed at Arques, near Rennes-le-Château.

In 1978, researcher Franck Marie, like Pierre Jarnac in 1985, concluded that there was really nothing special about this tomb and that it had been dug in 1903 by the owner of the property, Jean Galibert, who had buried his mother and grandmother there.

Their remains were exhumed and reburied elsewhere, most likely in the village cemetery, when the property was sold to Louis Lawrence, an American from Connecticut who had immigrated to the region.

The latter, in turn, buried his mother and grandmother in the empty grave and had a tombstone bearing the inscription "*Et in Arcadia ego*" erected. Louis Lawrence's son, Adrien Bourrel, told Franck Marie and Pierre Jarnac that he had seen the tombstone erected in 1933, when he was a teenager. Nevertheless, a certain Pierre Plantard had the time to completely fabricate his "priory of Sion" while he was in prison and claimed that the tomb at Les Pontils had served as a model for Poussin's painting.

This tomb was finally demolished in 1988 by the owner of the property, with the authorization of the local authorities, so as to stop the visitors who came from around the world in search of esoteric revelations, in vain.

Thus, far from having any fabricated esoteric meaning, Poussin's painting and the phrase "*Et in Arcadia ego*" simply mean that death awaits us all one day.

ARCADIA: A TASTE OF PARADISE?

Arcadia is a mountainous region of Greece's central and eastern Peloponnese. In antiquity it was considered a primitive and idyllic place where shepherds lived in harmony with nature. In this respect it symbolised a golden age echoed by numerous literary and artistic works: Virgil's *Bucolics* or Ovid's *Fasti* (Calendar), for example.

The ancient region, rediscovered during the Renaissance and the 17th century, notably through Poussin's painting *Les Bergers d'Arcadie* (The Arcadian Shepherds), is traversed by the Alpheus River which is said to run underground to the sea and resurface in Sicily, where its waters mingle with the fountain of Arethusa. As Alpheus was a sacred river-god, the mythological son of the Titan Oceanus and his sister Tethys, whose underground streams symbolised the hidden traditions of esoteric knowledge, some have wrongly established a link between Arcadia and esotericism.

The name Arcadia comes from Arcas, itself from the ancient Greek *arktos*, meaning "bear". Arcas, king of Arcadia, was in Greek mythology the son of Zeus and the nymph Callisto. The legend goes that Callisto had offended the goddess Artemis, the huntress, who changed her into a bear during a hunt. Callisto, killed in the chase, was placed among the stars by Zeus and became the *Ursa Major* (Great Bear) constellation, while her son Arcas was transformed into *Ursa Minor* on his death.

MASS IN ARAMAIC AT SANTA MARIA CHURCH ⓲ IN CAMPO MARZIO

45/A Via di Campo Marzio
• Mass in Aramaic: Sundays at 10:30am
• Metro: A – Spagna or Barberini

Mass in the language of Jesus

Hidden away in one of the most frequented parts of the historic centre, Santa Maria in Campo Marzio is an Eastern Catholic church of the Syrian-Antiochene rite but obedient to Rome, in which mass is celebrated in Aramaic at 10:30 every Sunday morning. The often sparse congregation and the blend of three languages in which the mass is said (Aramaic, Arabic and Italian), together with the majestic architecture of the church, creates an ambience especially propitious to contemplation. After the service, worshippers are commonly invited to take coffee with the Patriarch.

The church dates back to the 8th century, when nuns fleeing from Constantinople during the persecution arrived in Rome and founded a convent. It was then acquired by the Benedictine nuns and enlarged to the size it is today, becoming one of the most important convents in the city.

The entrance from the street leads to a splendid courtyard with a distinctive tau cross shape, an oasis of peace within the bustling city centre. It was designed by De Rossi, who was also responsible for reconstructing the church at the end of the 17th century. At the end of the courtyard, a very beautiful

cloister with a central fountain can be glimpsed through a glass door, as well as one side of the church of San Gregorio Nazianzeno with its delicate little Romanesque belfry. This part of the complex is not open to visitors as it is managed by the Italian Chamber of Deputies, which has undertaken major restoration work. The convent had fallen into serious disrepair and was expropriated after 1870, since when it has been occupied by various public offices.

N

Palazzo di Giustizia

PIAZZA
DEI TRIBUNALI

Castel Sant' Angelo

Marzio

Scrofa

Tevere

Lungotevere

PONTE UMBERTO I

PIAZZA
PONTE UMBERTO I

Via

di

Tore

Via di Tore di Nona

Nona

dell' Orso

Via

②

V. dei Portoghesi

della

Lungotevere

di

Via

dei

①

PIAZZA
SAN SALVATORE
IN LAURO

Via Maschero d'Oro

③

San Agostino

PIAZZA SANT'
APPOLINARE

PIAZZA
SAN AGOSTINO

④

Via

Coronati

PIAZZA
DI TOR
SANGUIGNA

PIAZZA
CINQUE
LUNE

PONTE SANT' ANGELO

Via
Paola

Banco di Santo Spirito

del

Via

Corso

Panico

Via del

LARGO
TASSONI

Via dei Banchi Nuovi

Santa Maria della Pace

Vittorio

Via di Monte Giordano

PIAZZA
DELL'OROLOGIO

PIAZZA
DEL
FICO

V. della
Pace

Via di Tor Millina

Palazzo Madama

LARGO
TONIOLO

⑭

Corso

del

PIAZZA

Palazzo Sacchetti

⑤

Via

dei

Emanuele II

Banchi

Vecchi

⑨

⑩-⑪

del

Governo

Sora

Via di Parione

PARIONE

NAVONA

Vecchio

⑬

**Fontana
dei Quattro
Fiumi**

Virginia Vecchia

⑥

Via del Gonfalone

⑦

Chiesa Nuova

⑫

PIAZZA
CHIESA NUOVA

Corso

del

PIAZZA
DI PASQUINO

PIAZZA
SANT' EUSTACHIO

PIAZZA
SANT' EUSTACHIO

V. dei
Canestrari

V. di Sediari

⑧

Giulia

Via

Via

del

Vittorio

PIAZZA
SAN PANTALEO

Rinascimento

Via Teatro Valle

Via San Filippo Neri

PONTE G. MAZZINI

Lungotevere

Via Sant' Eligio

Via della Barchetta

Pellegrino

PIAZZA
DELLA
CANCELLERIA

Baullari

Emanuele II

PIAZZA
SANT' ANDREA
DELLA VALLE

⑮

LARGO
DEI
CHIAVARI

Via di Montoro

Cappellari

dei

LARGO
DEL PALLARO

farina

REGOLA

Via della

di

PIAZZA
PARADISO

PIAZZA
CAMPO DE' FIORI

Via

Monserrato

⑯

Via in Caterina

PIAZZA
FARNESE

dei

PIAZZA
DEI SATIRI

PIAZZA
DEL
LIBRARI

Via del Monte della

Via

Palazzo Farnese

⑱

⑰

Giulia

Via del Mascherone

PIAZZA DELLA
QUERCIA

⑲

LARGO DEI
LIBRARI

㉒

Giubbonari

Villa Farnesina

Viccolo del Polverone

⑳

PIAZZA DEL
MONTE DI PIETÁ

㉑

Via degli Specchi

PIAZZA
BENEDETTO
CAIROLI

della

Lungotevere

Via

Lungara

della

Tebaldi

Palazzo Spada

Via dei Pertinari

㉓

Conservatorio

Via del delle

Arenula

Porta Settimiana

Farnesina

PONTE SISTO

PIAZZA
SAN VICENZO
PALLOTTI

Lungotevere

dei

Zoccolette

Vallati

Via

PONTE GARIBALDI

Via

Garibaldi

Via

PIAZZA
TRILUSSA

Benedetta

Lungotevere

Raffaello

Sanzio

Santa Maria della Scala

della

Scala

TRASTEVERE

0   100   200 m

CENTRE WEST

PICENI HOSPICE

❶

15 Piazza San Salvatore in Lauro
• Open Mon-Fri 7:30am-1pm and 3:30pm-7pm, Sat 9am-12pm
and 4pm-8pm, Sun 9am-12pm

A hidden cloister of unexpected beauty

The Ospizio dei Piceni (Piceni Hospice), with its various buildings, courtyard, garden and cloister, is a practically unknown complex of extraordinary beauty.

Annexed to the much better known church of San Salvatore in Lauro, Piceni Hospice was one of the most important hospices in the city, where many people from the Marches region stayed when they came to Rome to live or simply to visit. The Confraternity of the Piceni, who took over the church and adjacent monastic complex in 1669, offered assistance to people from their region for many years.

The entrance is via the church's first porch on the left. A few steps and you find yourself inside a spectacular 15th-century cloister with an overhead loggia. Beside the cloister is a small courtyard with a fountain and a beautiful portico that leads to the chapter house. Some important tombs, such as that of Pope Eugene IV, are also found here.

Apart from its historic importance and the artistic and architectural beauty that has been highlighted by long and careful restoration work, the hospice conceals another marvel.

On ascending the 16th-century staircase you can visit a superb place consisting of two vaulted rooms and a raised wing over the garden portico, with a beautiful trussed ceiling.

It houses a museum donated by the painter Umberto Mastroianni, with over a hundred works dating back to his most significant and productive periods. The door next to the Mastroianni Museum is the entrance to the Emilio Greco Foundation. The Pio Sodalizio dei Piceni foundation also organises exhibitions and musical and theatrical performances.

PALAZZO SCAPUCCI

18 Via dei Portoghesi
• Metro: A – Spagna or Barberini

Monkey business

Palazzo Scapucci, which owes its name to the noble Roman family that owned it during the 16th and 17th centuries, encompasses a four-storey brick tower of medieval origin, restored on several occasions, with beautiful marble-framed windows. At its top, a strange statue will intrigue curious passers-by.

The tower owes its name to a legendary Roman anecdote, made famous by American novelist Nathaniel Hawthorne in *The Marble Faun*, according to which a pet monkey is supposed to have snatched the newborn son of the owners from his cradle and brought him to the top of the tower, jumping and playing dangerously amongst the battlements. It is said that the parents' desperate prayers to the Virgin Mary were heard (they promised to build a shrine in her honour if the child were saved) and the monkey brought him down safe and sound. The statue of the Virgin and the lamp at the top of the tower, both of which are visible from the street, date back to that time.

TOMB OF SAINT ANICETUS

3

Palazzo Altemps
4 Piazza di Sant'Apollinare
• Open Tuesday to Sunday 9am-7:45pm

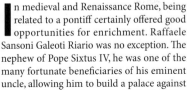

> *The only pope laid to rest in a private residence*

In medieval and Renaissance Rome, being related to a pontiff certainly offered good opportunities for enrichment. Raffaele Sansoni Galeoti Riario was no exception. The nephew of Pope Sixtus IV, he was one of the many fortunate beneficiaries of his eminent uncle, allowing him to build a palace against the walls that ran along Via dei Soldati between the river and what is now Piazza Navona.

Palazzo Riaro changed hands several times, with each owner making substantial modifications, before ending up as the property of the German-born Cardinal Mark Sittich von Hohenems, who had Italianised his name to Altemps. The cardinal rebuilt the palace from top to bottom, giving it the form it has today. A great collector and patron of the arts, he was nevertheless considered an "upstart" and could not compete with the patrician families whose past was inseparably linked to that of the Eternal City. What then could be better than a saint – if not in the family, at least in your palace – to add a little lustre that might be lacking from your family name?

Pope Clement VIII, who was in Altemps' debt for his unwavering support during his election to the papacy, responded positively to Duke Giovanni Angelo's request to gather the remains of Saint Anicetus, pope and martyr, found in the catacombs of Saint Sebastian in 1602. He had the remains transferred to an antique urn that had, according to tradition, contained the bones of Emperor Severus Alexander. Ever since then, the tomb of Anicetus, the eleventh pope, has lain below the altar in the private chapel of the Altemps family, decorated by Leoni and Pomarancio. This is the only example of a pope laid to rest in a private residence.

WHY IS VIA DEI SOLDATI (STREET OF THE SOLDIERS) SO NAMED?

Rome was anything but a quiet city. The relentless struggles for influence between the great Roman families quickly degenerated into street brawls and even armed conflict.

They eventually took control over entire neighbourhoods, dividing Rome into many small fiefdoms.

Near the Umberto I bridge over the Tiber was a system of fortifications that separated the Orsinis from the Colonnas. The route patrolled by the militia was thus known as the "Street of the Soldiers".

TOUR OF THE ANGELICA LIBRARY

8 Piazza S. Agostino
- Tel: 06 6840801 or 06 68408034 • E-mail: b-ange@beniculturali.it
- Director: Marina Panetta
- Group visits by arrangement or during exhibitions and concerts.
- Open Monday to Friday 8:30am-6:45pm and Saturday 8:30am-1:45pm
- Closed Sundays and the second and third weeks in August

Rome's oldest public library

The Biblioteca Angelica is the oldest public library in Rome and one of the first to be founded in Europe. The ensemble has a rare beauty and the enigmatic atmosphere is so hushed that it gives the impression of going back in time.

Book lovers can enjoy these marvellous reading rooms and the precious manuscripts preserved herein during the exhibitions, concerts, and guided tours that are regularly organised.

The library is named after an Augustinian bishop, Angelo Rocca, who was in charge of the Vatican printing presses during the pontificate of Sixtus V and left his precious library to the brothers of the convent of Saint Augustine at the end of the 16th century. Rocca wanted anyone to be able to use the library – an outlandish idea at the time.

In 1661, Lukas Holste, then curator of the Vatican library, bequeathed his prodigious collection of printed volumes. In 1762, the acquisition of the books of Cardinal Domenico Passionei doubled this heritage, adding the works that the cardinal had personally acquired during his travels in Protestant countries. This explains why the library contains copies of forbidden texts, the importance of which has been crucial for understanding the Reformation and the Counter-Reformation.

It was around this time that the architect Luigi Vanvitelli was commissioned to restructure the library, particularly its spectacular reading room where scholars still gather today.

Over 200,000 volumes are preserved here, half of which were published between the 15th and the 18th centuries. The most important sections of the library are devoted to the history of the Reformation and the Counter-Reformation and to Augustinian thought, as well as to Dante, Petrarch and Boccaccio, theatre from the 15th to the 18th centuries, Italian and foreign journals of the 17th and 18th centuries, and works on Rome itself. This is also the location of rare books of great artistic value, notably a 9th-century manuscript of the Liber Memorialis from Remiremont Abbey in France, an illuminated codex to Dante's *Divine Comedy* dating from the 14th century, as well as two *mappemondes* (maps of the world) from 1603, the only ones in Italy.

> Since 1940, the library has also been the headquarters of the Italian literary academy, or Accademia dell'Arcadia (see page 199).

PRIVATE TOUR OF PALAZZO SACCHETTI

66 Via Giulia
• Visits on request reserved for cultural associations or groups, Monday to Friday

A jewel waiting to be discovered

The sumptuous Sacchetti Palace is still the residence of the family of that name, which explains why it is less famous than other Roman palaces, even though it was built and decorated by such renowned artists as Antonio da Sangallo and Francesco Salviati.

On the death of Sangallo, the original owner, the palace was bought by Cardinal Ricci di Montepulciano, who commissioned Nanni di Baccio Bigio to make some alterations, including the masterful Sala dei Mappamondi, with its walls frescoed by Salviati depicting scenes from the Old and New Testaments. The allegorical and mythological decorations of the majestic gallery were carried out by Giacomo Rocca.

In the middle of the 17th century, the palace passed into the hands of Cardinal Giulio Sacchetti, member of a family of Florentine merchants and bankers, who wasted no time in carving out a prominent position for himself in Roman society and acquiring the title of marquis, buying up vast properties in the Latium countryside and throwing himself enthusiastically into the business of artistic patronage.

Cardinal Giulio did not make many changes when he moved into this splendid palace, but he began to collect hundreds of precious objects, archaeological artefacts, and contemporary works of art, including some twenty paintings by Pietro da Cortona. Only two works remain from this remarkable collection, *Adam and Eve* and *The Holy Family*. The others have been dispersed, the fortunes of the Sacchetti family having sharply declined at the beginning of the 18th century following their dazzling rise up to the time of Cardinal Giulio, who at one point almost became pope.

At the side of the palace overlooking the Tiber, a recently restored nymphaeum still embellishes the garden, which used to run right down to the water before the construction of the quays. Within a small arcade are two niches with an ornamental basin and satyrs portrayed lifting a section of drapery to reveal an imaginary view of Rome. Above, the framed family coat of arms can be seen, surmounted by ephebes. In addition to the stucco, imitation marble, and mosaics, the artistic techniques used here are highly original: real shells embedded at various points alternate with festoons of fruit and flowers covered with coloured glass designs, not to mention the *tartari*, chalk formations imitating stalactites and stalagmites.

THE "SOFAS" ON VIA GIULIA

Via Giulia, from the junction of Via del Gonfalone as far as Vicolo del Cefalo

> **Remains of an aborted project**

Only the base remains of the grandiose construction project for Palazzo dei Tribunali, designed by Bramante (see below). These huge blocks of travertine give an idea of the size of the building that was planned to bring together in one place the law courts of the papal government. The stones are now incorporated into the walls of the buildings for some 100 metres, and project out into the street. As they vaguely resemble large cushions and give passers-by a chance to sit down, they soon came to be known as the "sofas" on Via Giulia.

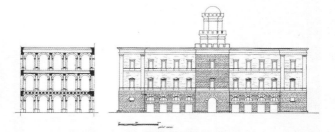

A FAILED PROJECT

Bramante and Pope Julius II della Rovere wished to make the new street the city's main artery. They planned it as long, straight, majestic and prestigious, according to the canons of the Renaissance — which it undoubtedly is.

They also saw it as the heart of a new administrative district: the papal law courts were to be set up here and bourgeois residences would be built along the street. On this point their plans came to nothing.

The courts never saw the light of day and the administration remained on the Campidoglio. Although some fine mansions were built, others were divided into rented apartments or small shops. A hundred and fifty years later, Pope Innocent X Pamphilj even had Rome's new prison built there (now, ironically, the anti-mafia headquarters), permanently laying to rest the monumental designs of his distant predecessor.

CRIMINOLOGY MUSEUM

29 Via del Gonfalone
• Tel: 06 68300234
• Open Tuesday to Saturday, 9am-1pm, Tuesday and Thursday,
2:30pm-6:30pm
• Admission: €2
• Bus: 23, 116, 116T, 271, 280, 870

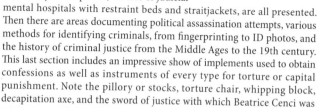

Crime and punishment

This exceptional museum offers a detailed and fascinating reconstruction of the history of crime.

On the first floor, in the section devoted to the 19th century, studies of criminal anthropology, scientific police techniques, the history of the prison, the rise of judicial mental hospitals with restraint beds and straitjackets, are all presented. Then there are areas documenting political assassination attempts, various methods for identifying criminals, from fingerprinting to ID photos, and the history of criminal justice from the Middle Ages to the 19th century. This last section includes an impressive show of implements used to obtain confessions as well as instruments of every type for torture or capital punishment. Note the pillory or stocks, torture chair, whipping block, decapitation axe, and the sword of justice with which Beatrice Cenci was

beheaded in 1599.

There are also plenty of whips and chains for punishing and transporting prisoners to hard labour camps.

On the second floor there is a display of finds from Italian prisons from the 1930s to the 1990s, evidence of perverse and criminal behaviour, such as espionage, organised crime (objects belonging to Salvatore Giuliano and Gaspare Pisciotta, Gennaro Cuocolo's ring, Pupetta Maresca's guns), terrorism, gambling and forgery of works of art.

Finally, a special area covers murders and news stories that caused a public stir in the 1940s and 1950s.

GONFALONE ORATORY ⑧

32/A Via del Gonfalone
• Tel: 06 6875952, 06 68805637, 06 9066572
• Opening times: During concerts, or on request
• Bus: 23, 116, 116T, 271, 280, 870

A little-known marvel

This small marvel of the 16th century, hidden at the end of one of the many intersections of Via Giulia, once belonged to the important Archconfraternity of the Gonfalone. The oratory, which was restored between 1998 and 2002, remains almost unknown even though it is used today as a concert hall. It is however an extraordinary example of Roman Mannerism.

Although the building's small façade, by Domenico Castelli, is not particularly impressive, the interior is superb with its walls completely covered with an extraordinary cycle of frescoes featuring the Passion of Christ in twelve parts. They were painted in 1573 by Federico Zuccari, Livio Agresti, Cesare Nebbia, Bertoja, Raffaellino Da Reggio and Marco Pino. Wooden choir benches encircle the room. Also note the ceiling of carved and gilded wood, the work of Ambrogio Bonazzini dating from 1568.

Gonfalone means "standard" or "banner" and refers to the fact that, in the 14th century, Archconfraternity members used to raise the standard of the pope (who resided in Avignon at the time), as a sign of support for his sovereignty over Rome. The confraternity, whose members wore a white habit and blue hood, was also known for the organisation of processions and other religious ceremonies. Their representations of Christ's Passion were so realistic that the popes had to put a stop to them in order to prevent crowd violence towards the Jews.

The Archconfraternity of the Gonfalone was dissolved at the end of the 19th century and the oratory fell into disuse, ending up in such a dilapidated state that it was used by refuse collectors as a storage area until a musician discovered this treasure and decided to use it as a concert hall.

MONUMENTAL HALL OF THE VALLICELLIANA ❾ LIBRARY

18 Piazza della Chiesa Nuova
• To organise a free guided tour of the monumental hall and a programme of temporary exhibitions, e-mail the following address: b-vall.servizi@beniculturali.it; alternatively, fax 06 6893868
• For further information contact Maria Teresa Erba on 06 68802671
• E-mail: mariateresa.erba@beniculturali.it
• Closed: 13-25 August and public holidays

A saint's library

Few people are familiar with the majestic monumental hall of the Biblioteca Vallicelliana, which forms part of the Institute of the Oratory of Saint Philip Neri (the Oratorians are a congregation of secular priests). On crossing the threshold, it is difficult not to fall under the spell of this vast rectangular chamber, the true dimensions of which are invisible from the outside, illuminated as it is by sixteen overhanging windows.

Decorated with stucco, wood panelling, and the monochrome canvases of G.B. Romanelli, the ceiling is exceptionally luminous. Spiral staircases have been concealed in the four corners of the hall to avoid breaking the homogeneity of the book-covered walls. The splendid wooden bookshelves dating from the 17th century are divided into two levels by a gallery supported by columns. The earliest documents relating to the order, founded by the Florentine priest Filippo (Philip) Neri in 1565, date back to 1581, but the growing number of adherents and the need for space to store the ever-increasing donations required an extension. Francesco Borromini carried out this work from 1637 to 1652. Following the rules of their order, the Oratorians attach great importance to books; each meal, for example, is accompanied by a reading or commentary on a sacred text. The library, originally made up of the personal collection of the founding saint, has been constantly enriched over the years to arrive at the present total of some 130,000 volumes, including rare manuscripts, incunabula, illustrated books and musical scores. Most texts are concerned with history or theology, but philosophy, law, botany, astronomy, architecture and medicine are also represented, and there is an exceptional collection of engravings and photographs.

THE LIBRARY TRAPDOOR

Saint Philip Neri asserted that music was a "fisher of souls" and the best form of spiritual diversion. Thus in the library there is a trapdoor that communicates with the oratory below, so that the music being played could be heard and inspire the readers above.

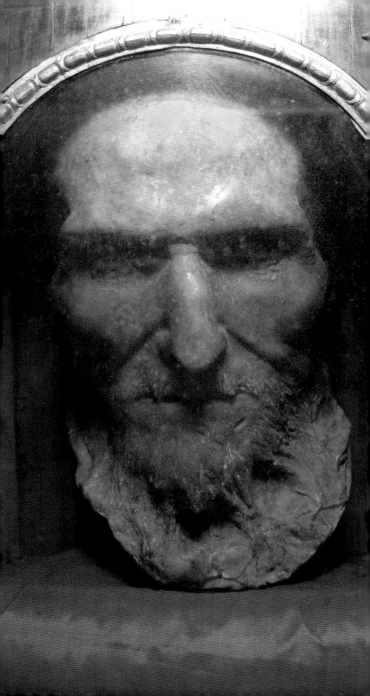

THE SECRET ROOMS OF SAINT PHILIP NERI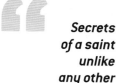

Church of Santa Maria in Vallicella (Chiesa Nuova)
Piazza della Chiesa Nuova
• Tel.: 06 688 04695
• E-mail: mauriziobotta@hotmail.com
• Pre-booked guided tours Tuesdays, Thursday and Saturdays from
10am to 12pm • Duration: about 30 min

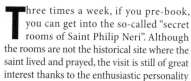

Secrets of a saint unlike any other

Three times a week, if you pre-book, you can get into the so-called "secret rooms of Saint Philip Neri". Although the rooms are not the historical site where the saint lived and prayed, the visit is still of great interest thanks to the enthusiastic personality of Father Maurizio Botta, a Filippini (from Filippo, the Italian name of the order's founder) who shows all the visitors round. You will also discover some particularly impressive aspects of the life of this saint, who is little known to the general public.

The tour begins in the red room, where a number of saintly relics are displayed as well as an attractive outline of the saint's standard (17th century) which the faithful carried during the seven churches pilgrimage. In the reproduction of Saint Philip's chapel, you can see a lovely Guercino painting, *The Vision of Saint Philip Neri*.

Notable works on the upper floor include a fine fresco by Pietro da Cortona (*The Ecstasy of Saint Philip*) and a Guido Reni painting of *Saint Philip Contemplating the Virgin*.

WHY DOES THE FAÇADE OF THE ORATORY OF SAINT PHILIP NERI CURVE INWARDS? Borromini's façade for the Filippini convent (notably the home of the oratory) was designed to be in harmony with the adjoining church. Its curve is reminiscent of the human body, arms outstretched, as if to welcome all those who cross its threshold.

The façade of the church of Santa Maria in Vallicella is embellished with statues of Saint Gregory to the left and Saint Jerome to the right. They are associated respectively with Pope Gregory XIII, who gave the church to Saint Philip, and the convent of San Girolamo della Carità (see page 85) where he spent many years.

SPIRITUAL CONCERTS IN CHIESA NUOVA SACRISTY
Once a month, from October to June, spiritual concerts in the revived tradition of Saint Philip Neri take place at 9pm in the superb sacristy of Chiesa Nuova. Admission is free, and pre-booking essential: padre.rocco@hotmail.com or musicaperduta@gmail.com. Entrance at 3 Via di Chiesa Nuova.

SAINT PHILIP NERI: A SAINT WHOSE HEART DOUBLED IN SIZE AS HE RECEIVED THE HOLY SPIRIT

Founder of the Congregation of the Oratory, also known as the Congregation of Filippinis after his forename, Saint Philip Neri (1515-1595) was often referred to as the joyful saint because of his cheerful disposition. Inspired by the early Christian communities, he wanted to anchor an intense spiritual life in daily routine based on prayer (he was one of the first to gather around him laymen with whom he prayed), reading, meditating on the word of God, and praising the Lord, mainly through chant and music. According to him, music was a special way of reaching people's hearts and bringing them to God (see article on the trapdoor in the Vallicelliana Library for listening to music from the oratory below, page 69). Thus he became one of the most avid defenders of the rebirth of sacred music. In 1544, while the saint was praying in the catacombs of Saint Sebastian over the tombs of the early martyrs, his heart was suddenly seized with immense joy and an intense light shone down on him. Raising his eyes, he saw a ball of fire which descended to his mouth and penetrated his chest. His heart, in contact with the flames, instantly dilated. The violence of the impact broke two of his ribs. The Holy Spirit had come to the saint, just as it had to the Apostles at Pentecost. In the 17th century, a scientific autopsy on his body confirmed that his was twice the size of any other human heart. Nothing was the same again for Saint Philip. The beating of his heart was so strong that it could be heard some distance away and the heat that constantly devoured him meant he could face the rigours of winter in his shirtsleeves. The symbol of the congregation today, a heart in flames, is based on this episode of his life. While looking after the sick, the poor and the infirm, he also took care to spend time with young people, wishing to stop them from falling into

boredom and depression. He often gathered a group around him and while always reminding them that life was to be lived joyfully, when the din became too loud one day, he is supposed to have said "Quieten down a bit, my friends, if you can!" His great spiritual gifts even enabled him to bring a child back to life for a few moments (see page 83).

SAINT PHILIP NERI AND THE PILGRIMAGE TO THE SEVEN CHURCHES OF ROME

Bringing the early pilgrimages to Rome to the tombs of Saint Paul and Saint Peter back into fashion, Saint Philip Neri and his followers began to visit the principal centres of worship in the city. Over time, these informal visits grew into a veritable pilgrimage around the seven major churches of Rome: San Pietro in Vaticano, San Paolo fuori le mura, San Sebastiano fuori le mura, San Giovanni in Laterano, Santa Croce in Gerusalemme, San Lorenzo fuori le mura and Santa Maria Maggiore. Each journey represented one of the seven stages of Christ's Passion. The pilgrimage still takes place today – enquire at Chiesa Nuova.

THE MOTORISED RUBENS

Church of Santa Maria in Vallicella (Chiesa Nuova)
Piazza della Chiesa Nuova
• Open in winter from 7:30am-12pm and 4:30pm-7:15pm (7:30pm in summer)
• Masses in winter at 8am, 9am, 10am and 6:30pm (8am, 10am and 7pm in summer), Sundays at 10am, 11am, 12pm, 12:45pm, and 6:30pm (10am, 11am, 12pm and 7pm in summer)
• The Rubens painting slides down after the evening mass on Saturday and is raised again on Sunday evening after mass

A painting that disappears once a week

Once a week, after the Saturday evening mass, Chiesa Nuova worshippers can take part in a very strange spectacle: the sexton lets down a Rubens painting by remote control to reveal a miraculous icon of the Virgin Mary behind it.

The source of this phenomenon dates back to the early 16th century.

At that time, a fresco depicting the Virgin and Child was on view outside, on the façade of a public bathhouse where the apse of the church now stands. In 1535, an unbeliever threw a stone at the image of the Virgin, who astonishingly began to bleed. The image was placed inside the original Vallicella church for safekeeping. When the new church was built, following the installation of Saint Philip Neri's Congregation of the Oratory, the sacred image was in the first chapel to the right. But the

conditions for conservation of the fresco rapidly deteriorated and to safeguard it the decision was made to place it behind the high altar. In 1606, Rubens was commissioned to paint a canvas that would serve to protect the image of the Virgin.

A first attempt failed, but in 1608 Rubens produced a work entitled *Angels Adoring the Madonna Vallicelliana*, which incorporated a special feature – a panel that could be removed to reveal behind it the miraculous Holy image it was intended to protect.

THE COVER OF THE "TERRINA" FOUNTAIN ⑫

Piazza della Chiesa Nuova
• Bus: 64 – Chiesa Nuova stop

*A Fountain
on the Move*

Designed by the architect Giacomo della Porta at the end of 16th century, the fountain known to the ancient Romans as the "Terrina" is today situated in the Piazza della Chiesa Nuova, opposite the Church of Santa Maria in Vallicella. The fountain attracts the attention because of its curious shape, resembling a teapot. There is an interesting inscription, now almost completely worn away, carved around the border of the travertine cover: "AMA DIO E NON FALLIRE FA DEL BENE E LASSA DIRE MDCXXII" (Love God, never fail to do good and let others say what they will, 1622). What appears at first sight to be a proverb was in fact a warning addressed to those who witnessed the executions (such as that of Giordano Bruno) that took place in the nearby Piazza Campo de' Fiori, the fountain's original location.

The spouts from which the water gushed were in the shape of a rose, probably because this flower appeared on the coat of arms of the Riario family, who owned the nearby Palace of the Chancellery (Palazzo della Cancelleria) (1485).

The edge of the marble basin used to be decorated with four bronze dolphins, made earlier for the famous fountain in the Piazza Mattei (also designed by Giacomo della Porta) but never used. (The upper basin of the Piazza Mattei fountain was left unadorned until 1658, when, following restoration work commissioned by Pope Alexander VII, the four famous turtles were placed there.) In 1622 the bronze dolphins were dismantled and the fountain was covered with an enormous travertine lid, giving it the appearance of a tureen. The cover was probably installed in order to prevent waste from the market from obstructing the spouts of the fountain.

When, in 1889, the monument to Giordano Bruno was erected in the centre of the Piazza Campo de' Fiori, the fountain was dismantled and placed in a city store until it was reinstalled, in 1924, on the Piazza della Chiesa Nuova. A new fountain, similar to the 16th-century version, appeared on the west side of the Piazza Campo de' Fiori.

Unusually, the fountain sits below the level of the piazza. The architect decided to position it this way because the pressure of the Aqua Virgo Aqueduct was relatively low at this point.

PALAZZO PAMPHILJ

Brazilian Embassy
14 Piazza Navona
• Free tours on registration with Embassy website (lengthy waiting list)
• www.ambasciatadelbrasile.it • Tel: 06 683981

The main gallery of the Brazilian Embassy

Palazzo Pamphilj, built in the 17th century, has accommodated the Brazilian Embassy since 1920. Twice a month, visitors who have booked ahead are shown round the seven magnificent chambers on the first floor (*piano nobile*), where biblical and mythological subjects alternate in the work of the most famous artists of the time: Giacinto Gimignani, Agostino Tassi (who went down in history as the rapist of Artemisia Gentileschi), Andrea Camassei, Gaspard Dughet and Giacinto Brandi.

The highlight of the visit is the main gallery, which is over 30 m wide and overlooks Piazza Navona. Designed by Francesco Borromini and decorated (1651-1654) by Pietro da Cortona, whose fresco cycle depicts scenes from the life of Aeneas, this privileged environment was designed to welcome and

impress even the most distinguished guests of the Pamphilj family.

Although the Pamphilj had owned houses on this side of Piazza Navona since the 15th century, it was not until two centuries later that the family had its moment of glory, when Cardinal Giovanni Battista was elected to the pontifical throne as Innocent X in 1644. This taciturn and wary pope was little loved by the public on whom he imposed heavy taxes to satisfy his architectural ambitions. As soon as he became pontiff, he commissioned Girolamo Rainaldi to build this magnificent palace as well as the church of Sant'Agnese in Agone (the family's private chapel), two projects on which Borromini subsequently worked.

The palazzo is also linked to Donna Olimpia Maidalchini, the pope's sister-in-law and one of the most influential women of her time. An authoritarian and hated figure, all kinds of sordid acts were attributed to her (it was said that she ran Rome's brothels); her ghost is still believed to haunt Piazza Navona. This powerful woman, nicknamed "Pimpaccia" (a pejorative diminutive of Olimpia) as well as "she-pope", was probably no worse than her male contemporaries but she was never forgiven for her influence over Innocent X (she was reputed to be his mistress). She was also renowned for her greed – it is said that on the pope's death she stole two chests filled with gold meant for his funeral expenses. In the end, Innocent X was buried without pomp and ceremony in the crypt of Saint Agnes, the place he had built by starving the people.

PRIVATE TOUR OF PALAZZO PATRIZI

Piazza San Luigi dei Francesi
• By appointment only, contact Corso Patrizi Montoro
• Tel: 06 6869737 or 347 5476534

> *The secrecy of private palaces*

I f you prefer the secret charm of opulent private residences to museums, do not miss the Patrizi Palace in the Sant'Eustachio district (rione). The palace stands on land originally occupied by a simple building that was acquired by Giovanni Francesco Aldobrandini in 1596. Giacomo della Porta is probably the architect of the present façade, commissioned by Donna Olimpia Aldobrandini and built by Carlo Maderno.

The marquises of Patrizi, originally from Siena but related to noble Roman families, bought the palace in 1642 and had major alterations carried out, such as refurbishing the grand staircase under the direction of Gian Battista Mola, and the addition of a third storey, cornice, attic, and chapel. Two members of the family, Costanzo Patrizi (1589-1624) and Giovanni Battista Patrizi (1658-1727), were treasurers to the pope and keen patrons of the arts. It is to them that we owe most of the paintings in the family collection displayed in the rooms furnished with 17th- and 18th-century antiques, and in the dining room, where a splendid Meissen porcelain dinner service can also be seen.

The fact that it once included masterpieces such as Orazio Gentileschi's *Cupid and Psyche* (now in the Hermitage Museum, St Petersburg) or Caravaggio's *Supper at Emmaus* (now in the Brera Museum, Milan) gives a clear idea of the importance of the original collection, but several other remarkable works still remain at the palace.

The tour, with the master of the house as guide, covers the second floor – the historical residence of the Patrizi family – tracing their fortunes in papal Rome and giving a real sense of the past splendours of this luxurious dwelling.

DINNER FOR TWO IN THE PATRIZI PALACE
The Patrizi family, who still live in their eponymous palace, offer the possibility of hiring the premises for a romantic dinner.

THE PRIVATE CHAPEL OF PALAZZO MASSIMO ALLE COLONNE

141 Corso Vittorio Emanuele II
• Open once a year, 16 March, 7am-1pm

Commemorating a miracle by Saint Philip Neri

The private chapel of the Massimo family, dedicated to Saint Philip Neri in commemoration of one of his miracles, can only be visited once a year, on 16 March.

Paolo Massimo, the young son of Prince Fabrizio, died on 16 March 1583. Saint Philip was a friend of the family. Scarcely had he heard the news when he rushed to the boy's side to give him the last rites. He began to pray beside the body and the constant repetition of his name finally brought the boy round. The two spoke together, little Paolo claiming that he was happy to die because that would allow him to be reunited with his mother and sister in Heaven. Saint Philip then placed his hand on the boy's head and said to him, "Go, with my blessing and pray to God for me". At these words, Paolo expired.

This story remained a secret until 1595, the year that Saint Philip was canonised, on the occasion of which Prince Fabrizio decided to reveal all. The miracle had taken place in the young boy's bedroom before it was converted into a chapel, which was restored and embellished over the centuries. Rectangular in shape, with a barrel vault, it contains eight marble columns supporting a decorated architrave, and three altars in polychrome marble. Pope Clement XI bequeathed the relics of Saint Clement the martyr to the main altar and in 1839, on the anniversary of the miracle, Gregory XVI promoted the chapel to the rank of church and opened it to the public once a year.

On that particular day, throughout the morning, the family allows people to go into the part of the palace housing the chapel. As the hours pass the few early morning habitués – close friends of the family or the saint's devotees – are replaced by a constant flow of curious visitors, fascinated and moved by the mysterious, reverential atmosphere characterising this ceremony, which is both intimate and solemn.

In the 16th century, the Massimo family owned three adjoining buildings, all of which are still standing today. The oldest of these is known as the Massimo Istoriato ("historiated" or illustrated) palace, because of the monochrome decorations of the Daniele da Volterra school gracing the façade overlooking Piazza de' Massimi. The Massimo di Pirro palace owes its name to a case of mistaken identity of a statue of Mars. The best known is however the Massimo alle Colonne, with its superb concave façade by Corso Vittorio, which Baldassarre Peruzzi built over the ruins of the *cavea* (tiered semicircular seating) of the Emperor Domitian's theatre.

CAPPELLA SPADA

San Girolamo della Carità
62 Via Monserrato
• Access from Piazza Santa Caterina della Rota
• Open Sundays 10:30am-12:30pm

Near Piazza Farnese, the church of San Girolamo della Carità is home to an unusual and little-known masterpiece of Baroque art, long attributed to Borromini.

> *Pivoting angel's wings lead to a little-known masterpiece*

The Spada chapel is the first on the right on entering the church by the main portal. It was decorated at the request of an influential Oratorian,* Virgilio Spada, who probably commissioned the architect Francesco Righi.

This chapel, whose originality lies in its superb polychrome marble, is separated from the church by a remarkable balustrade designed by Antonio Giorgetti, a pupil of Bernini. It consists of two statues of kneeling angels holding up a great sheet of jasper. Their wings are of wood, and those on the right pivot on hinges to allow access to the chapel. There is not much of note architecturally, but mosaic lovers will be enchanted by the interior. The veined jasper and precious marble suggest damask cloth embroidered with flowers, acanthus leaves, lilies, stars and swords, as if flowing over the floor and the smooth walls of the chapel. The last three of these motifs (lily, star and sword) are the symbols of the Spada family (*spada* being Italian for sword).

On either side of the altar (a simple block also decorated with mosaics of precious marble) are statues of Bernardino Spada (by Ercole Ferrata) and Giovanni Spada (by Cosimo Fancelli) recumbent on their respective tombs.

Tradition has it that this church was built on the very spot where the house of the widow Paula (who, in the 4th century AD, gave shelter to Saint Jerome) once stood. This was the house that Domenico Castelli rebuilt around the mid-17th century.

Before leaving the church, do not overlook the small and beautiful Antamoro chapel to the left of the high altar, the only work in Rome by Filippo Juvarra, and the statue of Saint Philip Neri by Pierre Legros.

SAINT PHILIP NERI'S CELL AT SAN GIROLAMO DELLA CARITÀ
Saint Philip lived for some thirty years in the convent of San Girolamo della Carità (an annex of the church).
His cell, which has been turned into a chapel, can still be seen. To book a visit, call 06 6879786.

* Member of the Congregation of Saint Philip Neri

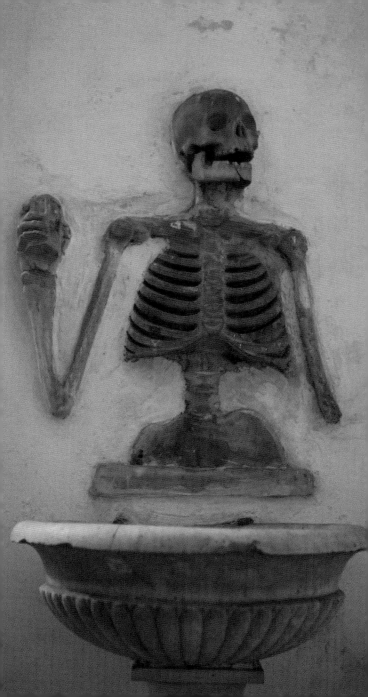

HYPOGEUM CEMETERY OF SANTA MARIA DELL'ORAZIONE E MORTE CHURCH

262 Via Giulia
- E-mail: billa.sapia@tiscali.it
- Daily tours, 4pm-6pm; Sundays, 4pm-7pm

"My turn today, yours tomorrow"

The church of Santa Maria dell'Orazione e Morte, seat of the arch brotherhood of the same name, overlooks Via Giulia opposite the Farnese arch. The façade bears a plaque featuring a skeleton who warns passers-by: *Hodie mihi, cras tibi* (literally, "Today for me, tomorrow for you").

Inside, having noted the decorations rich in necrological symbols, you enter the crypt via the sacristy, to the left of the master altar. You can also visit the remains of the ancient cemetery, the greater part of which was destroyed around 1870 during the construction of the barrier walls along the Tiber, the river waters having flooded the cells on more than one occasion. Two plaques still indicate the different levels that the water had reached inside the cemetery.

From 1552 to 1896, the brotherhood gathered over 8,000 bodies, a fair number of which were buried in this crypt. Wherever a body was found without a grave, in the depths of a bog, thrown up by the Tiber or the sea, or lying in the brush, the members of the brotherhood would recover it for holy burial.

Today, these galleries are like a boneyard in which the decorative artwork, crosses, sculptures and lamps have been made from bones and skeletons. In addition, the name of the deceased has been engraved on certain exposed skulls, with the date and sometimes the cause of death together with the place where the body was found.

ESOTERIC SYMBOLS AT PALAZZO FALCONIERI 🔞

Accademia d'Ungheria (Hungarian Academy)
1 Via Giulia
• Visits by appointment
• Reservations: 06 6889671
• Fax: 06 68805292

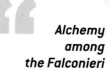

*Alchemy
among
the Falconieri*

Along the quiet Via Giulia, next to the church of Santa Maria dell'Orazione e Morte (Saint Mary of Prayer and Death), curious figures with a falcon's head and woman's breasts stand guard over Palazzo Falconieri. They are probably by Francesco Borromini, who in 1646 designed the beautiful three-arched loggia facing the Tiber.

The falcon's head is a dual allusion to the name Orazio Falconieri, who rebuilt the palace in the 17th century: the falcon was the symbol of the Falconieri (Italian for "falconers") family of Florentine origin; and the Egyptian god Horus (falcon-headed) recalled the name Orazio.

The figure of the falcon with its apparently female breasts is also an alchemical symbol of the "mercurial water" used in philosophical distillation in which the metal is washed to purify it (phase of alchemical sublimation).

Borromini also left his mark on the ceilings of the four salons on the first floor, decorated in stuccowork with symbolic elements of great complexity that fit into the alchemical tradition. The stuccos, which were originally in monochrome, were coloured in 1781 on the occasion of the marriage of Costanza Falconieri.

In the red salon, three intersecting laurel wreaths at the centre, traversed by sunbeams, symbolise the Trinity.

In the blue salon, the central oval shows a globe set upon the Earth with a sceptre arising from it (the axis of the world) and surmounted by an all-seeing eye (God). Behind the globe is the Ouroboros (tail-devouring snake), symbol of the eternal cycle of nature and the universal manifestation of God (see page 92) and a laurel wreath signifying the union of heaven (God) and Earth (man).

The last two salons, which are both green, have elegant decorations inspired by plant life.

Visitors should definitely go out onto the terrace for a magnificent view over the city, including the nearby gardens of Palazzo Farnese.

Palazzo Falconieri, which was the residence of Cardinal Fesch in the early 19th century, has been the seat of the Hungarian Academy since 1927.

See pages 92 and 93 for more on the Ouroboros.

THE OUROBOROS: A SYMBOL OF DIVINE ILLUMINATION

 The figure of a coiled serpent biting its own tail is sometimes found in iconography and literature. This symbol is traditionally known as the Ouroboros, a Greek word derived from the Coptic and Hebrew languages – *ouro* is Coptic for "king" and *ob* Hebrew for "serpent" – meaning "royal serpent". Thus the reptile raising its head above its body is used as a symbol of mystical illumination: for Eastern peoples, it represents the divine fire they call Kundalini.

Kundalini is the origin of the association that Western medicine of the Middle Ages and Renaissance made between, on the one hand, the body heat that rises from the base of the spine to the top of the head and, on the other, the *venena bibas* ("ingested venom" mentioned by Saint Benedict of Nursia) of the snake whose bite can only be treated by an equally potent poison. Just as the Eastern techniques of spiritual awakening, Dzogchen and Mahamudra, show how a meditating person must learn to "bite his tail like the serpent", the theme of the Ouroboros and ingested venom is a reminder that spiritual awareness can only result from a devout life: by elevating your consciousness onto a mental plane surpassing the ordinary, you search within to truly find yourself as an eternal being.

The Greeks popularised the word *ouroboros* in its literal sense of "serpent biting its tail". They acquired this image from the Phoenicians through contact with the Hebrews, who had themselves adopted it from Egypt where the Ouroboros featured on a stele dated as early as 1600 BC. There it represented the sun god Ra (Light), who resurrects life from the darkness of the night (synonymous with death), going back to the theme of eternal return, life, death, and the renewal of existence, as well as the reincarnation of souls in successive human bodies until they have reached their evolutionary peak, which will leave them perfect, both physically and spiritually – a theme dear to Eastern peoples.

In this sense, the serpent swallowing itself can also be interpreted as an interruption of the cycle of human development (represented by the serpent) in order to enter the cycle of spiritual evolution (represented by the circle).

Pythagoras associated the serpent with the mathematical concept of infinity, coiled up as zero – the abstract number used to denote eternity, which becomes reality when the Ouroboros is depicted turning around on itself.

Gnostic Christians identified it with the Holy Spirit revealed through wisdom to be the Creator of all things visible and invisible, and whose ultimate expression on Earth is Christ. For this reason, the symbol is associated in Greek Gnostic literature with the phrase *hen to pan* ("The All is One"); it was commonly adopted in the 4th and 5th centuries as a protective amulet against evil spirits and venomous snakebites. This amulet was known as Abraxas, the name of a god in the original Gnostic pantheon that the Egyptians recognised as Serapis. It became one of the most famous magical talismans of the Middle Ages.

Greek alchemists very quickly espoused the figure of the Ouroboros (or Uroboros) and so it reached the Hermetic philosophers of Alexandria – among them, Arab thinkers who studied and disseminated this image in their schools of Hermeticism and alchemy.

These schools were known and sought out by medieval Christians. There is even historical evidence that members of the Order of the Knights Templar, as well as other Christian mystics, travelled to Cairo, Syria and even Jerusalem to be initiated into the Hermetic sciences.

THE OPTICAL ILLUSION OF THE FOUNTAIN IN THE PIAZZA CAPODIFERRO ⓳

Piazza Capodiferro
• Tram: 8 – Arenula/Ministry of Justice stop

Borromini's other secret optical illusion

The "forced perspective" gallery commissioned by Francesco Borromini (1599–1667) in the Palazzo Spada is famous throughout the world. However, the elegant fountain in the Piazza Capodiferro – comprising the bust of a woman, an ancient sarcophagus and a small basin – also forms an optical illusion that is both spectacular and relatively unknown, the work of a great architect and sculptor from Ticino.

A supreme exponent of Roman Baroque, Borromini was commissioned by Cardinal Bernardino Spada to remodel his palace, the current seat of the Italian Council of State. He altered the interior of the complex, where he also created his famous perspective gallery outside. He was responsible for altering the grounds in front of the palace, which were in a neglected state. Here the great architect created his remarkable optical illusion, which was only revealed at the end of the 20th century.

The discovery was made during the restoration of the Palazzo Ossoli in the early 1990s. The restorers noticed that the façade of the building, near the Palazzo Spada, was completely covered with several layers of paint that hid an immense fresco, depicting a fake façade made of travertine blocks, known as "bossage" (the bosses in question were stones protruding from the building). At the centre of this *trompe-l'œil* façade, Borromini had carved out a (real) niche in which the "Erma" was placed – the bust of "a woman who, when she squeezed her breasts, caused water to gush out into the basin over which she stood". All trace of the original statue has been lost (a replacement was made in 1996 by the sculptor Giuseppe Ducrot).

Borromini needed one final element to complete his illusion: a special observation point. Since the Palazzo Spada also had an entrance on Via Giulia, he made sure that the path taken by visitors to the palazzo coincided with the optical axis in the direction of the fountain outside the palace. It may seem implausible, but this "guided view" penetrates through the courtyards of the palace, giving the observer the illusion of seeing the fountain inside the building, whereas in reality it is situated on the outside.

THE "NOBLE FLOOR" OF PALAZZO SPADA

13 Piazza Capo di Ferro
• Tel. 06 6832409
• Open the first Sunday of every month at 10:30am, 11:30am and 12:30pm
• Admission: €6 + entry ticket to Galleria Spada
• Tram: 8

> *A splendid palace open once a month*

Many curious passers-by go inside the courtyard of Palazzo Spada to admire the famous optical illusion created by Borromini, while lovers of 17th- and 18th-century paintings will have already contemplated those in the Spada Gallery, but very few also know of the palace's sumptuous *piano nobile* (literally "noble floor" in Italian – the main floor). The seat of the State Council, it is normally closed to the public except on the first Sunday of the month.

The palace, which was built at the behest of Cardinal Girolamo Capodiferro from 1548 onwards by the architect Bartolomeo Baronino, already had extraordinary paintings and stucco decorations decorating the Galleria degli Stucchi (Stucco Gallery) and the Sala delle Quattro Stagioni (Four Seasons Hall) of the main floor in 1550. Another extremely rich stucco decoration (by Giulio Mazzoni, Diego di Fiandra, Tommaso del Bosco and Leonardo Sormani) adorned the inner courtyard and the façade.

Cardinal Bernardino Spada acquired the palace in 1632, and commissioned painters, sculptors and architects with a series of new work. He extended the left wing of the palace onto Vicolo dell'Arco and the right wing onto Vicolo del Polverone, and created a painting gallery in four halls of the left wing of the main floor (these halls have remained intact and today are open to the public), but above all he gave expression to his passion for optics and astronomy.

The walls of the Salone di Pompeo (Pompey Hall), next to the Four Seasons Hall, are painted with distorted architectural perspectives. The adjoining Corridor of the Meridian, a catoptric sundial based on reflected light and not on shadow, was constructed by Father Emmanuel Maignan (see below) in 1644 or 1646, depending on the source.

There is another catoptric sundial at the convent of Trinità dei Monti (see page 27 for more information on this type of sundial).

THE MONTE DI PIETÀ CHAPEL

Piazza del Monte di Pietà
- Opening times: Mornings for private visits. Advance reservation is necessary by contacting Giovanni Innocenti by telephone at 06 67078495, or by fax at 06 67078112
- Tram: 8

A hidden Baroque jewel

Hidden behind a gate in the inner courtyard of the Palazzo del Monte di Pietà, this chapel covered in polychrome marble and stucco decorations is a jewel of Baroque architecture that remains almost unknown.

In 1639, the Monte di Pietà Archconfraternity commissioned Francesco Peperelli, an architect active in Rome during the first half of the 17th century, to carry out restructuring work on both the palace and the chapel. Giovanni Antonio de' Rossi took over from Peperelli, who died in 1641, and finished the work while respecting the original project.

On entering the small square atrium leading to the chapel, built between 1700 and 1702, one is struck by the beauty of the relief work by Michele Maglia in the centre of the oval-shaped vault, featuring the Eternal Father in Heaven surrounded by angels and garlands of flowers in golden stucco, by Andrea Berrettoni, Giovanni Maria Galli da Bibiena and Filippo Ferrari.

The atrium leads to the chapel, also oval-shaped. The gold stucco decorations and the shimmering colours of the marble covering the walls contrast with the white of the statues in their niches and the bas-reliefs on the altar and on the two side doors.

The statues representing the theological virtues Faith, Hope and Charity were the work of Francesco Moderati, Augusto Cornacchini and Giuseppe Mazzuoli respectively, and are accompanied by a contribution from Bernardino Cametti, symbolising *Alms* given by the confraternity to the needy. The extraordinary bas-relief on the altar is of a unique shape. It was created by Domenico Guidi in 1676 and it represents *Mercy*.

The two other beautiful bas-reliefs on the left and right sides of the altar represent *Tobias and the Angel*, a work by Pierre Le Gros, and *Joseph in Egypt*, by Jean-Baptiste Théodon.

The vault was decorated in 1696, based on a project by the architect Francesco Bizzacheri, with cornices, shells and plant ornaments in gilded stucco that join up with white stucco medallions by Michele Maglia, Lorenzo Ottoni and Simone Giorgini, depicting the main events surrounding the birth of the Monte di Pietà.

BEES AT THE CASA GRANDE

At the junction of Via dell'Arco del Monte and Via dei Giubbonari

> ## *Barberini bees on the family's main residence*

From the Via dei Giubbonari shopping street, the Casa Grande – the first palace built by the Barberini family – almost goes unnoticed. Their emblem of three bees features only at one corner of the building on the second floor, as a reminder that here stands a grand property of the prestigious Roman dynasty.

The Casa Grande grew out of the cumulative purchase of nearby properties and so has never been detached from the other buildings, as was Palazzo Farnese for example. This is why the first-floor windows and doors overlooking the street are of different sizes and shapes. The building is only unified from the first floor upwards. The properties purchased one after the other were not demolished but altered and adapted to the structure to which they were attached. This residence clearly shows the "cannibalisation" of Roman palazzos within their surroundings (which would become less obvious over time).

The presence of the Barberinis is also marked at the main entrance, in Piazza del Monte di Pietà, by bees on a frieze.

ABANDONMENT OF A GREAT PALACE

At a time when a residence acquired prestige and dignity if it was part of a larger urban plan, the Casa Grande seemed rather cramped in the narrow crowded streets of the Regola neighbourhood. A fire providentially led to the creation of the small Piazza dei Librai, and another space was opened up in front of Monte di Pietà, but the Barberinis' great project was to run a street through to the church of Sant'Andrea della Valle, where the family still have a chapel. Unfortunately for them, the Theatre of Pompey stands between the two, so nothing could be done. The family relocated to the Quirinal Hill, and the palazzo was sold and passed from hand to hand until the municipality took it over. It now accommodates offices, schools and the historic city-centre office of the Italian Communist Party.

THE ABANDONED INFANTS BAS-RELIEF ㉓

22 Via delle Zoccolette

Abandoned girls destined to become prostitutes?

A remarkable bas-relief set into the wall of 22 Via delle Zoccolette shows two swaddled infants. It commemorates an orphanage, now demolished, that used to take in abandoned children and give them an education.

The Palazzo dei "Cento Preti", built in 1576 by Domenico Fontana on the banks of the Tiber, was run by the congregation of that name as a hospice for beggars who had dedicated their life to Saint Francis. When the congregation moved elsewhere in 1715, the hospice became a church hospital, but the rear section giving onto Via delle Zoccolette was used as an orphanage. Among other domestic duties, girls learned embroidery, which could, if they had the opportunity, help them find a husband.

The name of the street also comes from the former orphanage, *zoccolette* meaning abandoned infants in the Roman dialect.

There are two versions of the source of this name. According to the first, the street is named after the little clogs (*zoccoli*) that the children wore, whereas the second more common theory is that *zoccolette* used to designate

prostitutes in Rome, as it does in the Neapolitan dialect.

The term, through sympathy rather than malice, is thought to have been extended to the abandoned young girls who were condemned to end up walking the streets themselves, if they found neither work nor husband. Or the name could simply be due to the fact that some of the abandoned children were born to prostitutes.

For further information on abandoned children, see the article on the foundlings' wheel (see page 191).

CENTRE SOUTH

CRYPT OF THE PAPAL ENTRAILS

①

Church of Santi Vincenzo e Anastasio
73 Vicolo dei Modelli
• Open daily 9am-8pm

> **A practice
> that lasted
> from 1590 until
> the time of Pius X**

The church of Saints Vincent and Anastasius, which was built opposite the Trevi Fountain as a parish church to serve what was then the pontifical Quirinal Palace nearby, has the distinction of preserving the entrails and hearts (or more precisely the *praecordium*, the lower thorax over the heart) extracted from the bodies of popes at the time of embalming. They are kept in porphyry urns, jealously guarded in a crypt behind the apse.

The remains belong to twenty-three popes, as listed on two marble plaques on the wall. Sixtus V, who died in 1590, was the first to "inaugurate" this practice, which continued until the death of Leo XIII in 1903. Pope Pius X (1903-1914) put an end to it.

The operation took place at the Quirinal Palace in the so-called Sala del Balcone (Balcony Room), from where the election of the new pontiff was also announced. On the very evening of embalming, the viscera were solemnly carried to the church by the pope's personal chaplain and placed in the crypt. Only Pope Innocent XI asked that his urn should be deposited in another part of the church, in the chapel of the Vergine delle Grazie (Our Lady of Graces), whom he particularly revered.

A HIDDEN DOOR

On the extreme left of the façade, behind the last column, lies a small door that leads to what is surely Rome's smallest shop.

The door is so narrow that you have to go in sideways and the shop can only accommodate one person at a time.

A shoemaker once worked here whose tasks included resoling the sandals of the church brethren and consequently he was exempted from rent. A florist took over from him.

Today, street vendors use it to store their goods.

A LAY WOMAN ON A CHURCH FAÇADE

On the façade of the church of Saints Vincent and Anastasius, note the statues of women, their arms raised in triumph and bearing the emblem of Cardinal Jules Mazarin, who had the church built.

The presence of these female figures with their naked torsos is quite a shock. Also questionable is the female portrait bust in the foreground. Seemingly, although this is not proven, it represents one of the cardinal's nieces, Marie Mancini, mistress of King Louis XIV, or perhaps her sister Hortense, known for her amorous affairs. Whatever the truth, this is a very rare example of the figure of a lay woman on a church façade.

THE STAG OF SANT'EUSTACHIO CHURCH ❷

Piazza Sant'Eustachio

> **A stag's head in place of Christ's cross**

A vigilant pedestrian looking upwards in Piazza Sant'Eustachio might notice a curious detail: instead of the traditional Christian cross that surmounts churches the world over, the church of Sant'Eustachio is crowned with a stag's head, with a cross on top of it.

This curiosity owes its existence to the life of St Eustace, who converted to Christianity when he encountered a stag with a crucifix between its antlers.

SAINT EUSTACE

Martyred in Rome around AD 130, St Eustace was originally named Placidus. After his conversion he took the name Eustace (Latin Eustachius), which signifies "constancy". His feast day is 20 September, believed to be the day of his death.

On his way to hunt in the forest one day, Placidus, a well-respected Roman soldier, came across a herd of deer, one of which seemed larger and more splendid than the others. He approached the herd to kill the stag and noticed that he bore a crucifix in his antlers. A divine voice spoke to the soldier, saying that it had come to save him. In the face of this miracle, and because his wife had had a similar dream the night before, the whole family was baptized.

Returning the next morning to the scene of the miracle, Eustace once again had a vision of Christ, who informed the saint that he was going to be put to the test but that Christ would never forsake him.

A few days later, plague overwhelmed the region. St Eustace lost his troops and his home was raided. He and his family fled to Egypt. His wife was held for ransom by the owner of the boat making the crossing, but Eustace journeyed on with his two children who were soon taken by wild animals, one by a lion and the other by a wolf. After some years, the family was finally reunited. His wife had not after all been defiled by the boat's captain, and the children had been saved by villagers. After refusing to sacrifice to pagan gods, however, the family was put to death by the Emperor Hadrian.

The same miracle was later attributed to St Hubert, who became patron saint of hunters.

ROSE PETALS AT THE PANTHEON ❸

Church of Santa Maria dei Martiri (Pantheon)
• Pentecostal Mass

> *A shower
> of red petals
> from the Pantheon
> oculus*

At the Pentecostal Mass celebrated in the church of the Pantheon, the faithful are treated to an amazing spectacle. At the end of the service, thousands of red rose petals rain down on them through the central opening in the vault. This Christian tradition, which is rarely practised today, dates back many centuries to when the early Christians associated the rose with the Holy Spirit and the colour red with the blood shed by Christ for the redemption of mankind. At Pentecost, which is celebrated fifty days after Easter, red petals symbolising the descent of the Holy Spirit were thrown from the ceilings of churches upon the believers below. This explains why the festival was also known as "Easter dew". After being suspended for many years, the ceremony was reintroduced at the Pantheon in 1995.

NEARBY

PLAQUE CONDEMNING THE "VILE TAVERNS AND THEIR LOATHSOME UGLINESS" ❹
Piazza della Rotonda

The superb Piazza della Rotonda is heaving with restaurants. This phenomenon is not new and Pope Pius VII (1800-1823) had already tried to solve the problem. A large marble plaque still testifies to his efforts in this direction. The gist of the proclamation is: "Pius VII, *pontifex maximus*, in the twenty-third year of his pontificate, on the square in front of M. Agrippa's Pantheon, occupied by vile taverns, justifies their providential demolition on account of their loathsome ugliness". And it goes on: "and orders that the view should be left unhindered". This explicit message is a reminder of Pius VII's urban renewal schemes. Ironically, the marble slab is now fixed above one of the restaurants that have once again invaded the square.

SCAR ON A MARBLE COLUMN

Via della Spada di Orlando

⑤

A small street leading into Piazza Capranica, near the Pantheon, bears traces of the knight Roland (Orlando in Italian) when he passed through Rome. Actually, it's more than just a trace; it's a "scar" left by his legendary sword Durandal on a marble column.

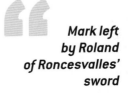

> *Mark left by Roland of Roncesvalles' sword*

Charlemagne's paladin, who was visiting the city, was engaged in a brawl with some Roman knights. Given their number, Roland was forced to draw his sword – his attackers soon fled. During the fight, one of his blows struck a block of marble and split it in two. Today it is still easy to imagine Durandal's magical powers – or Roland's strength – in this little street that was subsequently named "Street of the Sword of Roland".

This marble column belongs to a larger group which includes the remains of a nearby ancient wall, clearly visible where it slightly encroaches on the street from the overhanging medieval building. These are the ruins of the Temple of Matidia, built by Emperor Hadrian in AD 119 in honour of his mother-in-law.

Two other columns, an impressive 1.7 metres in diameter and 17 metres high, are incorporated in the façade of the house at No. 17 Piazza Capranica.

ACCADEMIA D'ARMI MUSUMECI GRECO

87 Via del Seminario
• To book a visit, email accademia@accademiagreco.it, call Monday to
Friday between 4pm and 7pm (06 6791846) or ask at the entrance
• Tram: 8; Bus: 64 – Torre Argentina

*A shrine
to fencing*

On the first floor of No. 87 Via del
Seminario is one of the oldest arms
schools in the world, a meeting place
for fencing enthusiasts who come here to
train. Dozens of awards, prizes, vintage
photos and portraits – including the mafia
boss Salvatore Greco in an eye-catching Garibaldian red shirt – hang on the
walls. The room where fencers can cross swords on three different platforms
is decorated with an extensive collection of blades and, on the wood-panelled
walls, there are traces of past cuts and thrusts that had missed their targets.

The most disparate characters, such as Gabriele D'Annunzio, Mussolini,
Roman dialect poet Trilussa and President of the Italian Republic Luigi
Einaudi, have passed through here as spectators or students, united by their
passion for the noble art.

It is also here that the best-known actors of the past seventy years, from
Tyrone Power to Errol Flynn, Gina Lollobrigida to Charlton Heston, Burt
Lancaster to Richard Burton, have learned to handle their weapons for big-
budget films.

The current master-at-arms, Renzo Musumeci Greco, represents the fourth
generation of a family that has made fencing its *raison d'être*.

This all began in 1878, when the Garibaldian hero Marquis Salvatore Greco
dei Chiaramonte decided to open an arms academy in a 15th-century palace
near the Pantheon. His sons, Agesilao and Aurelio, took over the business and
passed it on to their sister's son, Enzo. In the late 1930s, Enzo developed the
master-at-arms role for the cinema: it was the early days of great epic films

and actors had to learn the basic
techniques of wielding a sword
or sabre. In the 1970s Renzo
took over the school founded
by his great-grandfather and
developed the business to cover
theatre, musicals, opera and TV
soaps.

THE CHURCH OF SANT'IGNAZIO

Piazza di Sant'Ignazio
- Opening times: Monday to Sunday 7:30am-12:30pm and 3pm-7:30pm
- Metro: A – Spagna or Barberini
- Bus: 116, 116T

A flat dome

Founded by Cardinal Ludovisi in 1626 and built in several phases until 1662, the church of Sant'Ignazio has a peculiar aspect that goes unnoticed by almost all visitors: the cupola, which at first glance is nothing special as regards its decoration and dimensions, was in fact never built because of technical problems. The circular space for the dome, which is in fact flat, was painted using the *trompe-l'oeil* technique by Father Andrea Pozzo. This work, known as the *Gloria di Sant'Ignazio* (Glory of Saint Ignatius) was painted in the vault of the nave with impressive perspective. The sensation felt once inside the church is strange, walking from the centre of the nave in the direction of the altar while looking at the skylight of the cupola. Little by little as you approach, the initial perspective no longer works and you realise that there is, in fact, no cupola.

NEARBY

THE APARTMENTS OF SAINT ALOYSIUS GONZAGA
- Tours by appointment (tel: 06 6794406), minimum 2 € per person

A lift next to the sacristy entrance of the church of Sant'Ignazio (Saint Ignatius of Loyola) leads to the apartments of Saint Aloysius Gonzaga. The way up there is an unforgettable experience, with a wonderful view over the Roman roofs overlooking the courtyard of the Collegio Romano: on the top floor are the rooms reserved for Jesuit students at the time when Gonzaga lived there, from 1587 to 1590. The first part of the visit takes in what used to be the students' recreation room, now decorated with scenes from the life of the saint. Next are the chapel and other rooms with altars, in one of which his relics are kept in a glass case.

THE MONUMENTAL HALL OF COLLEGIO ROMANO

9

27 Via del Collegio Romano
• Tel: 06 6797877
• Open Tuesdays, Wednesdays and Thursdays 9:30am-1:30pm

" *An exceptional, little-known library*

Lovers of art or archaeology, ancient books and great Baroque library enthusiasts, will take great pleasure in exploring the spectacular Sala Crociera (cruciform hall) of Collegio Romano, or even studying in the sumptuous reading room attached to it.

The immense hall in the form of a cross, as its name indicates, is disconcertingly beautiful. The walls that form the arms of the cross are entirely covered in books, most of them ancient and rare. The superb shelving where they are stacked was built especially for the library in the 17th century, at the time when the hall was the main library of the college founded by Saint Ignatius of Loyola and modelled on the University of Paris.

More recently, this hall and the adjoining reading room were part of the National Library of Rome, until the latter moved into its present site at Castro Pretorio.

Since 1989, these halls have been occupied by the Library of Archaeology and History of Art, and the collection includes a vast number of volumes donated by archaeologists, art and architecture historians, as well as a collection of art gallery catalogues, with sections devoted to theatre, music, heraldry and Oriental art, besides an exceptional collection of catalogues from the principal salerooms dating from the 19th century onwards.

MUSEO ATHANASIUS KIRCHER

Collegio Romano
4 Piazza del Collegio Romano
• Tel: 06 6792425
• E-mail: rmpc080007@istruzione.it
• Guided tours can be booked by writing to the Ennio Quirino Visconti
Liceo (15 days before requested date of visit)

> *Remains of a fantastic cabinet of curiosities*

The Roman College was built between 1582 and 1584 by the architect Bartolomeo Ammannati (although some attribute it to the Jesuit Giuseppe Valeriani) thanks to Pope Gregory XIII, the "founding father and protector" of the institution. It was the seat of one of the largest universities of Baroque Rome, inspired by the free school of grammar and Christian doctrine conceived in 1551 by Ignatius of Loyola, founder of the Jesuits. Today the buildings are shared by the Visconti high school, the Ministry of Culture and the research unit for climatology and meteorology.

Among its teachers, the college – which was witness to the learned debates between Galileo and Segneri – counted scientists such as Clavius, who helped draw up the Gregorian calendar, and Athanasius Kircher, polymath and creator in 1651 of a *Wunderkammer*, a cabinet of curiosities that was famous throughout Europe. In the Athanasius Kircher Museum works of art rubbed shoulders with scientific instruments, specimens from the natural world and all kinds of rare and curious objects, such as a stone from the tower of Babel, obviously of rather dubious authenticity ...

The collections were dispersed for the first time during the suppression of the Jesuits (1773) and were then scattered throughout various Roman museums during the fascist era. Today only a fraction of them can be seen in the small high-school museum that was opened in 1870 and enriched by acquisitions of the 18th and 19th centuries. The great hall houses mineralogical and natural specimens (such as the skeleton of a newborn child), most of which came from the Antonio Neviani collection.

A room on the top floor has an interesting collection of scientific instruments, an 18th-century sperm pouch (!) and most notably the six wooden obelisks used by Kircher to illustrate his Egyptology lessons. Three of these are faithful scale models of the obelisks at the Lateran, Flaminio and Villa Medici. The fourth is an invention of Kircher's and bears a dedication to Pope Clement IX, beneath which an earlier dedication to Queen Christina of Sweden has been found. The other two obelisks have no inscriptions. As a known expert on the subject, Kircher collaborated with Bernini on the Fontana dei Quattro Fiumi (Fountain of the Four Rivers) in Piazza Navona and was convinced he had found the secret of interpreting hieroglyphs.

BIBLIOTECA CASANATENSE ⑪

52 Via Sant'Ignazio
• Tel: 06 69760328 or 06 69760334
• promozione.casanatense@biblioroma.sbn.it
• Closed Sundays, 2nd and 3rd weeks of August
• Free guided tours on request

A sumptuous monumental hall

With the exception of employees and a few researchers, hardly anyone knows that the sumptuous Casanatense Library is open regularly to the public for regular exhibitions, conferences, performances and concerts, and can even be visited free of charge upon request.

This library was founded by the Dominican friars of the Monastery of Santa Maria sopra Minerva in Rome at the request of Cardinal Girolamo Casanate, and inaugurated in 1701 in a structure within the Minerva cloister specially designed by the architect A. M. Borioni.

To the 25,000 original volumes that the cardinal bequeathed to the library were added many others acquired by the Dominicans over the years. Through their contacts with the main European booksellers, they sought out both antique and modern volumes to build up a "universal library" of texts on

theology, economics and Roman law, as well as other scientific and artistic works.

In 1884, the Dominican librarians were finally replaced by civil servants when the library was forfeited to the Italian state. Since then it has formed part of the Ministry of Culture with a collection of over 350,000 works.

The splendid *salone* (hall), measuring 60.15 by 15.30 metres, is home to some 55,000 illustrated works dating from the 16th to the 18th centuries, displayed on magnificent wooden shelves built by the sculptor Marchesi and the gilder Cantoni to a design by Borioni. The shelving, divided by a single gallery halfway up, covers the walls from floor to ceiling, bathed in a perfectly uniform flood of light from the windows pierced in the vaulting above.

The coat of arms of the Casanate family can be seen (a tower surmounted by an eight-pointed star), the same symbol found on the library decorations and stamped on each object in the collection. This includes two magnificent 18th-century globes (the Earth and the Heavens), drawn in pen and wash by Abbot Moroncelli, a celebrated cosmographer, geographer and topographer, as well as an ancient copper armillary sphere surmounting the statue of Cardinal Casanate, created in 1708 by the French sculptor Pierre Le Gros.

> Note, to the right of the entrance, the series of *trompe-l'œil* works that forms part of a door, often left open, behind which is concealed a spiral staircase.

THE HIDDEN SYMBOLISM OF BERNINI'S ELEPHANT-OBELISK ⓬

Piazza della Minerva

> **A symbol of the resurrection of the body**

Although Bernini's curious elephant-obelisk is of course famous in Rome, its symbolism is much less well-known. Why did Bernini design such an unusual sculpture? What does it signify? Bernini's design for the base of the obelisk, a stone elephant, is very similar to an engraving that appeared in *Hypnerotomachia Poliphili* (Poliphilo's Dream of the Strife of Love), the extraordinary Renaissance *roman-à-clef* published in Venice in 1499 (portraying well-known real people disguised as fictional characters — see the following double-page spread). While for the Egyptians, the obelisk symbolised the "divine rays of the Sun", the great mass of the elephant symbolised the Earth. With its trunk, it draws up water (the rain) which flows through the interior; the Earth is nourished, and with the help of the Sun (the obelisk) which traverses the Earth (the elephant), the grain is fertilised, so that it can be reborn and flourish. In the text that inspired Bernini, the reader enters the elephant, inside of which a man and a woman are represented. The full force of the symbol is thus revealed: besides the grain which is reborn and fertilised, the elephant-obelisk symbolises the resurrection of the body, a belief transmitted by the Egyptians (notably in the Book of the Dead) to the Hebrews and Christians to become a central element of Christianity. At the Last Judgment (like the biblical Jonah who emerges from the belly of the whale), man will leave the Earth to rise again from the dead. Pope Alexander VII, who commissioned the monument from Bernini in 1667, to be erected on the site of a former Temple of Isis, possessed a copy (annotated in his own hand) of *Hypnerotomachia Poliphili* and it was he who had the Latin phrase inscribed on the base recalling the immense wisdom passed down from ancient Egypt.* Remember that in Christian doctrine, the resurrection of Christ foreshadows that of all men and women at the Last Judgment. Finally, the Bernini sculpture also bears an eight-pointed star. The figure 8, for Christians, is the symbol of resurrection.

There is another elephant bearing an Egyptian obelisk at Catania, Sicily.

*Sapientis Ægypti / insculptas obelisco figuras / ab elephanto / belluarum fortissima / gestari quisquis hic vides / documentum intellige / robustae mentis esse / solidam sapientiam sustinere [These symbols of the science of Egypt, which you see engraved on the obelisk borne by the elephant, the most powerful of all animals, take them as the precept that a strong mind is needed to support a solid knowledge]

THE UNREQUITED LOVE OF LORENZO DE' MEDICI: AN INSPIRATION FOR POLIPHILO AND SHAKESPEARE?

The doomed love affair of Lorenzo de' Medici and Lucrezia Donati (who was married to Niccolo Ardinghelli against her will) seems to have directly inspired Poliphilo's quest: same name, same events, same timescale (1462-1464) ...

The love life of Lorenzo the Magnificent is also thought to have provided the material for Francesco Cei, a poet close to Lorenzo, in his poem *Giulia e Romeo* which directly inspired Shakespeare to write the famous *Romeo and Juliet*.

POLIPHILO'S DREAM OF THE STRIFE OF LOVE, AN EXTRAORDINARY HUMANIST ROMANCE THAT DIRECTLY INSPIRED THE GARDENS OF VERSAILLES, BOBOLI (FLORENCE) AND BERNINI'S CELEBRATED ELEPHANT-OBELISK IN ROME

Printed by Aldus Manutius in Venice in 1499, *Hypnerotomachia Poliphili* (Poliphilo's Dream of the Strife of Love) is perhaps the most complex *roman-à-clef* ever published. Illustrated with around 170 exquisite woodcuts, it is also considered one of the finest examples of early printing. The book, written in a mixture of Italian, Latin, Greek, Hebrew, Arabic, Spanish, Venetian and a few other dialects, was long considered anonymous. Recent research, however, chiefly led by Emanuela Kretzulesco,* has pointed to Francesco Colonna, as the decorative first letters of each of the 38 chapters spell out the following phrase: *Poliam Frater Franciscus Columna peramavit* ("Brother Francesco Colonna dearly loved Polia"). A nephew of Cardinal Prospero Colonna, Francesco Colonna was part of the circle of Enlightenment figures that included Cardinal Bessarion, the future Pope Pius II and Nicholas V, known as the Renaissance Pope, opposed to the succeeding popes and in particular to Alexander VI Borgia. At a time when the Borgias, against the advice of Pius II and Nicholas V, were seeking to grant the pontiff temporal as well as spiritual power, and the papacy was embarking on a dark period of its history, *Poliphilo's Dream* was consequently rendered deliberately obscure in order to escape papal censure. More than a story of Poliphilo's love for Lucrezia, the book is a spiritual quest of a philosopher passionately devoted to divine wisdom (Athena Polias). Developing humanist themes, he transmitted in a cryptic way the spiritual testament of a circle of theologians united around Nicholas V, who had undertaken comparative studies of religious traditions going back to ancient Greece and Egypt with great openness of mind, thus reviving the heritage of Pope Sylvester II (Gerbert of Aurillac). In concurrence with the Florentine Platonic Academy of the Medici and Marsilio Ficino, this group notably included the architect Leon Battista Alberti and Prospero Colonna, as well as being a great inspiration to Pico della Mirandola, Leonardo da Vinci, Nicolaus Copernicus, Giordano Bruno and Galileo.

Poliphilo's Dream reveals that the best way to know God is through Nature, divine creation. With the help of the codes held in the *Hyeroglyphica* of Horus Apollo (Horapollo), it also illuminates the spiritual road that leads there. In an absolutely extraordinary fashion for anyone interested in understanding the background against which *Poliphilo's Dream* evolved, it is clear that it also closely inspired the gardens of Versailles or Boboli in Florence, as well as Bernini's celebrated elephant-obelisk in Rome through the numerous symbols scattered along Poliphilo's route.

WHAT DOES *HYPNEROTOMACHIA* MEAN?

The etymology of the term *Hypnerotomachia* is based on the following Greek words: *hypnos* (sleep), *eros* (love), and *mache* (fight).

*Les Jardins du songe. Poliphile et la mystique de la Renaissance. Paris, Magma (only in French and Spanish).

FLOOD PLAQUES
AT THE CHURCH OF SANTA MARIA SOPRA MINERVA

Piazza della Minerva

> *Why are there so many flood plaques at Santa Maria sopra Minerva?*

The right-hand wall of the main façade of Santa Maria sopra Minerva, almost on the corner of Via Caterina da Siena, is dotted with plaques commemorating past floods in the neighbourhood. As the church stands close to the Pantheon, in one of the lowest parts of the city, it was very susceptible to flooding.

Although the Pantheon is not very near the river, flood water often reached Piazza della Rotonda (the square in front of the Pantheon) via the Cloaca Maxima, the famous sewer of ancient Rome (whose system of underground drains still exists today).

THE OLDEST FLOOD PLAQUE IN ROME

The small arch at the end of Via dell'Arco dei Banchi, near the river on the opposite bank to Castel Sant'Angelo, still bears, on its left side, what may be Rome's oldest surviving evidence of a Tiber flood. A marble plaque gives not only the level reached by the water, but also the exact date and duration of the event: "As far as here the Tiber came but, agitated, it quickly subsided, in the year of Our Lord 1277 ... the 7th day of the month of November." This plaque was formerly on the wall of the church of Santi Celso e Giuliano (Saints Celsus and Julian).

122 COMMEMORATIVE FLOOD PLAQUES

It is estimated that in 1937 Rome had 122 plaques commemorating its floods, most dating from the 16th and 17th centuries. Many were lost to urban development but you can still see some interesting examples around the city. Sometimes they consist of a single line and a date (such as the plaque on the church of San Bartolomeo on the Isola Tiberina dating from 1937). But they can also be more elaborate – perhaps triangular or rectangular, with a boat motif or with a hand to indicate the level the water had reached (as in Via Antonio Canova and Via dell'Arancio), with the date and perhaps a brief comment.

WHY WERE THERE SUCH FREQUENT FLOODS?

As the riverbanks had no protective walls, Rome was regularly flooded during the rainy season, especially as the river varied in width as it flowed through the city.

There were two points at which the flow was restricted. The first was near Castel Sant'Angelo, where Pope Alexander VI had added a large tower in the late 15th century (demolished in 1628).

These alterations on the west bank had left a small pile of earth and two of the bridge's arches were blocked.

The current was particularly strong at this point because of the two bends in the river, but although the bridge had not been reinforced since the 2nd century, Ponte Sant'Angelo, built to the exacting standards of the time, withstood it.

The second narrow spot was near Villa Farnesina, the Farnese family's grand property in Trastevere, where extensions to the gardens had over the years encroached on the river.

Huge numbers of boats were also moored all along the banks. When the river was in flood, some would break away and jam under the nearest bridge, clogging up the stream and aggravating the problem.

After the last series of floods in 1870 (recorded on numerous plaques), the decision was taken to build the *muraglioni* (high protective walls), about 12 metres high; construction began in 1876.

The water-level gauge at Largo San Rocco (see page 39) and the columns of the former port of Ripetta (see page 41) also carry flood records.

HIDDEN SYMBOLISM OF THE TOMB OF ANDREA BREGNO

⓮

Church of Santa Maria sopra Minerva
Piazza della Minerva

> *A "Masonic" grave in a Roman Catholic church?*

Andrea Bregno (1418-1506) was the major representative of Lombard sculpture in the 15th century. His epitaph – probably the work of Luigi Capponi (1506) – compares him with the Greek sculptor Polyclitus of Argos (*c.* 460-410 BC), testimony to the immense reputation he had acquired.

His tomb in the church of Santa Maria sopra Minerva (left aisle, not far from the altar) has some remarkable symbols: to the left of his portrait bust, an open compass standing upright on a set-square is the starting point for a plumbline that passes through a lozenge containing a six-pointed star and pierces the central square of a set of three.

Symbolically, the compass represents the Spirit or supreme Spiritual Condition and the line is the one that aligns the Spiritual World to the Physical World. The hexagram (formed from two intersecting triangles) symbolises the World of the Soul or the equilibrium between the two states of Spirit and Matter. Finally, the triple square is the classic primitive representation of the Terrestrial Paradise linked to the Heavenly Jerusalem (or Spiritual World), indicated by the compass.

The message of this allegorical group seems to be that Andrea Bregno, having lived in the beauty of the Terrestrial Paradise (as borne out by his many sublime artistic works), has returned to the Heavenly Jerusalem.

To the right of Bregno's bust, the compass (in its medieval form) over a set-square and ruler, all of which are again connected by a plumbline and level, represents the perfection of his work in equilibrium and the absence of inaccuracy and discord.

The plumbline motif is repeated vertically on the identical side friezes, running through various instruments of the sculptor's art (mallet, ruler, hammer, chisel, etc.): a lovely allegory and a reminder that Bregno was a master sculptor and architect, his work always totally accurate and perfect.

Although nowadays this symbolism reminds us of the conventional Masonic symbols, in Bregno's time they were principally the symbols used by the master masons of the late Middle Ages, who paved the way for modern Freemasonry.

SANCTUARY OF OUR LADY OF THE SMALL ARCH

Via di San Marcello
• Opening times: Monday to Saturday 6pm - 8pm for the recital of the rosary; Sunday 11am and 7pm for mass

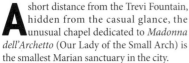

Virgin's eyes

A short distance from the Trevi Fountain, hidden from the casual glance, the unusual chapel dedicated to *Madonna dell'Archetto* (Our Lady of the Small Arch) is the smallest Marian sanctuary in the city.

The narrow street that joined Via di San Marcello to Via Dell'Archetto had a picture of the Virgin Mary painted on its wall. Domenico Muratori, a painter from Bologna and a student of Carracci, painted this picture for the marchioness Savorelli Papazzurri in 1690.

In 1696, the Virgin miraculously moved her eyes and the owner decided to display her within the street's arch for public veneration. In 1751, it was decided to close the entrances to the street with two gates, in order to protect the precious offerings that had accumulated. In 1796, the miracle, which was witnessed by several people, took place again and was recognised by the Church. In the middle of

the 19th century, the street was finally closed off completely and made into a chapel. The Savorelli Papazzurri family commissioned the architect Virginio Vespignani to build a small sanctuary, a jewel of neo-Renaissance art. It was solemnly inaugurated on 31 May 1851. The small temple, declared a national art monument and yet relatively unknown, contains sculptures by Luigi Simonetti and encaustic paintings by Costantino Brumidi, who, using the same technique, also painted the *Apotheosis of George Washington* fresco and became known as the "Michelangelo of the United States Capitol".

HIDDEN MESSAGE OF THE HOLY APOSTLES ⓰

Basilica dei Santi Apostoli
Piazza dei Santi Apostoli

> *A discreet tribute to spare the pope's susceptibilities ...*

The ancient basilica of the Holy Apostles has been altered several times, even rebuilt, and Pope Sixtus IV added the imposing portico that opens onto the square. It is now crowned with 13 statues of Jesus and the Apostles. A letter is engraved on the pedestal of each statue, forming a strange series as these letters do not use the traditional abbreviations found on ancient monuments and, *a priori*, have no connection with the figures of the saints above.

The series of letters (**F L D L C S O T C E C V B**) is actually a "tribute" to

Cardinal Lorenzo Brancati di Lauria, tutor at the monastery of Santi Apostoli, who donated the sculptures.

This theologian, who was close to Pope Alexander VII and adviser to the "Congregation of the Apostolic Visitation", was librarian at the Vatican and he commissioned and paid for the statues. Although his gift was probably disinterested, as the donor he still wished to go down in posterity, so rather than having an inscription that was too ostentatious or self-serving and might have hurt the pontifical feelings, he devised this little puzzle:

Frater Laurentius De Laureolo Consultor Sancti Officii Theologus Cardinalis Episcopus Custos Vaticanae Bibliothecae (Brother Lorenzo de Laureolo, adviser, theologian of the Holy Office, cardinal, bishop, librarian of the Vatican library).

Michelangelo was laid to rest for a time at Santi Apostoli before his tomb was moved to the basilica of Santa Croce in Florence, which is a sort of pantheon to "illustrious Italians".

PRINCESS ISABELLE'S APARTMENT

Colonna Gallery
66 Piazza Santi Apostoli
• Tel: 06 6784350 or 06 6794362
• Colonna Gallery is open on Saturday mornings from 9am - 1pm
• The apartments are open for private visits every day, all year round except August, for a minimum of 10 people. Specialised guides available on request
• Admission: €7
• Metro: A – Spagna or B – Colosseo

A fantastic private visit

The gallery of Palazzo Colonna is certainly one of the most precious of Italy's artistic treasures and only insiders know that since 1946 it has been open to visitors once a week. Its extraordinary beauty can be enjoyed on Saturday mornings, by going through a small entrance hidden in the beautiful Via della Pilotta. Nor do many people know that while on private visits to the gallery, you can gain access to the rest of the palace. By contacting the palace administration and booking a private visit, it is possible to admire, alone and undisturbed, parts of the palace that are closed to the public: the gallery, a series of adjacent rooms and the apartment of Princess Isabelle Sursock Colonna, who lived here until the end of the 1980s. This last visit is a unique experience: in the rooms of the apartment facing the interior garden some extraordinary art is to be found, such as the frescoes by the renowned painter Bernardino di Betto, known as Pinturicchio, refined works of Flemish masters, including engravings by Jan Bruegel the Elder, the rich collection of views by Gaspard Van Wittel, known in Italy as di Vanvitelli, and the decorations of Gaspard Dughet, Crescenzio Onofri, Cavalier Tempesta, Giacinto Gimignani and Carlo Cesi.

THE PALAZZO COLONNA CANNON BALL

Fired from the Janiculum Hill during a confrontation between French troops and Garibaldi's soldiers defending the Roman Republic in 1849, a cannon ball can amazingly still be seen on the grand staircase linking the two levels of the Palazzo Colonna gallery.
The projectile shattered one of the great windows and flew across the gallery before wedging itself in the steps, where the palace owners have left it as a reminder of the incident.

THE HOLY FACE OF JESUS AT SANTO STEFANO DEL CACCO

Church of Santo Stefano del Cacco
26 Via Santo Stefano del Cacco
• Tel: 338 3478858
• Opening times: The first Tuesday of the month at 4:30pm for veneration of the Holy Face and on Sundays at 11:30am for mass

> *A sacred image left on the moon in 1968*

On the first Tuesday of the month, at 4:30pm, a remarkable ceremony takes place in the first chapel of the left aisle of the church, during which the icon known as the Holy Face of Jesus is venerated.

Strictly speaking, this image was painted in 1945 by Gertrude Mariani (Sister Zeffirina of the Sacred Heart), based on a miraculous vision said to have been experienced by Sister Pierina De Micheli.

On 31 May 1938, in Milan, she had had a dazzling apparition of the Virgin Mary holding in her hand a medal on which the face of Christ was imprinted. The Virgin told the nun that this medal would allow whoever carried it and came each Tuesday to pray before the Holy Sacrament, to protect themselves against evil and enjoy the mercy of Jesus.

Jesus had already appeared to Sister Pierina De Micheli in 1932 and 1937, asking her to pray while contemplating his face.

The cult of the medal of the Holy Face was approved in August 1940 by the Archbishop of Milan and spread by, among others, Abbot Ildebrando Gregori, a Sylvestrine Benedictine monk who had been the spiritual father of Pierina De Micheli since 1940. In 1968, with the blessing of Pope Paul VI, a medal of the Holy Face was deposited on the moon by the American astronauts.

This beautiful church is commonly known as Santo Stefano del Cacco (Saint Stephen of the Monkey) because of an ancient Egyptian statue of the god Thoth represented with a dog's head, thought to be a monkey (*macacco*), which was found nearby (now exhibited in the Vatican Museums). The actual name of the church is Santo Stefano de Pinea: the marble pine-cone that can be seen on top of the belltower alludes to the name of the district.

The church, which probably dates back to the 9th century, has kept its basilica form with three naves divided by two rows of columns, and in the underground crypt there are still a number of very interesting tombstones. Pope Pius IV entrusted the church to the Sylvestrine monks in 1563. Its current appearance is the result of restoration work carried out in 1607.

BERARDI'S WATER CLOCK

Palazzo Berardi
62 Via del Gesù

A rare and curious mechanism

Stop in front of the open gate of Palazzo Berardi, in La Pigna district, to see a superb and theatrical water clock (hydrochronometer) in the courtyard. It was installed in 1870 by the Dominican scholar Giovan Battista Embriaco, head of the nearby Minerva convent. The clock was not his first attempt as he had already successfully presented two prototypes at the Paris Universal Exposition of 1867. This curious mechanism, which is still in working order, sits at the centre of a shell surrounded by four caryatids supporting two marble busts. The whole structure acts as a fountain and water feature.

There is another water clock on the Pincio (see page 19).

THE IRREGULAR FAÇADE OF PALAZZO ALTIERI ⓴

Palazzo Altieri
Piazza del Gesù and Via del Plebiscito

"You won't get your hands on my house!"

It must have been very difficult for an ordinary citizen to oppose the urban projects and home improvements of the great aristocratic Roman families. When a Farnese, a Chigi or a Colonna decided to enlarge a palace, build a new street or erect a church to the greater glory of God (and incidentally their own), the rights of small property-owners in the neighbourhood did not carry much weight. It was better to sell up than suffer the violent and not always legal means of persuasion. As these expansionist projects generally coincided with the election of a family member to the throne of Saint Peter, it was difficult to find a sympathetic ear to register any complaints. However, one woman did manage to thwart the plans of one of the most powerful families of the time during the construction of Palazzo Altieri, which opens onto Piazza del Gesù and Via del Plebiscito.

The Altieri family had been living in the district since the 14th century and already occupied an imposing building that was demolished when Cardinal Giovambattista Altieri began to build his new palace. The election of his uncle Emilio Altieri to the papacy as Clement X changed things and went down in history as one of the most outrageous examples of nepotism: Clement transferred the huge sum of 1,200,000 ecus from the papal accounts to those of his family and friends. Part of this money was then used to enlarge the newly built palace. The cardinal, who was anxious to have it finished before his ailing uncle died, kept the builders on the job round the clock, working by torchlight. The new wing of the palace was completed in the record time of six years.

Nevertheless there is one curious feature. The beautiful alignment of the windows marked with a star – the Altieri heraldic symbol – is broken and then resumes. Here lived an old woman who rejected all offers to buy her modest home, even though they were much higher than the actual value of the house.

The pope himself intervened but she refused to budge. Has popular memory idealised the resistance of this ordinary woman? Did the scandal of the costly building work do the rest? The Altieri no longer insisted, the work continued, and the house was incorporated into the new building. At this point, the façade has an unusual curve; and a small window and door that are completely out of line with the rest still interrupt the flow of the superb ground-floor windows. Nobody has touched the façade since.

THE BOARDED-UP WINDOW AT PALAZZO MATTEI

Palazzo Mattei
19 Piazza Mattei

A room with no view

There is a curious legend that Duke Mattei once lost a substantial part of his fortune. Hearing of this, his future father-in-law refused to give his daughter's hand in marriage.

So the duke decided to show the father that he had lost none of his power or noblesse, and overnight had the celebrated Fountain of the Turtles built in front of the palazzo.

The palazzo was part of what was known as the Mattei district, and today its façade still forms one of the sides of the pretty square of the same name. The next day, the duke invited his beautiful fiancée and her father to his palace to put matters right. He asked them to lean out of a little window from which there was a perfect view of the sumptuous fountain and declared: "Look what the unfortunate Duke Mattei can do in a few hours!"

The young woman's father offered his apologies and finally gave his approval to the marriage. As a souvenir of this memorable day, the duke had the window boarded up so that nobody else could appear at it. And you can still see it like that today.

The fountain was built around 1585 by the Florentine Taddeo Landini according to a design by Giacomo della Porta. It seems that on the original sketches the bronze ephebi were meant to be pushing dolphins in the upper basin, rather than the bronze turtles to which the fountain owes its name. These turtles, attributed to Bernini, were added later but have since been replaced by copies and the originals preserved in the Capitoline Museums.

WHY IS IT OFTEN WINDY IN PIAZZA DEL GESÙ?

Popular tradition holds that the square in front of the Jesuit Chiesa del Gesù is often very windy. According to a story told by Stendhal, one day the Wind, out walking with the Devil, came to the church of the Jesuits. The Devil, who had a mission to accomplish there, asked the Wind to wait for him a moment and went into the church. The Wind readily agreed, waiting one day, then two. Legend says it is still waiting there ...

THE *PIANO NOBILE*
OF PALAZZO MATTEI DI GIOVE

32 Via Michelangelo Caetani
- Tel: 06 68801613
- The loggia and interior can be visited on request by emailing the American Studies Center at info@centrostudiamericani.org
- Free entry to the courtyard
- Tram: 8 – Torre Argentina; Bus: 40, 64, 119, 492, 780 – Botteghe Oscure

Hidden treasures

There is nothing in the plain façade of Palazzo Mattei to indicate that the building conceals two spectacular treasures: a splendid collection of antiques in the courtyard and a series of stunning frescoes inside.

Although the Mattei family was one of the richest in 16th- and 17th-century Rome, they lived austerely except for their two great passions: collecting artefacts from ancient Rome and having their palace decorated by great painters. The finest frescoes can be seen on the first floor (*piano nobile*), home since 1932 to the American Studies Center. Access is through a beautiful loggia, protected by an elegant trellis, from which there is an unusual view of the two spectacular courtyards: the perimeter walls feature a collection of busts, statues, sarcophagi, inscriptions and Roman coins that are the envy of the city's most important museums. But be careful! Many of these pieces are Renaissance reproductions that are difficult to distinguish from the originals.

In the library, as you stroll through the halls overflowing with books, you can admire the ceilings decorated by great 17th-century masters. Following the wishes of their patrons, the frescoes are all on biblical themes. Domenichino, Francesco Albani and Giovanni Lanfranco worked here, as did the young Pietro da Cortona, who decorated the gallery with frescoes on the stories of Solomon – his first commission in Rome. There is also a small chapel with frescoes by Il Pomarancio.

Designed by the architect Carlo Maderno and completed over twenty years from 1598 for Asdrubale Mattei, husband of Constance Gonzaga and son of Alessandro Mattei, Duke of Monte Giove, Palazzo Mattei became the property of the Italian State in 1938. Today, in addition to the American Studies Center, it houses the Italian Institute of Modern and Contemporary History, with its own library, and the National Record Library.

In 1822, when the celebrated poet Giacomo Leopardi stayed there, he wrote to his brother, telling him about the "horrible disorder, confusion, mediocrity, unbearable pettiness, unspeakable neglect and all the other appalling qualities that prevail in this house". Admiring the building now, we can only assume that it's a question of taste.

INSTITUTE OF THE ITALIAN ENCYCLOPAEDIA ㉓

Palazzo Mattei di Paganica
4 Piazza dell'Enciclopedia Italiana
• Library open weekdays 9.30am-6pm
• Visits to the Sala Igea and the Sala Rossa can be arranged through numerous cultural associations, including Roma Sotterranea (www.romasotterranea.it)
• Tram 8, Torre Argentina stop; bus 40, 64, 119, 492 and 780, Botteghe Oscure stop

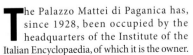

Hidden wonders

The Palazzo Mattei di Paganica has, since 1928, been occupied by the headquarters of the Institute of the Italian Encyclopaedia, of which it is the owner. During the week, the institute's beautiful library is open to the public. The other rooms in the palace, which are all magnificent, may be visited under the aegis of a number of cultural associations.

Behind the large entrance to no. 4 on the square (previously known as Via Paganica) and at the end of a narrow porch, one arrives at an enormous cloister whose loggias are built in two different styles. On the ground floor stands the Sala Igea (Hygieia Room), protected by large windows, whose arches are covered with mythological grotesques.

On the *piano nobile* (the first floor), the halls are painted with frescoes. These include episodes from the life of Joshua and David, as well as scenes from *Jerusalem Delivered* by Tasso, produced between 1593 and 1596 by Giovanni de' Vecchi. In addition, the Sala Rossa (Red Room) contains the bas-relief that inspired the institute's logo: an eagle with outspread wings, the work of Alberto Gerardi (1929). Coffered ceilings with polygonal frames from the middle of the 16th century, embellished with pictorial decorations dating from the 17th century, look down on the inside of the loggia and the main hall. The latter, illuminated by the original chandelier, is used as the magnificent reading room of the institute's library, which contains about 100,000 books.

The palace was constructed in 1540 on the initiative of the Duke of Paganica, Ludovico Mattei, and was designed by Nanni di Baccio Bigio. The building rests partly on the structure of the Balbo Theatre and certain radial partitions in the *cavea*, the *opus reticulatum* and *quadratum*, are still visible in the basements.

In 1640 the palace was enlarged on the side adjoining Via delle Botteghe Oscure. In 1927 it was acquired by Giovanni Treccani, founder of the Institute of the Italian Encyclopaedia. He then established the institute's headquarters in this building, which it has occupied almost continuously ever since. The German occupation of Rome and the establishment of the Italian Social Republic led to the closure of the institute, the laying-off of employees and the relocation to Bergamo of a large part of its archives, photographs and manuscripts. However, from late 1944 onwards, the work undertaken in the Paganica Palace has continued without a break.

OUTLINE OF THE FORMER GHETTO FOUNTAIN ㉔

Piazza Giudia – Piazza delle Cinque Scole
• Tram: 8 – Via Arenula; Bus: 64, Largo Argentina

A fountain's long journey

Not until 1930, after a long journey, was the fountain designed in 1593 by the renowned Roman architect and sculptor Giacomo della Porta erected in Piazza delle Cinque Scole. Originally it stood at the heart of the vibrant Jewish ghetto, a hundred metres from its current location in Piazza Giudia. Today, a beautiful marble outline on the cobbled square marks its former position.

In 1555 Paul IV promulgated his papal bull *Cum nimis absurdum*, which stated that Roman Jews should not enjoy the same rights as other citizens: "… these very Jews have insolently invaded Rome … to the extent that not only have they mingled with Christians (even when close to their churches) and wearing no identifying garments, but to dwell in homes, indeed, even in the more noble … conducting business from their houses and in the streets and dealing in real estate; they even have nurses and housemaids and other Christians as hired servants."

Jews were required to wear distinctive clothing and to live together in the same neighbourhood, the ghetto, bounded by the Tiber, the Theatre of Marcellus, the Portico of Octavia and Piazza Giudia.

In 1581, Pope Gregory XIII wanted to bring drinking water to the Campo Marzio district as well as the ghetto, but the project ground to a halt at what is now Piazza Mattei, where the nobleman Muzio Mattei was granted permission to build the so-called Fontana delle Tartarughe (Turtle Fountain, see page 141) directly in front of his residence. In 1591, the Acqua Felice (Happy Waters) at last flowed into the main square of the ghetto, Piazza Giudia.

The fountain, which was built of recycled marble from the Temple of Serapis on the Quirinal, was completed in 1593 and erected near the gallows where condemned Jews were hanged. The upper basin, supported by a pillar, has four gorgon's heads with water flowing through their open mouths, while the main basin features the coats of arms of magistrates sitting in the year 1593.

In the 1880s the ghetto was demolished, and the whole area was reconstructed with the opening of thoroughfares such as Via Arenula, profoundly changing the earlier townscape. Pending a new location, the fountain remained in storage for many years. In 1924, the basin and pillar were reused for a fountain opposite the church of Sant'Onofrio sul Gianicolo. In 1930 the original fountain was finally reassembled on the present site.

INSCRIPTION AT PALAZZO MANILI

1-2 Via del Portico d'Ottavia
• Bus: 8, 64, 46 – Largo Argentina

Lorenzo Manili's impossible dream

Palazzo Manili is a unique complex that incorporates several Renaissance buildings. It overlooks Piazza Giudia, one of Rome's most iconic spots, where there is still a vivid sense of the city's history: the Circus Flaminius, the Theatre of Marcellus, the Portico of Octavia, the Temple of Apollo, the medieval district, the fish market, the ghetto, executions, the Nazi deportations …

In 1468, Lorenzo Manili bought several buildings, probably with the intention of joining them into one. This enterprise was not a success, due perhaps to financial difficulties, but he still wanted to leave a trace of his overwhelming love for Rome, so he covered the façades of his buildings with a long inscription in capital letters resembling those of antiquity:

URBE ROMA IN PRISTINAM FORMA(M R)ENASCENTE LAUR. MANLIUS KARITATE ERGA PATRI(AM) (A)EDIS SUO NOMINE MANLIANAS PRO FORT(UN)AR(UM) MEDIOCRITATE AD FOR(UM)

IUDEOR(UM) SIBI POSTERISQ(UE) SUIS A FUND(AMENTIS) P(OSUIT).
AB URB(E) CON(DITA) M.M.CCXXI L AN(NO) M(ENSE) III D(IE) II
P(OSUIT) XI CAL(ENDAS) AUG(USTAS)

The text can be rendered as follows: "At the time when the city of Rome
was reborn in its ancient form, Lorenzo Manili, for love of his homeland, near
the forum of the Jews, for himself and for his descendants, built up from its
foundations this house, which bears the name *manliana*, at least within the
limits allowed by his mediocre wealth. 2221 years after the founding of Rome,
at the age of 50 years, 3 months and 2 days, he built this house on the eleventh
day before the beginning of August."

Manili also affixed fragments of reliefs to the façades. On some of the
windows to the left of the complex, those overlooking Piazza Costaguti, he had
carved the motto "HAVE ROMA" (Take care, Rome).

Manili's initiative – bizarre as it may seem – is important because it
demonstrates better than any book the cultural climate in Rome during the
flowering of humanism, when the language, literature, history and values of
the classical world were being rediscovered. It was a world that must have
seemed like a sort of golden age to Manili's contemporaries.

Had it been within his means, Manili might have built a new Colosseum.
Nevertheless he left this memorable inscription, witness to a wonderful and
impossible dream.

PALAZZO COSTAGUTI'S WALLED-UP ENTRANCE

29 Via della Reginella and Piazza Mattei

26

> *Why is the entrance to Palazzo Costaguti walled up?*

Originally, Palazzo Costaguti opened onto Via della Reginella and the square that was later named after the owners, the Costaguti (who still live there today). This is where the former main gateway stood, now walled up.

When the street was widened and incorporated into the ghetto, the palazzo had to be restructured: to avoid the restrictions enforced in the Jewish quarter, such as closing the gates at nightfall, the owners walled up the old gateway and opened another on the small Piazza Mattei. These later works explain why the original entrance is wedged at an angle on one of the narrowest walls of the building (with only two windows!). It is also why the finest rooms are on the side of the building that overlooks Via della Reginella.

A PALACE OF UNSUSPECTED MAGNIFICENCE

Palazzo Costaguti is one of Rome's grandest palaces. It is entered via a beautiful spiral staircase that leads to the *piano nobile*, which was decorated by the leading artists of the time, among whom were the brothers Taddeo and Federico Zuccari, Giuseppe Cesari (Cavaliere d'Arpino), Domenichino, Guercino and Gaspard Dughet. The palace is still privately owned: Don Diego Afan De Rivera Costaguti lives in part of it while the rest is rented out. As it is closed to the public you can only view it from the outside, unless you happen to see someone coming in or out so that you can glimpse inside.

MARBLE SLAB STIPULATING THE SIZE OF FISH

Church of Sant'Angelo in Pescheria (Portico of Octavia)

A bizarre privilege

From the Middle Ages until the early 19th century, the Portico of Octavia and the surrounding area was home to Rome's main fish market. The right pillar of the archway still bears remarkable testimony to this. A marble inscription, recording the maximum size of fish for sale, establishes a bizarre privilege: it states that the city administrators (known as the "conservatives") have a right to the head (as far as the first bones) of all fish over a certain size. Moreover, no one could claim they were either acting in good faith or in ignorance of the rule. In other words, it applies to all. The length in question was stipulated below. So the administrators were sure of getting the heads of all fish over 13 cm long. This long-lasting privilege was only abolished in 1799.

VESTIGES OF THE OLD FISH MARKET

The district has retained many traces of its not-so-distant past, particularly the name, Sant'Angelo in Pescheria or Sant'Angelo dei Pescivendoli (fish sellers). The church, chapels and oratory near the Roman arch all take up this theme. The oldest texts mention the neighbourhood as *"in foro piscium"*. Its emblem is an angel holding a set of scales in one hand and a sword in the other: rather than meting out justice, this could more prosaically refer to the weighing and filleting of fish. At No. 25 Via di Sant'Angelo in Pescheria, a plaque marks the former site of a market stall.

MONASTERO DI SANTA FRANCESCA ROMANA DI TOR DE' SPECCHI

32 Via del Teatro di Marcello
• Tel: 06 6793565
• Open 9 March only, 8am-11:45am and 3pm-5pm
• Admission: Free

> *A convent open one day a year*

Located at the foot of the Capitoline Hill, the ancient residence where St Frances of Rome founded the religious congregation known as the Oblates is today still a convent that contains a number of treasures virtually unknown to the public. Once a year, however, an open day is held to let visitors discover the superb cloister and antique frescoes.

A stone doorway surmounted by a 17th-century fresco leads to a hall formerly used as stables. It is here that the Scala Santa (Holy Stairs) is found, leading to a small oratory dating from the 15th century, whose four walls are decorated with an astounding sequence of frescoes executed in 1468 and attributed to Benozzo Gozzoli (although some suggest they were painted by Antoniazzo Romano or a disciple of Piero della Francesca). Among the scenes illustrating the life of St Frances is the very beautiful panel showing the Virgin enthroned between St Frances, the angel and St Benedict, as well as a curious representation of Hell painted in a niche.

The visit continues into a great hall, which must have served as the refectory, where another cycle of monochrome frescoes covers an entire wall, as well as a small room in the medieval Tor de' Specchi (Tower of Mirrors), where Frances cloistered herself to pray and meditate and where her clothes and relics are preserved today in a coffer.

On Via del Teatro di Marcello, another entrance leads to the part of the convent dating from the 17th century. Having crossed the first two rooms with their fresco paintings where the "parlour" or reception room was situated, visitors enter a magnificent cloister, difficult to envisage from the outside, probably designed by the Baroque architect, Carlo Maderno. It is embellished with arcades on three sides, an octagonal well constructed in pale travertine stone, beautiful potted lemon trees, tombstones and archaeological artefacts embedded in the walls, recalling the life of the saint and the history of the convent. The buildings surrounding the cloister were erected in the early years of the 17th century to increase the number of cells, reflecting the growth of the congregation.

After the cloister, still on the ground floor, the tour continues with another room and a chapel, before mounting a flight of stairs to view another beautiful frescoed room and the choir of the Santissima Annunziata.

CAGES OF THE WOLF AND THE EAGLE

Via del Teatro Marcello
• Bus: 63, 81, 83, 170, 715, 716

Caged animals

Historically, the wolf and the eagle are the two symbols of Rome. The wolf refers to the myth of the founding of the city, as putative mother of the twins Romulus and Remus, while the imperial eagle, sacred attribute of Jupiter, was the emblem of the Roman Empire. With outspread wings, it featured on the banners carried in war and during the Roman conquests.

On 28 August 1872 the city council, in a highly symbolic move aimed at reaffirming the greatness and supremacy of Rome and its ancient tradition, decided to introduce a live wolf into the Capitoline gardens – it was to be kept in a special cage as a symbol of the city.

The eagle was installed shortly afterwards, initially to the left of the steps where the monument to the 14th-century tribune Cola di Rienzo now stands. It was then moved along the rocks overlooking Via del Teatro Marcello, near the wolf.

Both the rusty cages can still be seen today. Until the 1970s they housed numerous specimens of these animals, although the idea was increasingly controversial. When the umpteenth wolf died on 28 June 1954, a number of animal lovers protested for the first time in eighty years in an attempt to stop a new animal being introduced. Despite heated arguments and impassioned press articles supporting one side or the other, on 15 November a young male wolf from the city zoo was shut up there in a small, damp cage. Although the animals were looked after in the post-war era by a guard nicknamed Luparo (wolf-man), who was responsible for feeding them and cleaning their cages, the controversy did not die down.

In August 1970, the tradition finally came to an end, when Mayor Clelio Darida ordered that the wolf should be moved to the zoo. The official version was that the cage would be refurbished in order to give "a better view of the animal" … but the wolf never went back.

The last eagle, which probably attracted much less attention from animal lovers, died in 1973 and has never been replaced.

The memory of the wolf pacing endlessly round its cage lingers in a typical Roman idiom: *"Me pari la lupa der Campidojio"* ("You look like the Capitoline wolf"), used for someone who is restless and impatient, unable to sit still.

HOLE IN THE FAÇADE
OF SANTA MARIA IN ARACOELI

Basilica of Santa Maria in Aracoeli

③⓪

*Reminder
of Rome's first
public clock*

In the 14th century, when the great European cities had already had public clocks for a long time (the tower on the Île de la Cité housed the first Parisian public clock in 1370), Rome was conspicuously lacking and had to wait until 1412.

The city's first public clock – made by master watchmaker Ludovico of Florence, who designed the mechanism, and master Pietro of Milan, who fitted it with a bell *pro horis pulsandis* – was set into the façade of Santa Maria in Aracoeli and inaugurated on 27 December 1412. The event was of such importance that a special corps of *moderatores horologii* was created: its first members came from the nobility and were responsible for the clock's operation and maintenance.

In 1806 the clock was moved to the tower of the Palazzo Senatorio (Palace of the Senators) on Piazza Campidoglio.

The hole in the church wall is thus the last, rather striking, reminder of the clock that used to be there.

In addition to the clock, the façade of the basilica of Santa Maria in Aracoeli was covered with mosaics and frescoes, now sadly missing. Each of the three doors was surmounted with a rosette. The middle rosette incorporating the Cross of Jerusalem was removed (and lost) by Pope Urban VIII, who replaced it with a stained-glass window decorated, of course, with the famous Barberini bees, symbol of the pope's family.

THE HIDDEN TREASURES OF ROMAN BANKS

UniCredit Banca di Roma • Via del Corso 374
Banca Finnat Euramerica, ABI (Associazione Bancaria Italiana) and Banco Popolare: Palazzo Altieri • Piazza del Gesù
BNL • Via Veneto 111 and 119
Banco di Sicilia. Palazzo Mancini • Via del Corso 270-272
Banca Antonveneta. Palazzo Rondinini • Via del Corso 518
Mediocredito Centrale. Villino Casati • Via Piemonte 51
• Open: first Saturday of October
• Admission free

Many Italians (and even more tourists) are unaware that for some years various palaces now occupied by banks have been open to the public one day each year. The open day is part of the *Invito a Palazzo* ["Invitation to the Palace"] event organized by the Italian Banking Association (ABI).

The banks taking part in this initiative form a circuit of guided tours through which lovers of hidden treasures of the arts can enjoy free access to historic palaces, villas and gardens usually inaccessible to the public.

The headquarters of the UniCredit Banca di Roma (Via del Corso) possesses a curious oval spiral staircase built in 1713 for the Marchese De Carolis by the famous Alessandro Specchi, architect of the palace and spiritual heir of Borromini. The frescoes and canvases gracing the first floor are the work of such artists as Giuseppe Bartolomeo Chiari, Sebastiano Conca and Andrea Procaccini.

In Piazza del Gesù, the Altieri Palace (by the celebrated architect Giovanni Antonio De Rossi), is also home to a number of masterpieces: the ceiling of the headquarters of the Banca Finnat Euramerica is decorated with a superb fresco by Canuti, *The Apotheosis of Romulus*, and that of the ABI with a Maratta fresco, *The Triumph of Clemency*, while the Banco Popolare's offices on the second floor are filled with sculptures, tapestries, valuable pieces of furniture and a large collection of sacred art, landscapes and scenes of everyday life.

BNL's head offices in Via Veneto were designed in the 1930s by the architect Piacentinin and the building's halls are filled with antique statues and a collection of paintings ranging from masterpieces by Lotto and Canaletto to more modern canvases of Corot and Morandi. Nor should the other banks be missed, including the Monte di Pietà with its chapel (see page 99), the headquarters of Banco di Sicilia in the Mancini Palace, or the offices of Banca Antonveneta in Rondinini Palace and the Mediocredito Centrale in the Casati Villa, former residence of the socialite Marchesa Luisa Casati Stampa, well-known for her romantic and intellectual relationship with the writer Gabriele D'Annunzio.

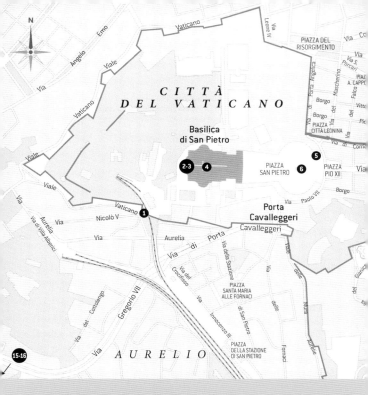

THE VATICAN
& SURROUNDING AREA

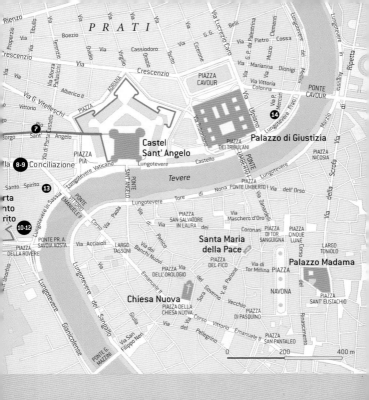

THE POPE'S RAILWAY

Via della Stazione Vaticana
• Open to the public

> *The shortest international railway in the world*

One thousand, two hundred and seventy metres – this is the total length of the Vatican railway built (following the Lateran Treaty of 11 February 1929) to link the Holy See with the Italian rail network via a junction with the nearby station of Roma San Pietro.

Construction work was finished in 1932. It involved erecting the 143-metre-long Gelsomino ("Jasmine") viaduct, built of masonry faced with travertine and brick. The track passes under a wide arch surmounted by the coat of arms of Pope Pius XI and goes through the Leonine Wall to enter the State of the Vatican City. A majestic sliding double gate – weighing over 35 tonnes – closes this passage, which is only open on rare occasions to allow a freight convoy through. A short distance beyond the gate is Vatican City station, opened in 1933 and now a shopping centre.

The track continues for another hundred metres or so to end in a cul-de-

sac: an 80-metre-long tunnel, with two parallel sidings used for shunting.

During the preparations for Jubilee 2000 at Roma San Pietro station, one of two tracks along the viaduct was taken up, to be replaced by a pleasant walkway with a fine view of the gate and an unusual perspective on *Er Cuppolone*, the immense dome of Saint Peter's.

SANCTVS.
LONGINVS.
MARTYR

THE LONGINUS LANCE AT SAINT PETER'S

Saint Peter's Basilica
• Open daily, 7am-7pm from April to October, and 7am-6pm from November to March

I n front of Bernini's baldachin, to the left seen from the church entrance, there is another statue by Bernini, in a similar style to the statue of Veronica (see page 167), representing Saint Longinus in the act of piercing the side of Christ on the Cross.

A mysterious and controversial lance

Although the church treasury possesses a fragment of this lance, the location where the main section is preserved is a closely guarded secret.

THE LANCE THAT PIERCED THE SIDE OF CHRIST ON THE CROSS: A FERVENTLY DISPUTED RELIC

According to the Gospel of Saint John, a Roman soldier pierced the side of Jesus with a lance to ensure that he was dead. Blood flowed from the wound, a symbol of his sacrifice, as did water, a symbol of his fecundity. Some also read into this scene the birth of the Church from the body of Christ, just as Eve had sprung from Adam's rib.

The apocryphal Gospel of Nicodemus (circa AD 450) adds a detail: the name of the soldier was Longinus, as shown by a miniature in a manuscript of the Laurentian Library at Florence, even though some believe that the name in Greek characters (ΛΟΓΙΝΟΧ), or LOGINOS, was simply derived from the word for "lance". Tradition says that Longinus, partially blind, was also touched by a drop of Christ's blood and water, which immediately restored his sight. The retrieval of this lance, not mentioned by the other evangelists, has been the object of intense competition to acquire such an important relic. Apparently taken to Constantinople in 615 to escape from the sack of Jerusalem by the Persians, the lance probably remained there until 1244, when it was presented to Saint Louis (the French king Louis IX) by the emperor Baldwin II together with Jesus' crown of thorns, which is still preserved in Notre-Dame Cathedral in Paris (see *Secret Paris* in this series of guides). The lance was later transferred to the Bibliothèque Nationale during the French Revolution and then disappeared. Note that meanwhile several copies have appeared: one has been spotted in Jerusalem, another in Constantinople and yet others are to be found in Cracow, Vienna, Budapest and Ejmiadzin in Armenia. The Armenian lance was said to have been recovered during the First Crusade: in 1098, a certain Pierre Barthelemy had a vision in which Saint Andrew showed him that the lance was in Saint Peter's Church at Antioch. The crusaders captured Antioch, found the lance in the predicted place, and then carried it off to Armenia.

THE VEIL OF VERONICA AT SAINT PETER'S ③

Saint Peter's Basilica
• Open daily, 7am-7pm from April to October, and 7am-6pm from
November to March

Very few visitors to Saint Peter's pay much attention to the statues around Bernini's baldachin in the central space of the basilica. Behind it, on the left (as seen from the entrance), is displayed a statue of Veronica, whose extraordinary history is virtually unknown. Her original veil (see box) is preserved above the statue.

> *A little-known rival to the Shroud of Turin?*

THE EXTRAORDINARY SAGA OF VERONICA'S VEIL

A great many churches possess a copy of a veil on which is imprinted the miraculous image of the face of Christ. The origin of this image is to be found in the Gospels of Mark [5: 25-34], Matthew [9: 20-22] and Luke [8: 43-48], which all relate the story of a woman who was healed of a haemorrhage by Jesus. Around the year 400, the Bishop of Lydia named her Berenike, a little before the apocryphal Gospel of Nicodemus [circa 450] finally referred to her as Veronica. The name seems to derive from "vero" and "icona", meaning "true image", while the personality of Veronica was embellished, gradually departing from the miraculously healed woman. In the 7th century, another apocryphal text, The Death of Pilate, spoke of Veronica as a confidante of Jesus to whom he had given the veil on which his face was imprinted.

Towards 1160, the canon of Saint Peter's Basilica in Rome, Pietro Mallius, put forward the hypothesis that this legend had arisen when, seeing Christ carrying his Cross to Golgotha, a woman removed her veil to wipe his brow and the image of his face was miraculously imprinted on it. This notion took root and little by little it was established as the true version of this rare and miraculous acheiropoieta [an image not made by the hand of man] [see page 171].

Still according to legend, Veronica's veil was first reported to be kept in Saint Peter's Basilica in 1287, although Pope Celestine III [1191-1198] had previously mentioned the existence of such a shroud. The veil may have been sold during the sack of Rome in 1527, but, as often happens with relics, it soon reappeared and was again noted in the relics hall in the 17th century, although some claimed that the face imprinted on the veil was that of a peasant named Manopello.

The cathedral of Jaen, in Spain, also claims to possess the authentic veil of Veronica.

THE CULT OF CHRISTIAN RELICS

Although rather neglected these days, with their devoted following greatly diminished in numbers, saints' relics had extraordinary success from the Middle Ages onwards.

Their presence today in numerous churches across Europe is a reminder of those exceptional times.

The cult of Christian relics goes back to the beginning of Christianity, to the deaths of the early martyrs and the creation of the first saints. The function of these relics was threefold: they bore witness to the example of a righteous and virtuous life to be copied or followed; they possessed a spiritual energy and power that could even work miracles (it was believed that the miraculous powers of the saints themselves was retained by their relics); and over time, with the rise of the contested practice of granting indulgences, relics bestowed indulgences on those who possessed them (see page 173).

As demand dictated supply, it was not long before unscrupulous parties were competing to invent their own relics, aided in their task by the Church which, for political reasons, canonised a great number of undeserving individuals (see opposite). Over-production went to absurd extremes: if one accepted the authenticity of all their relics, Mary

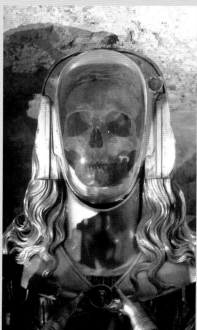

Magdalene would have had six bodies, and St Biagio a hundred arms.

These excesses, of course, raised suspicions and the popularity of relics gradually waned, although many people still believe that the true relic of a saint possesses spiritual power.

How else can one explain the numerous pilgrimages in the footsteps of Father Pio throughout Italy?

There are around 50,000 relics scattered around Europe, from some 5,000 saints.

Note that most of the world's other religions also worship relics, or used to do so.

21,441 RELICS FOR 39,924,120 YEARS OF INDULGENCES! The greatest collector of relics was Frederick III of Saxony (1463-1525), who procured 21,441 of them in all, 42 of which were fully preserved bodies of saints. Based on this unique collection, he calculated that he had amassed a grand total of 39,924,120 years and 220 days of indulgences! However, under the influence of Luther, who opposed indulgences, he abandoned the cult of relics in 1523.

WHEN SAINTS ARE NOT SO HOLY: SAINT GEORGE, SAINT CHRISTOPHER, AND SAINT PHILOMENA STRUCK FROM THE LIST ...

From the Middle Ages onwards, the pursuit of relics continued, as did their falsification. Not only relics were fabricated, however. Sometimes, even the saints themselves were a fabrication.

Recently – an event that passed almost without comment – the Church purged Saint George, Saint Christopher and Saint Philomena from its calendar, the very existence of all three now being in doubt.

The totally abusive canonisation of certain real personalities also took place, allowing the objects connected with them to feed the market for saintly relics.

For diplomatic reasons linked to the Counter-Reformation of the 16th century, canonisation was often based on political rather than religious or moral criteria. As a result of this *Realpolitik*, many rulers of the time were thus sanctified in a bid to ensure their subjects' allegiance to the Roman Catholic Church, then under pressure from the Protestant movement. Saint Stanislas of Poland, Saint Casimir of Lithuania, Saint Brigitte of Sweden, Saint Stephen of Hungary, Saint Margaret of Scotland, Saint Elizabeth of Portugal, Saint Wenceslas of Bohemia ... The list is long, indeed.

RELICS OF THE FEATHERS OF THE ARCHANGEL MICHAEL, THE BREATH OF JESUS, AND EVEN THE STARLIGHT THAT GUIDED THE THREE WISE MEN!

Leaving no stone unturned in their efforts to make money at the expense of the most naive believers, relic merchants showed unparalleled imagination in their quest for sacred paraphernalia and invented some fascinating objects, such as the horns of Moses or the feathers of the Archangel Michael, recorded as having been on sale at Mont-Saint-Michel in 1784.

The most highly prized relics were of course those of Christ. Unfortunately for relic hunters, as Christ had ascended to Heaven, his body was by definition no longer on Earth. Imagination again came to the rescue in the form of the quite extraordinary relic of the breath of Jesus (!) which was preserved in Wittenberg cathedral, Germany, in a glass phial.

The remains of Christ's foreskin, recuperated after his circumcision seven days after birth, and of his umbilical cord (!) were preserved at Latran, Rome (in the Sancta Sanctorum , see page 297) while bread from the Last Supper was kept at Gaming, Austria. Certain medieval texts lost to us today even spoke of the relic of the rays of the star that guided the Wise Men, also preserved at Latran.

ACHEIROPOIETIC WORKS OF ART

In Christian doctrine the Greek term *acheiropoieta* is used to describe works of art "not made by human hands". Although these artefacts are relatively rare, some can nevertheless be seen, for example at the legendary but mysterious Mount Athos in Greece. This semi-autonomous republic of Orthodox monks, isolated on a peninsula in north-eastern Greece and forbidden to women, children and female animals since the 11th century, is home to two acheiropoietic icons. One is kept at the Holy Monastery of Megisti Lavra, the other at the Holy Monastery of Iviron.

In France, the church of Notre-Dame-des-Miracles at Saint-Maur near Paris also possesses such an icon.

Similarly, the Holy Face of Edessa, in the church of St Bartholomew at Genoa, is said to have been painted by Christ himself (see photo opposite). The painting of Christ in the Sancta Sanctorum of the Latran, Rome, is said to be the work Saint Luke, but completed by angels. The Veil of Veronica at Saint Peter's in Rome is traditionally considered as an acheiropoieton in some quarters.

The famous *Volto Santo di Lucca* (Holy Face of Lucca), Tuscany, attributed to Nicodemus, who was present at Christ's crucifixion with Joseph of Arimathea, is also said to have been completed by angels (see *Secret Tuscany* in this collection of guides).

In Venice there are two acheiropoietic sculptures: one in the church of Santi Geremia e Lucia and the other in the church of San Marziale, both in Cannaregio.

In the Abruzzi region of Italy there is a *Volto Santo* at the village of Manoppello.

CHI. BACIA. QUESTA. CROCE.
. ACQUISTA . . GIORNI.
D'INDULGENZA.

RICORDO.
DEL. GIUBILEO
. 1886 .

INDULGENCES: "AS SOON AS THE MONEY CLINKS IN THE COLLECTION BOX, THE SOUL FLIES OUT OF PURGATORY."

In Roman Catholic doctrine, sins are erased by the sacrament of penance. But the confessional does not remove the pain of Purgatory, a place from which sinners hope to be liberated as quickly as possible. The length of time spent in Purgatory can be reduced or even written off completely by the granting of indulgences. These can be partial or full, depending on whether they free the penitent partially or totally from the duration of punishment for the sin in question. An indulgence is obtained in exchange for an act of piety (such as pilgrimage, prayer, mortification), carried out to this end in a spirit of repentance. Partial indulgences were traditionally counted in days, months or years. Contrary to what one might think, they do not correspond to an equivalent amount of direct remission from Purgatory, but indicate the remission corresponding to a particular penance. This practice, handed down from Roman law, goes back to the 3rd century, when it was important to bring back into the fold those Christians who had denied their religion because of persecution. "Simony" is a corruption of the practice of indulgence: the faithful made a bargain with the priest through an act of charity, which often took the form of a cash donation ... A notorious example dates from 1515: that year, the Dominican friar Johann Tetzel was responsible for the sale of indulgences in the name of the Archbishop of Mainz, Albrecht von Brandenburg, who deducted 50% of the money to cover his household expenses. The hugely cynical motto of the enterprising monk, who beat a drum to attract the crowds, was "As soon as the money clinks in the collection box, the soul flies out of Purgatory." It was against this background of scandal that Martin Luther intervened on 31 October 1517, the eve of All Saint's Day, posting his Ninety-five Theses denouncing the practice. The dispute over indulgences became one of the main causes of the schism between Protestants and Catholics.

In 1967, Pope Paul VI suppressed the references to a fixed number of days or years, but the indulgence itself, although perhaps less well known today, is still practised: during the millennium Jubilee celebrations, for example, indulgences were granted by Pope John Paul II. Protestants objected in vain. Five centuries may have gone by, but history repeats itself ...

Simony is the term used by Christians to refer to the buying or selling of pardons and other spiritual privileges. The practice owes its name to a certain Simon Magus, who practiced sorcery and wished to buy Saint Peter's ability to work miracles (Acts 8: 9-21), earning him the apostle's condemnation: "May your silver perish with you, because you have thought that the gift of God may be purchased with money!"

SOULS IN PURGATORY

While you can shorten your own stay in Purgatory (see above), it is also possible to alleviate the pain of souls already there, in what is known as the communion of saints.

When a living Christian prays for a soul in Purgatory, that soul sees its time reduced. Equally, a soul in Purgatory can intervene on behalf of a living person ...

SYMBOLS OF MOTHERHOOD ON THE HIGH ALTAR OF SAINT PETER'S ❹

Twisted columns of the baldachin
Saint Peter's Basilica
• Open 1 October to 31 March, 7am-6:30pm; 1 April to 30 September,
7am-7pm

The embellishment of Saint Peter's Basilica by successive popes, although always with the aim of glorifying the Church, was sometimes done for more personal reasons. It is hard to imagine today that the majestic sculpted canopy over the basilica's high altar is the result of a private vow by Pope Urban VIII Barberini.

> **Memories of the difficult pregnancy of Pope Urban VIII's niece**

A very dear niece of the pope, probably Anna Colonna, his nephew's wife, had a difficult pregnancy to the point that they feared for her life and that of the child. Urban VIII vowed to dedicate a majestic altar at Saint Peter's if she had a successful delivery. Which is exactly what happened.

The pope gave the commission to the greatest sculptor of the time, Bernini, who decided to hint at what lay behind the pope's donation of this monumental work. He did so on three of the four marble plinths that support the twisted columns of the canopy. The donor's coat of arms, with the three bees of the Barberini family, is engraved on the two outer sides of each plinth in such a way that it represents the different stages of pregnancy.

The shape of the first shield, which encircles the bees, is normal though slightly narrow and recalls a woman's belly. At the top is the smiling head of a woman, and below are stylised female reproductive organs.

But the coat of arms on the second plinth clearly highlights the changes that pregnancy brings about in a young woman. Her face is contorted with pain, the body (of the shield, but by extension of the woman) and organs are enlarged.

On the third shield the belly has flattened again and the face of a smiling baby takes the place of the woman's.

These Bernini sculptures, although obviously discreet, can be seen as an allegory of the pregnancy of the pope's niece.

SYMBOLISM OF THE FONTANELLA DELLE TRE TIARE

⑤

Largo del Colonnato

> ## *Triple tiara for a threefold symbol*

The Fountain of the Three Tiaras, designed by the Roman architect Pietro Lombardi in 1927, stands on a raised circular plinth divided into three, in the centre of which are three basins into which the water flows. The whole structure is surmounted by three papal tiaras arranged in a triangle. Under each is a set of pontifical keys.

These three tiaras represent the triple crown (*triregnum*), the papal crown shaped like a beehive that is placed on the pope's head during the coronation ceremony to mark the beginning of a pontificate. Popes can either wear the tiara of their predecessors or have a new one made. It is a non-liturgical ornament (the pope, like the bishops, wears a papal mitre for acts of worship) that is only used for papal processions and solemn acts of jurisdiction.

The first mention of the use of the triple crown goes back to the 8th century, although its ornamentation and shape kept evolving until the mid-14th century. The last pope to wear the *triregnum* regularly was Paul VI in 1963. Since then popes have rarely worn it, although with its crossed keys attached by a cord it remains a potent symbol of the papacy.

The origins of the papal tiara go back to Pope Sylvester I (314-335), who had received the crown of the Emperor Constantine as a sign of freedom and peace in the Church, the beginning of the Pax Romana. According to another source, it was Clovis I who gave the papal crown to Pope Symmachus in the church of Saint Martin of Tours, France, in the 5th century.

The lowest of the three tiers of the triple crown appeared at the base of the traditional white hat worn by popes in the 9th century, when they took on the temporal power of the Papal States. This crown was decorated with jewels to resemble those of kings and princes. The term "tiara" is mentioned for the first time in 1118, in the biography of Pope Paschal II, *Liber Pontificalis*.

A second tier was added to the first in 1301, during the pontificate of Boniface VIII at a time of conflict with Philip IV ("the Fair") of France, in order to demonstrate his spiritual authority over the royal power, and the crown was renamed the *biregnum*.

When the third tier was added – apparently during the reign of John XXII (1316-1334) – the crown took the name *triregnum*.

The three tiers were given the following papal attributes derived from the triple dimensions of Christ – priest, prophet and king: universal pastor (upper crown), supremacy of spiritual authority (middle crown) and domination of temporal power (lower crown), but also emperor of bodies, souls and minds, enjoying absolute sovereignty over Hell, Earth and Heaven.

The pontifical cord connects the three worlds, to which the keys give access.

WHY ARE THE KEYS A PAPAL SYMBOL?

It was Jesus Christ himself who conferred on Saint Peter, the first pope, the authority of the supreme head of the Church in the Gospel according to Saint Matthew (16:19): "And I will give unto thee the keys of the kingdom of heaven."

There are two keys: one gold (heavenly), the other silver (terrestrial), which symbolise the ability to open and close the gates of Paradise.

SAINT PETER'S MERIDIAN   ❻

Piazza San Pietro

A forgotten giant sundial

Since 1817, the famous obelisk of Saint Peter's Square – a red granite monolith over 25 metres high, or 40 metres if you count the base and the cross – is one of the world's largest gnomons marking a meridian (see the Place de la Concorde meridian in *Secret Paris*, in this series of guides). On the paving stones of the square is a strip of granite that forms a straight line linking a point to the right of the base of the obelisk to another point beyond the Maderno fountain.

At each end of this strip, two marble discs indicate the points where, at midday, the shadow of the cross is projected during the summer solstice (in the sign of Cancer) and the winter solstice (in the sign of Capricorn). Five more discs mark the passage of the sun through the other signs of the zodiac, arranged in pairs: Leo-Gemini, Virgo-Taurus, Libra-Aries, Scorpio-Pisces and Sagittarius-Aquarius.

The obelisk was probably erected at Heliopolis during the 12th dynasty (20th-18th centuries BC). Caligula had it brought to Rome in AD 37 to set off his private circus, on the Vatican hill, before it was taken over by Nero.

Several popes have attempted to embellish or otherwise make their mark on the obelisk. Sixtus V, for example, decided to add four lions to the base as a reference to the coat of arms of his family, the Peretti, and he donated the bronze ball that surmounts the obelisk, claimed to contain the ashes of Caesar,

to the municipality of Rome. Alexander VII crowned it with the Chigi symbols of mountains and stars, and Innocent XIII added the bronze eagles and the heraldic emblems of the Conti family.

The obelisk of Saint Peter's Square is the only one in Rome not to have collapsed. It even remained in its original position beside the basilica until 1586, when Sixtus V asked Domenico Fontana to move it to its present site.

PASSETTO ARCHES

❼

Borgo Sant'Angelo
• Bus: 23 – Via della Traspontina

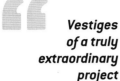

Vestiges of a truly extraordinary project

Along the street known as Borgo Sant'Angelo, behind the church of Santa Maria in Traspontina, the wall of Il Passetto is pierced by three arches bearing the arms of Pope Clement VIII (1592-1605). These openings, which today connect the districts of Borgo Sant'Angelo and Borgo Pio, look quite ordinary and yet they owe their existence to a truly extraordinary project, instigated by none other than Julius Caesar.

The history of Rome may be said to have begun in the 10th century BC, thanks to a shallow stretch of the river at the Isola Tiberina (Tiber Island), where easy access to both banks encouraged trade. Winter floods, however, often brought destruction and devastation to the city.

Julius Caesar recognised that the problem was caused by too many bends in

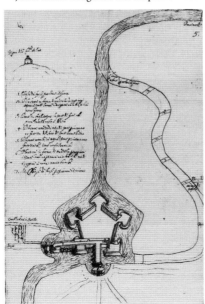

the river as it ran through the city, so his solution was to "correct" its course. He planned a perfectly straight new riverbed that would leave the original course at Monte Mario to rejoin it at Trastevere.

In imperial Rome, the river was properly maintained by a designated authority whose exclusive duties were to look after the river. In the Middle Ages, however, the strengthening of the ancient Roman bridges formed an additional barrier to the flow of water. Then on 25 December 1598 a flood of unprecedented magnitude led to disaster in the city: the Tiber rose almost 20 metres.

So Caesar's original project was resurrected by Clement VIII, who decided in 1599 to have a new riverbed dug: the river at Monte Mario was to be channelled into a "ditch" as far as Santo Spirito hospital, where it was supposed to meet up with the old course. The only obstacle was the Passetto di Borgo, which is why Clement VIII had three arches opened in the wall. However, the project remained dead in the water because the pope's advisers, worried about the proximity of the river and the newly built church of Santa Maria in Traspontina, suggested diverting the water into Castel Sant'Angelo's moat, so that it would flow directly into the original riverbed. That project met with no success either. The solution was only found after yet another destructive flood (1870), with the construction of the Lungotevere (the riverside quays) and the realisation of a dream.

HEADQUARTERS OF THE ORDER OF THE HOLY SEPULCHRE ❽

Palazzo della Rovere - 33 Via della Conciliazione
• For a guided tour of the Order's international headquarters: 06 0877347

> *A palace
> so beautiful
> that Charles VIII
> preferred it
> to the Vatican ...*

Since 1950, Hotel Columbus has occupied a wing of the Palazzo della Rovere, a magnificent 15th-century residence belonging to the Equestrian Order of the Holy Sepulchre of Jerusalem, where some little-known treasures are to be discovered. The five sumptuous rooms of the *piano nobile* (high-ceilinged main floor) house the administrative offices of the Order, but they can be toured in the company of a guide, booked in advance. Between 1480 and 1490, Cardinal Domenico della Rovere, nephew of Pope Sixtus IV, commissioned architect Baccio Pontelli to build this prodigious edifice on the narrow street that led from Saint Peter's Basilica to the Castel Sant'Angelo (Mausoleum of Hadrian). The decoration was carried out by the most celebrated artists of the time. It is said that this palace was so beautiful that Charles VIII preferred to stay there rather than at the Vatican. Several cardinals in their turn chose to live there until 1655, when the palace was bought by the Order of the Penitentiaries (a religious order charged with hearing the confessions of pilgrims who presented themselves at the basilica), which would remain there for the next 300 years. Looking out from the former doorway, two small 17th-century fountains can be seen, one adorned with an eagle and the other bearing the dragon of the Borghese family. The façade is known to have been decorated with 16th-century graffiti, now eroded by the ravages of time. The *piano nobile* opens onto a succession of rooms decorated by Pinturicchio and other painters of his school: the Hall of the Grand Master, the Hall of the Seasons or the Zodiac, the Hall of the Prophets and the Apostles, and finally the Hall of the Demigods, in perfect condition, with a superb wooden ceiling featuring figures painted on sheets of paper fixed to the beams. Pheasants peck at the ears of wheat under the English oak, the coat of arms of the Della Rovere, resplendent in the centre and at the four corners of the ceiling. Cardinal Alidosi had the chapel added in 1505. It is fitted with a beamed vault adorned with eagle and oak tree, the motifs of which are repeated, with the following motto: "Profit, O mortals, from your leisure, enlivened by nourishment in the shade of the oak". On the second floor of the hotel wing there are two rooms with frescoed ceilings commissioned by Cardinal Giovanni Salviati and painted by Francesco Salviati.

WHERE TO EAT NEARBY

RESTAURANT *LA VERANDA* ❾

73 Borgo Santo Spirito • Tel: 06 6872973
To appreciate the Palazzo della Rovere without staying at Hotel Columbus or visiting it, you can have a drink or dine at the Veranda restaurant, within the hotel. Whether seated in the garden or below the painted vaulted ceilings, the atmosphere is particularly romantic at night.

NATIONAL MUSEUM OF THE HISTORY OF MEDICINE

3 Lungotevere in Sassia
• Tel: 06 68352353
• From September to June, Monday, Wednesday and Friday 10am-12pm

A little museum of horrors

The museum, which was planned after the First World War to bring together medical material collected for the 1911 World Fair, was opened in 1933 in nine large rooms at the Pio Istituto di Santo Spirito (Pious Institute of the Holy Spirit). There is no other museum in Italy with as many artefacts relating to the history of medicine as this one. The visit starts in the Sala Alessandrina on the ground floor, with hand-painted anatomical tables from the 17th and 18th centuries hanging on the walls.

The Sala Flaiani contains the remains of one of the most important anatomical museums of Europe, the Museo di Santo Spirito (Museum of the Holy Spirit), founded in the 18th century by the great surgeon Flaiani. Here one can observe several anatomical preparations that have been kept unaltered over the centuries thanks to refined preservation techniques. These include skeletal alterations, examples of pathological anatomy, deformed foetuses, skulls and limbs affected by syphilis and mummified heads. In the centre of the room there is a mill in the form of a wooden temple, which was used to grind quinine.

The next hall is the Sala Capparoni, where a series of incredibly realistic Roman and Etruscan ex voto offerings are preserved along with other modern wax ex voto offerings, as well as a collection of Roman, medieval, Renaissance and 19th-century surgical instruments, and a phial of scorpion oil for poisonous animal bites and stings. There are also some snakes' tongues, a crown used for headaches, Renaissance first-aid kits, a collection of glass and ceramic recipients used to keep medicines and a 19th-century electrotherapy machine.

The Sala Carbonelli today houses fascinating and macabre objects and instruments: a collection of drills, saws for amputating from the 16th to the 19th centuries, anal and vaginal specula from the 15th to the 19th centuries, microscopes and glasses of all shapes and from all periods, the two glass beakers used by Avogadro to demonstrate the law of the compression of gases, a girl's hand metallised by a process that is still unknown, a huge wooden 17th-century press for extracting plant essences, and some stone and metal mortars for making medicinal potions. The reconstructions of an old pharmacy and the chemical-alchemical laboratory from the 17th century are beautiful. You can also admire a 16th-century walnut bookcase with over ten thousand books, prints and reviews concerning the history of medicine on its shelves.

MONUMENTAL COMPLEX OF SANTO SPIRITO IN SASSIA

1-2-3 Borgo Santo Spirito
• Individual guided tours Mondays at 10am and 3:30pm
• Reservations for group tours with qualified guide: 06 68352433 or 06 68210854

> *Rare visit to a former hospital*

Once a week, the remarkable architectural ensemble of Santo Spirito in Sassia is open to visitors.

On the initiative of the King of Wessex, the "Schola Sacorum" (Saxon School), a charitable institution for Saxon pilgrims on their way to visit Saint Peter's tomb in Rome, was created in the 8th century. The buildings, later destroyed by fire and pillaging, were reconstructed at the end of the 12th century on the orders of Pope Innocent III, who dedicated the main section to helping the sick, paupers and abandoned babies. Under the name Santo Spirito in Sassia, it grew into the most advanced hospital of its time. The grand rectangular gallery could receive up to a thousand people.

The tour begins in the Corsia Sistina (Sistine Ward), which Pope Sixtus IV added to the hospital two centuries later. The gallery, 120 metres in length and 13 metres high, is divided into two sections by a majestic tiburium, in the centre of which rises a very beautiful altar, the only work by Palladio to be found in Rome. The interior portal, finely carved in marble and attributed to Andrea Bregno, is called the Portale del Paradiso (Heaven's Door). Next to this entrance is the "foundlings' wheel" (see page 191). Sixtus IV had the walls of this gallery frescoed to the level of the windows to celebrate the establishment of the hospital and the merits of Innocent III, as well as for his own glory. He also ordered the construction of two buildings adjoining the superb cloisters, reserved respectively for the monks and nuns who worked at the institute (at present, only the priest's quarters are open to the public).

Around 1570, Monseigneur Cirillo, then Commander of the brotherhood, enlarged the hospital by building the Palazzo del Commendatore around a splendid courtyard. A grand staircase leads to the upper gallery where frescoes by Ercole Perillo entirely cover the upper part of the walls. This gallery leads into the Lancisiana library (18th century, currently under restoration), and the Commander's former apartment, decorated with sculptures, tapestries, antique furniture and frescoes by Jacopo and Francesco Zucchi telling the story of the hospital.

THE ITALIAN CLOCK OF THE PALAZZO DEL COMMENDATORE

3 Via Borgo di Santo Spirito

A huge and unusual clock dominates the courtyard of the former Santo Spirito architectural ensemble, set in the cornice of the Palazzo del Commendatore (Palace of the Commander, as the president of the charitable institution of Santo Spirito used to be known).

A clock with only six hours

This curious Baroque clock dates back to 1828 and has the particularity of possessing an "Italian" face, divided into six sections (see below). The clock face is encircled by a serpent biting its own tail, while a bronze lizard (symbol of death and resurrection) takes the place of a hand.

WHAT IS THE ORIGIN OF "ITALIAN" CLOCKS?

The subdivision of the day into hours goes back to antiquity and was probably introduced by the Chaldeans. Whereas the Babylonians and Chinese measured time in double hours, twelve *kaspars* a day for the former and twelve *tokis* for the latter, the Greeks and Romans divided the day into two equal parts of twelve hours each. As the time from sunrise to sunset varied with the season, daylight hours in summer were longer than the hours of darkness, while the reverse held true in winter.

The rigorous discipline of monastic orders, especially the Benedictines, led to a radical upheaval in ways of measuring time. The hour began to be calculated by sundials that did not show the hour, but the religious duty to be fulfilled at various moments of day and night (matins, vespers, etc.). At the end of the 13th century, mechanical clocks made their appearance in Europe. This was a true revolution, as from then on the hour had a fixed duration, to such an extent that by the end of the 14th century most towns had abandoned the solar hour indicated by a gnomon to organise themselves by the striking of the church tower clock.

The day began at sunset and was divided into twenty-four hours: consequently the clock faces were graduated from I to XXIV. However people soon got tired of counting twenty-four chimes, not to mention the innumerable errors that occurred.

So from the 15th century the system was modified so that the clock would strike only six times a day instead of twenty-four. Little time was wasted in applying this simplification and so clock faces began to be numbered I to VI, like that of San Niccolò castle. During the Napoleonic campaigns, "Italian" time was replaced by "French-style" time, where clocks were numbered I to XII and the day started at midnight.

THE FOUNDLINGS' WHEEL

Former hospital of Santo Spirito in Sassia
Borgo Santo Spirito
• Guided tours Mondays at 10am and 3pm

Backing onto the right-hand side of the Santo Spirito in Sassia complex, you can still see today a small construction fitted with a grille through which can be glimpsed a "foundlings' wheel" intended to discreetly receive unwanted newborn infants (see below).

> *For abandoning your child discreetly*

Before these wheels existed, the most common practice was "oblation" (offering to God), which was not considered abandonment since the parents "gave" their child to a convent that not only welcomed it but offered it a place in monastic life.

In Italy, the first wheel was installed at this hospital by Pope Innocent III in 1198. In the second half of the 19th century there were 1,200 "wheels" of this kind in Italy, but they were abolished from 1867 and finally disappeared in 1923.

WHAT IS A FOUNDLINGS' WHEEL?

It is said that in 787, Dateus, a priest in Milan, began placing a large basket outside his church so that abandoned infants could be left there. More organised initiatives for the reception of abandoned children were begun by the Hospice des Chanoines in Marseille from 1188 onwards, with Pope Innocent III (1198-1216) later giving the practice the Church's benediction; he had been horrified by the terrible sight of the bodies of abandoned infants floating in the Tiber and was determined to do something to save them.

So the doors of convents were equipped with a sort of rotating cradle which made it possible for parents to leave their infant anonymously and without exposing it to the elements. The infant was left in the outside section of the cradle, and then the parent rang a bell so that the nuns could activate the mechanism and bring the child inside. Access to the "turntable" was, however, protected by a grille so narrow that only newborn infants would fit through ...

Abandoned during the 19th century, the system had to be readopted after some twenty years at various places in Europe due to the sharp upturn in the number of infants abandoned.

You can see historic foundling wheels at the Vatican, Pisa and Florence (see the *Secret Tuscany* guide from the same publisher), in Bayonne and in Barcelona (see the *Secret Barcelona* guide).

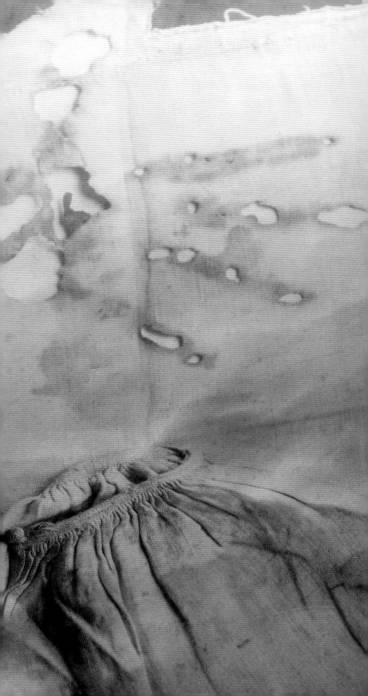

MUSEUM OF THE SOULS IN PURGATORY

12 Lungotevere Prati
• Tel: 06 68806517
• 7.30am-11am, 4pm-7pm
• Admission: Free

*Traces of
the netherworld*

The church of the Sacro Cuore del Suffragio (Sacred Heart of Suffrage) was built at the behest of father Victor Jouet, a French priest from Marseille, who acquired a large plot of building land in Lungotevere Prati in 1893. The peculiarity of this building, which was designed by Giuseppe Gualandi, is that it is entirely built in Gothic style, so much so that some have called it the "small dome of Milan".

In 1897 a fire broke out in a chapel that no longer exists, dedicated to Our Lady of the Rosary, and when the fire was extinguished, faithful bystanders noticed that on one side of the altar there was the image of a face, which, it was said, belonged to a soul in Purgatory. This amazing event prompted Father Jouet to try to find other testimonies concerning the souls in Purgatory. The result of his research is the collection that is preserved today in a showcase hanging on the wall of a small corridor leading to the sacristy.

The collection consists of about a dozen disturbing relics in the form of writing material, fabrics, books and photos that testify to presumed contact between the living and souls in Purgatory. These signs have been left by the souls of the deceased asking for prayers and indulgence.

The relics found here are quite enigmatic: the imprint of three fingers left in 1871 on Maria Zaganti's book of devotion by the deceased Palmira Rastelli who was asking for a holy mass to be said for her, the photo of an imprint by the deceased Mrs Leleux burned into the sleeve of her son Giuseppe's shirt during her apparition in 1789 in Wodecq in Belgium, the burned imprint of Sister Maria di San Luigi Gonzaga's finger when she appeared to Sister Maria of the Sacred Heart in 1894, and finally the imprint left on Margherita Demmerle's book by her mother-in-law who appeared 30 years after her death, in the parish of Ellinghen in 1815.

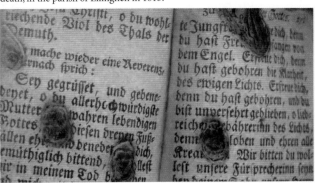

PALAZZETTO BIANCO

28 Via di San Fabiano
• Bus: 916, Gregorio VII or San Damaso

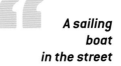

*A sailing
boat
in the street*

I
n a side street off Via Gregorio VII, standing between the Vatican and Piazza Pio XI among more anonymous buildings, is an architecturally avant-garde white residence with modern lines and a very unusual shape. It was designed to fit a narrow triangular space of less than 900 square metres.

The project, which dates back to 1990, is the joint work of the renowned psychiatrist and artist Massimo Fagioli and the architect Paola Rossi: a unique combination where Fagioli took on the role of designer and illustrator and Rossi that of interpreter and director. For administrative and planning reasons, construction did not commence until 2004-2005.

The two sides of the building could not be more different: facing the street is a hymn to the vertical – a curved, cliff-like wall with five floors pierced at regular intervals by twelve small square windows that illuminate the sleeping quarters. On the ground floor, an "indent" in the wall marks the entrance.

The rear of the building, looking onto the hill, consists of rows of projecting balconies, each slightly larger than the one on the floor below. The tall windows give onto the living space of the apartments (there are two on each floor).

This small building – whatever you think of it – really grabs the attention of the (rare) passer-by. Young architectural students can often be seen gazing up admiringly at the white sail on Via di San Fabiano.

NEARBY

THE OPTICAL ILLUSION OF VIA PICCOLOMINI

Via Piccolomini • Bus: 982

After a stroll to Villa Pamphili, it is worthwhile going to Via Piccolomini to enjoy an excellent and surprising view of Saint Peter's cupola, much better even than that from the piazza opposite the basilica. The transformation of the shape of Saint Peter's from Michelangelo's Greek-cross design to Maderno's Latin cross in fact meant that the façade advances so much that a large part of the cupola is hidden from view from Via della Conciliazione. Via Piccolomini however, offers a complete view of the gem and a curious optical illusion that few people notice. Arriving from Villa Pamphili, the cupola, which is visible in the background, seems huge and takes up the entire field of vision. But moving towards the cupola, you notice that contrary to what should logically happen, the cupola shrinks surprisingly until it becomes tiny.

GIANICOLO

BOSCO PARRASIO

0

32 Via di Porta San Pancrazio
- Tel: 06 4872607
- E-mail: giovannarak@gmail.com
- Opening times: contact Accademia dell'Arcadia, 8 Piazza San Agostino
- Bus: 115, 870

The arcadian grove

Bosco Parrasio, former home of the Accademia dell'Arcadia (Academy of Arcadia - an Italian literary academy), is a beautiful garden attributed to Francesco de Sanctis, who also designed the Spanish Steps of Trinità dei Monti. Antonio Canevari, responsible for carrying out the work, found an ingenious solution to the problem posed by the sloping land, dividing it into three levels, joined by concave and convex flights of steps. On the upper level, there is an oval theatre with three rows of seats and a marble lectern, where poets would read their verses. The *Serbatoio* (literally reservoir or tank) building in the background housed the academy's archives and secretarial office. It was restructured in 1838 by Giovanni Azzurri, giving it a semi-circular façade, on which the academy's laws and the inscription *Deo nato sacrum* are displayed. This Latin inscription is a reminder that the garden is dedicated to the Baby Jesus. On the middle level a grotto was constructed, and on the lower level a large marble

edicola (shrine) with an inscription dating from 1726 commemorates the donation from the King of Portugal that made the project possible. This place knew a period of glory thanks to the presence of great men among its academicians, such as the poet Pietro Metastasio and the philosopher Giambattista Vico. At the end of the 18th century, with the decline of the Arcadians, it was abandoned, but reopened in 1839, after restoration work. Bosco Parrasio still belongs to the academy.

The name *Parrasio* comes from an area in southern Arcadia, Parrasia.

THE *ACCADEMIA DELL'ARCADIA*

In 1690 a group of Italian intellectuals who had been part of Queen Christina of Sweden's circle, concerned about the neglected state of literature, founded the Accademia dell'Arcadia in homage to *Arcadia* (1504), a pastoral romance by Jacopo Sannazaro, and to the Greek region of Arcadia, with the objective of returning to the purity of the classical texts as a reaction against Baroque "bad taste". The president took the name of Great Keeper, in reference to the role of shepherd, the members became known as *pastorelli* and *pastorelle* (young male and female shepherds) and Baby Jesus, born among shepherds, was declared protector of the academy. For years the Arcadians would meet in one garden or another, until, in 1726, they founded their permanent headquarters at the foot of Janiculum Hill, alongside the gardens of Palazzo Corsini, former residence of Queen Christina, acquired through the beneficence of John V, King of Portugal, who donated 4,000 escudos to the institution.

ARCADIA: AN ESOTERIC TASTE OF PARADISE?

Arcadia is a mountainous region of Greece's central and eastern Peloponnese.

In antiquity it was considered a primitive and idyllic place where shepherds lived in harmony with nature. In this respect it symbolised a golden age echoed by numerous literary and artistic works: Virgil's *Bucolics* or Ovid's *Fasti* ("Calendar"), for example.

Rediscovered during the Renaissance and 17th century, Arcadia again came to signify the ideal, although for many scholars it represented much more.

The ancient region was celebrated in the 17th century by the French painter Poussin and his canvas *Les Bergers d'Arcadie* ("The Arcadian Shepherds"), now in the Louvre in Paris, in which many see a hidden esoteric message. (See also page 46, Poussin's tomb).

The Alpheus River winds its way through Arcadia and is said to run underground to the sea and resurface in Sicily, where its waters mingle with the fountain of Arethusa.

Alpheus was a sacred river-god, the mythological son of the Titan Oceanus and his sister Tethys, whose underground streams symbolised the hidden traditions of esoteric knowledge.

So this knowledge, which is transmitted to certain artists, was found in the work of Leonardo da Vinci, Botticelli and Poussin, among others.

The name Arcadia comes from Arcas, itself from the ancient Greek *arktos*, meaning "bear". In Greek mythology, Arcas, king of Arcadia, was the son of Zeus and the nymph Callisto. The legend goes that Callisto had offended the goddess Artemis, the huntress, who changed her into a bear during a hunt. Callisto, killed in the chase, was placed among the stars by Zeus and became the *Ursa Major* (Great Bear) constellation, while her son Arcas was transformed into *Ursa Minor* on his death.

NEARBY

JANICULUM HILL: THE TRUE LOCATION OF SAINT PETER'S CRUCIFIXION? ❷
Tempietto de Bramante - 2 Piazza San Pietro in Montorio
• Opening times: April to September, 9:30am-12:30pm and 4pm-6pm
(2pm-4pm from October to March), except Mondays

According to one tradition, different of course from the official version which maintains that these events took place on the hill of the Vatican, the apostle Saint Peter may actually have been crucified on the hill called Janiculum, at the site where the Tempietto de Bramante now stands. Janiculum was indeed used back in those times as a site for the crucifixion of criminals and slaves. Saint Peter, who had put an end to the magical practices of Simon Magus (see page 267), was responsible for the latter's death. Consequently considered by some to be an assassin, he is said to have been crucified at the exact spot of the well behind the Bramante monument. The bas-reliefs featured here recall that Saint Peter supposedly asked to be crucified head down, as he felt himself unworthy of being crucified in a manner similar to Christ.

THE VIA GARIBALDI LATRINES ❸
Via G. Garibaldi (near Piazza San Pietro in Montorio)
• Visits on request, by telephoning the Cultural Heritage department of the Municipality of Rome (*Sovraintendenza Comunale ai Beni Culturali*) at 06 0608, alternatively through cultural associations such as *Roma Sotterranea* (www.romasotterranea.it).

In 1963, the collapse of a retaining wall next to the church of San Pietro in Montorio revealed an unexpected public facility: Roman latrines dating from the end of the 2nd century AD. You can reach them by pushing your way through the undergrowth to find a little door. Inside, the walls are decorated with frescoes of geometric patterns in green and red. The illustrations include plant motifs and an ibex. These artworks are nevertheless of rather less interest than the vast quantity of later graffiti representing animals, obscene symbols and human figures, as well as Latin or Greek examples of lavatory humour. All these spontaneous expressions are a clear sign that subversive graffiti is nothing new. On the other hand, there is no trace of any stone lavatory seats, so they were probably made from wood. Below, a canal has been dug to evacuate waste to the sewers. Under the tiles another canal can be glimpsed, smaller than the first, where clean water probably ran for use in sponging down the latrines. The black and white tiles with geometric motifs have only been preserved on a small portion of the floor.

BORROMINI'S STAIRCASE ❹
Crypt of the monastery of Santa Maria dei Sette Dolori
Hotel Donna Camilla Savelli - 27 Via Garibaldi • Tel: 06 588861

At the foot of Janiculum Hill, there is also the monastery of Santa Maria dei Sette Dolori with its adjoining church, whose façade has never been completed due to lack of funds. The crypt of the monastery, now transformed into an elegant hotel, conceals solid ancient and medieval walls which form the foundations of the church. Here, Borromini in his genius did not alter the existing structures, but simply added a grand staircase, opening another dimension for viewing the walls in rough masonry, the beaten earth floor and a row of beams with barrels resting on them. In the future, the crypt will probably be opened to the public as plans are afoot to convert this space, without making any major changes, for wine tastings.

MINISTERO PER I BENI CULTURALI E AMBIENTALI

SOPRINTENDENZA PER I BENI AMBIENTALI ED ARCHITETTONICI DI ROMA

PROIETTILE DI CANNONE DA 140
DELL'ARTIGLIERIA FRANCESE
– MEMORIA BELLICA –
DEI BOMBARDAMENTI
DEL GIUGNO 1849 –
QUI' TROVATO E RIPOSTO
IN RICORDO
DELL'EROICA RESISTENZA DELLA REPUBBLICA ROMANA
E DEI GRAVI DANNI ALLORA SOFFERTI
DA QUESTA INSIGNE CAPPELLA
– ORA NUOVAMENTE RESTAURATA –
OPERA DI CARLO MADERNO

A. D. MDCCCCXCV

SAN PIETRO IN MONTORIO'S CANNON BALL ❺

Outside wall of the church of San Pietro in Montorio
Via Garibaldi

I f you look to the left on the façade of the church of San Pietro in Montorio, you will see a strange plaque with a sphere attached to it. Step closer to read the inscription and you will discover a French artillery cannon ball found at this very spot. It commemorates the 1849 battles during which the independent republic of Rome put up a heroic defence.

An unusual souvenir of the fighting on Janiculum Hill in 1849

1849 was a decisive year for the Risorgimento, the ideological and political movement behind Italian unification. In Rome, papal rule foundered in the face of popular pro-democracy uprisings, and the pope was obliged to flee the city. The republic was proclaimed on 9 February. The conservative European regimes offered help to restore temporal power while Garibaldi and his followers disembarked at Rome to defend the new republic. He was entrusted with the defence of Janiculum Hill, the point most exposed to the French army offensive.

GARIBALDI: SAVIOUR OF TASSO'S BELL

It was in 1595 that the smallest bell of the church of Sant'Onofrio al Gianicolo had come to be known as "Tasso's bell". On 25 April of that year, its melancholy peals accompanied the death throes and announced the end – at the age of only 51 – of the celebrated poet who was being cared for in the neighbouring convent.

In spring 1849, this bell was almost destroyed during the rioting that gripped the capital. The order had gone out to confiscate all church bells to make cannons, and as it was not far from the fighting Sant'Onofrio was one of the first churches to be requisitioned by the military.

The story goes that the Father Superior vainly begged the officer in charge to take whatever he liked except the little bell, but he would not be moved, until Garibaldi arrived in the nick of time. As a last resort, the priest appealed directly to the general.

Moved by his supplications, or perhaps by the sad early death of a great poet, Garibaldi ordered that Tasso's bell be spared.

Thus it can still be seen today, as well as the tomb and the convent cell where the unfortunate author of the immortal *Gerusalemme liberata* died.

AMERICAN ACADEMY IN ROME

5 Via Angelo Masina
- Tel: 06 58461
- info@aarome.org
- Open to the public for exhibitions, concerts, lectures and more
- Programme available at www.aarome.org

T he American Academy, even more discreet than other similar Roman institutions, accepts some thirty artists and researchers per year, as well as around forty short-stay students.

Artists' workshops inspired by the pavilions of the 1893 Chicago World's Fair

The project to set up an American Academy in Rome emerged following the Chicago Columbian Exposition of 1893 and was based on the idea of a group led by two architects: Charles Follen McKim, who designed some of the buildings of Columbia University (1893) and the Pierpont Morgan Library (1903) in New York; and Daniel Burnham, responsible for the Flatiron Building in New York (1902). These men attached great significance to European classical culture, and would convince the biggest New York financiers of the time (J.P. Morgan, John D. Rockefeller and Henry Clay Frick) to make substantial donations to establish the American Academy in Rome in 1894.

Today, the artists' workshops in front of the outer façade are reminiscent of the pavilions of the 1893 Expo, while the academy's main building, designed by McKim, Mead and White, was inspired by Renaissance villas with a *piano nobile* (main floor) and a courtyard ornamented with the remains of antique sculptures.

The beautiful Villa Aurelia was built for Cardinal Girolamo Farnese in 1650. In 1849, Garibaldi set up his headquarters there to defend the Roman Republic against the French armies, whose artillery almost destroyed the villa and its gardens in their victorious battle. After major restoration work, the villa was bequeathed to the American Academy in 1909. Conferences and concerts are regularly held there.

In the gardens, the Casa Rustica stands on the site of the 16th-century casino of Cardinal Malvasia. On 14 April 1611, the Academia dei Lincei held a grand reception there in honour of Galileo, whose guests could view the heavens through the telescope he had invented. The casino was demolished in 1849 and replaced by the Casa Rustica, which houses maps produced by NASA representing the sky on 14 April 1611. The building was used as a tavern until the 1920s (the inscription "VINO" can still be seen), when it was bought by the Academy.

THE FAÇADE OF "MICHELANGELO'S HOUSE" ❼

Passeggiata del Gianicolo

A façade that was moved three times

While strolling along the Passeggiata del Gianicolo (Janiculum Walk), just opposite the statue of Ciceruacchio ("the chubby one", the nickname of Angelo Brunetti), you will come across a beautiful 16th-century façade with a plaque bearing this inscription: QUESTA FACCIATA DELLA CASA DETTA DI MICHELANGELO GIÀ IN VIA DELLE TRE PILE DEMOLITA NELL'ANNO MCMXXX FU RICOSTRUITA AD ORNAMENTO DELLA PASSEGGIATA PUBBLICA XXI APRILE MCMXLI.[1]

What was said to be "Michelangelo's house" stood near the first bend in Via delle Tre Pile, the lane that climbs up to the right of the Cordonata (flight of steps designed by Michelangelo leading to Piazza d'Aracoeli) on the Capitoline Hill. In 1872 the building was demolished, but the architectural elements of the façade were purchased by the architect Domenico Jannetti, who recycled them in a new construction in Via delle Tre Pile. Then, during 1930s construction work on the Capitoline Hill, Jannetti's building was in turn demolished, but once again the 16th-century façade was preserved. It was dismantled and stored in a municipal depot, only to be reused in 1941 to conceal a large water tank at the end of the Passeggiata del Gianicolo from the gaze of the Romans.

It is extraordinary that this façade has been attributed to Michelangelo's house: he lived elsewhere, in the Macel de' Corvi district, as borne out by the inscription at the junction of Piazza Venezia and Via dei Fornari which translates as: "On this site stood the house consecrated by the occupancy and death of the divine Michelangelo."

Michelangelo did indeed live in Macel de' Corvi until his death on 18 February 1564. The house was then bought by Daniele da Volterra, one of his pupils, nicknamed "*braghettone*" (breeches-maker) because at the height of the Counter-Reformation he was responsible for covering up the nudity of several figures (painted by his master) in the Sistine Chapel's *Last Judgment* fresco.

Between the late 19th and early 20th centuries, the south and east sides of Piazza Venezia were demolished to make way for the Altare della Patria, also known as the Monumento Nazionale a Vittorio Emanuele II, built in honour of King Victor Emmanuel.

The main consequence of this work was the destruction of the medieval district where Michelangelo's house stood. The only record we have of this area's special charm comes from a number of engravings and old photographs.

1: This façade of the house said to be Michelangelo's formerly in Via delle Tre Pile and demolished in 1930 was rebuilt to grace the public highway 21 April 1941.

A STATUE FACING THE OTHER WAY AT THE REQUEST OF THE VATICAN

On the Janiculum Hill, at one of the sites with the best views of Rome, an equestrian statue of Garibaldi stands on a high marble plinth, dominating the city spread out at his feet. This bronze monument by the artist Enrico Gallori, erected in 1895, has however had its ups and downs. Under Mussolini's dictatorship it was replaced by fascist symbols, but was eventually reinstalled in 1943, although in a different position, giving rise to a string of political interpretations.

When the monument was first erected, the "Hero of the Two Worlds" did indeed face the Vatican in a rather provocative way. At the time, the relationship between the fledgling Italian state and the Holy See was extremely tense and the Church felt that the unification of Italy was detrimental to its interests.

With the signing of the Lateran Treaty in 1929 and the establishment of normal relations between the two states, the Holy See asked that the statue should face the city: the request was granted. The Romans were greatly amused, joking that now it is the horse's turn to show its backside to the Vatican!

A crown on the steps to the right of the plinth is a reminder that the Republican Garibaldi was the first Grand Master of Italian Freemasonry.

VILLA LANTE

8

10 Passeggiata del Gianicolo
• Tel: 06 68801674
• E-mail: info@irfrome.org
• Visits on request from Monday to Friday, 9am-12pm
Amici di Villa Lante al Gianicolo association: €25 annual membership
includes invitations to conferences, concerts and exhibitions
• Bus: 115, 870

An unbeatable view

Villa Lante on Janiculum Hill, one of the best-preserved 16th-century Roman villas, is a priceless example of the work of Raphael's school in Rome. It offers an exceptional view, perhaps the most beautiful in the city.

The villa, with its three arches, four antique columns in purple-veined Phrygian marble and a stucco-decorated vault, is nevertheless little known, as it is not visible from the street.

Its construction dates back to when Baldassare Turini, Pope Leo X's datarius (papal official), bought some 2 hectares of land on Janiculum Hill, covered in vineyards and gardens at the time, as a summer residence and to welcome other officials and the literati.

Giulio Romano, Raphael's favourite student, was the architect, and other artists from the school carried out the pictorial decoration. The original decoration of the salon, with its imitation marble and precious stones, was discovered and restored in the 1970s on part of the walls, whereas elsewhere the neoclassical work by the renowned architect Valadier was retained. The famous graffiti "A dì 6 de maggio 1527 fo la presa di Roma", representing the sacking of Rome, is still visible in the salon.

In 1551 the property went to the Lante family, who lived in a palazzo in Piazza Sant'Eustachio. The size of the villa's garden was reduced in 1640, when Pope Urban VIII decided to build the Janiculum defensive wall and in exchange gave the Lante family the villa in Bagnaia, close to Viterbo, with its spectacular park filled with fountains.

At the beginning of the 19th century, the Lante family sold part of their property, including the villa, which passed to Prince Camillo Borghese, husband of Napoleon's sister Pauline, who in turn sold it a few years later to the order of nuns of the Sacred Heart of Jesus. The frescoes in the salon, which were not part of the sale, were removed from the ceiling and now can be found in Palazzo Zuccari. At the end of the 19th century, the nuns rented the villa to the German archaeologist Wolfgang Helbig and his wife, the Russian princess Nadine Schahawskoy, who converted it into a much-frequented cultural centre.

MONASTERY OF SANT'ONOFRIO

9

2 Piazza Sant'Onofrio

The entrance door of Sant'Onofrio monastery bears a rather unusual red cross. The monastery is in fact the religious headquarters of the Order of the Holy Sepulchre of Jerusalem. Far from being an esoteric order, this is one of the last remaining Catholic chivalric orders surviving today (see opposite). Its characteristic emblem recalls the five wounds of Christ on the Cross (see opposite).

THE CROSS OF THE ORDER OF THE HOLY SEPULCHRE OF JERUSALEM

The insignia of the order is the red Jerusalem cross or cross potent (with

crossbars), surrounded by four smaller crosses. These five crosses now serve as a reminder of the five wounds of Christ on the Cross, even though they originally signified that the Word of Christ had spread in four directions around the world.

The symbolism is also of resurrection. The colour red, representing life, strength and blood, was chosen to commemorate the wounds inflicted on Christ.

In the East, the cross is golden, symbolising the immense value of Christ's Passion.

ORDER OF THE HOLY SEPULCHRE OF JERUSALEM

The Order of the Holy Sepulchre of Jerusalem is a military and religious chivalric order of knighthood thought to have been founded by Duke Godfrey of Bouillon, victor of the First Crusade in 1099 at Jerusalem, or even, according to other sources, by Charlemagne (in 808). With its headquarters in Rome at Sant'Onofrio monastery on Janiculum Hill, the order has thirty-five branches around the world. There are some 18,000 Knights and Ladies of the Holy Sepulchre, whose principal aim is to encourage and propagate their faith in the Holy Land, under the authority of the pope. The order owes its name to the Holy Cross of Jerusalem, the sanctuary built around the supposed site of Christ's crucifixion and the place where he is thought to have been buried and resurrected.

Today the order runs forty-four Catholic schools in and around Jerusalem, bringing together some 15,000 pupils, both Christian and Muslim.

In France, the order is the guardian of the holy relic of Christ's crown of thorns (see *Secret Paris* in this series of guides).

NEARBY

THE BELFRY OF SAN GIACOMO ALLA LUNGARA ⑩
12 Lungotevere della Farnesina

Walking along Via della Lungara towards Porta Settimiana, on the corner with Salita del Buon Pastore, the small church of San Giacomo rises in front of you, with a convent annexed to it. The church dates back to the 9th century and it has a small and beautiful belfry, decorated with marble medallions, enclosed by rows of zigzagging brick. It is now hemmed in between later buildings, and is only visible from Lungotevere. The belfry has the peculiarity of being the only remaining Romanesque belfry in Rome with one opening. It was built in the 13th century, when Pope Innocent IV gave the church to the Sylvestrine nuns. Parts of the masonry in bare brick possibly belonged to an older, already existing tower.

HERMETIC FRESCOES OF VILLA FARNESINA

230 Via della Lungara
• Open every day except Sundays and public holidays, 9am-1pm (last admission 12:40pm)
• Admission charge

The "lucky star" of Agostino Chigi

Villa Farnesina was built between 1508 and 1511 by Baldassare Peruzzi for the Sienese banker Agostino Chigi (1466-1520), then the richest man in Rome. It was later sold to the Farnese family, who gave it their name (see page 217 for the villa's history).

Chigi was interested in the mythological and esoteric themes for which there was quite a craze at this period of the Italian Renaissance. He asked Peruzzi (1481-1536) to paint a fresco of his horoscope, following a mythological and astrological journey. The result is a unique work that can still be seen today.

Conscious of being born "under a lucky star", Chigi wanted his good fortune to be represented in his home by the favourable conjunctions of the stars on the day of his birth. In a work probably dated 1 December 1466, on

the vaulted ceiling of the room on the ground floor of the villa (now the Galatea Room), Peruzzi sketched out the complete cycle of constellations and the planets aligned in a specific astrological pattern, symbolised by classical mythological figures on a background of intense blue sky.

Thus to illustrate the moment of Chigi's birth, he painted the constellation of the Great Bear aligned with those of Pegasus and Leo. In the centre of the ceiling vault is the fluttering winged figure of Fame. Perseus seizes and beheads the Gorgon, and from his blood springs Pegasus, the mythical winged horse of the constellation of the same name. Nearby, a chariot pulled by magnificent bulls carries a young girl up to heaven: Callisto, a nymph beloved of Jupiter whom he transformed into the constellation of Ursa Major (Great Bear) to escape the wrath of his wife Hera, who in a fit of jealousy had changed her into a she-bear. In the next hexagon Hercules battles the Nemean Lion, suggesting the constellation of Leo.

Europa (who took the form of a bull after being abducted by Zeus), shown together with the symbolic representation of the ram, indicates that at the time of Chigi's birth the planet Jupiter (Zeus) was in the sign of Aries. The Sun in Sagittarius is represented by Apollo near a centaur ready to let fly his arrow. The transit of the planet Venus in the constellation of Capricorn is illustrated by the goddess at the centre of a shell surrounded by doves and accompanied by the unicorn.

The artist continues the mythological story through signs of the Zodiac linked to Chigi: Gemini is denoted by the fable of the love of Zeus – in the form of a swan – for Leda, Queen of Sparta. From their union were born the Dioscuri (Sons of Zeus), the twins (Gemini) Castor and Pollux. Hercules, bitten by a scorpion while fighting the monstrous Hydra, represents Scorpio; while Ganymede is ravished by Jupiter disguised as an eagle that carries him off to Olympus to be the cupbearer of the gods, symbolising Aquarius. The traditional sequence of the signs of the Zodiac ends with Pisces, where Eros and Psyche are transformed, according to myth, to escape the monstrous Typhon.

The depiction of a favourable event as a ceiling fresco was more than just decoration, it had a real esoteric objective. According to the Egyptian tradition of hermeticism, rediscovered during the Renaissance (see following double-page spread), the positive energy represented by the fresco was supposed to pour into the room and into the entire house in which it was painted, as well as on the occupants.

HERMES TRISMEGISTUS AND HERMETISM: ATTRACTING CELESTIAL ENERGY TO EARTH BY REPRODUCING THE COSMIC ORDER

Hermes Trismegistus, which in Latin means "thrice-great Hermes", is the name given by the neo-Platonists, alchemists, and hermetists to the Egyptian god *Thot*, *Hermes* to the Greeks. In the Old Testament, he is also identified with the patriarch Enoch. In their respective cultures, all three were considered to be the creators of phonetic writing, theurgical magic, and messianic prophetism.

Thot was connected to the lunar cycles whose phases expressed the harmony of the universe. Egyptian writings refer to him as "twice great" because he was the god of the Word and of Wisdom. In the syncretic atmosphere of the Roman Empire, the epithet of the Egyptian god *Thot* was given to the Greek god *Hermes*, but this time was "thrice great" (*trismegistus*) for the Word, Wisdom and his duty as Messenger of all the gods of the Elysium or of Olympus. The Romans associated him with *Mercury*, the planet that mediates between the Earth and the Sun, which is a function that Kabbalistic Jews called *Metraton*, the "perpendicular measure between the Earth and the Sun".

In Hellenic Egypt, *Hermes* was the "scribe and messenger of the gods" and was believed to be the author of a collection of sacred texts, called *hermetic*, that contained teachings about art, science, religion and philosophy – the *Corpus Hermeticum* – the objective of which was the deification of humanity through knowledge of God. These texts, which were probably written by a group belonging to the *Hermetic School* of ancient Egypt, thus express the knowledge accumulated over time by attributing it to the god of Wisdom, who is in all points similar to the Hindu god *Ganesh*. The *Corpus Hermeticum*, which probably dates from the 1st to the 3rd centuries AD, represented the source of inspiration of hermetic and neo-Platonic thought during the Renaissance. Even though Swiss scholar Casaubon had apparently proved the contrary in the 17th century, people

continued to believe that the text dated back to Egyptian antiquity before Moses and that it announced the coming of Christianity.

According to Clement of Alexandria, it contained 42 books divided into six volumes. The first treated the education of priests; the second, the rites of the temple; the third, geology, geography, botany and agriculture; the fourth, astronomy and astrology, mathematics and architecture; the fifth contained hymns to the glory of the gods and a guide of political action for kings; the sixth was a medical text.

It is generally believed that Hermes Trismegistus invented a card game full of esoteric symbols, of which the first 22 were made of blades of gold and the 56 others of blades of silver – the *tarot* or "Book of Thot". Hermes is also attributed with writing the *Book of the Dead* or "Book of the Exit towards the Light", as well as the famous alchemy text *The Emerald Table*, works that had a strong influence on the alchemy and magic practised in medieval Europe.

In medieval Europe, especially between the 5th and 14th centuries, hermetism was also a School of Hermeneutics that interpreted certain poems of antiquity and various enigmatic myths and works of art as allegorical treaties of alchemy or hermetic science. For this reason, the term *hermetism* still designates the esoteric nature of a text, work, word or action, in that they possess an occult meaning that requires a hermeneutic, or in other words a philosophical science, to correctly interpret the hidden meaning of the object of study.

Hermetic principles were adopted and applied by the Roman *Colegium Fabrorum*, associations of the architects of civil, military and religious constructions. This knowledge was transmitted in the 12th century to the Christian *builder-monks*, the builders of the grand Roman and Gothic edifices of Europe, who executed their work according to the principles of sacred architecture, true to the model of sacred geometry. It is the direct legacy of volumes three and four of the *Corpus Hermeticum*, according to which cities and buildings were constructed in interrelation with specific planets and constellations, so that the design of the Heavens could be reproduced on Earth, thus favouring cosmic or sidereal energies. All of this was done with the purpose of achieving the hermetic principle that states: "Everything above is like everything below".

During the European Renaissance (16th and 17th centuries), hermetism was replaced by humanism. Forms were rationalised and the transcendental ignored. It was the end of the traditional society and the beginning of a profane, Baroque and pre-modernist society, paving the way for the arrival of the materialism and atheism that dominates the modern world. There were, however, some exceptions to this predominant rule in Europe. In Portugal, in the 16th century, the *Master Builders*, the heirs of the builder-monks, founded the Manueline style according to the hermetic rules of sacred architecture. The influence of the *Free Builders* continued into the 18th century and their greatest work was the restoration of Lisbon after the earthquake of 1755. That is why Pombal's Lisbon is designed and constructed according to the geometric and architectural measures of the Tradition handed down by Hermes Trismegistus (see *Secret Lisbon*).

THE FACE AT VILLA FARNESINA

230 Via della Lungara
• Open every day except Sundays and public holidays, 9am-1pm (last admission 12:40pm)
• Admission charge

> **Michelangelo's alleged gift to Raphael**

The banker Agostino Chigi entrusted the decoration of his Roman residence on the far side of the Tiber to the most renowned artists of the time: Peruzzi (who was also the architect) as well as Sebastiano del Piombo, Il Sodoma and Raphael. The only exception was Michelangelo as he was fully occupied with papal projects.

In the loggia featuring Raphael's *Triumph of Galatea* fresco is a magnificent charcoal study of a head that has long been attributed to Michelangelo. There have been several rumours about the origin of this drawing. It was said that Michelangelo was extremely curious about how the work was going, but Raphael had banned anyone from entering the loggia he was painting. To deceive the guards, Michelangelo disguised himself as a peddler and managed to enter the room where Raphael had been working. Then, unable to resist the temptation, he grabbed a stick of charcoal and drew a superb and imposing face in an unpainted alcove. Another version of the story is that Michelangelo wanted to see his pupil Daniele da Volterra, who was working on the Farnesina site. Not finding him, he climbed on the scaffolding to draw the head in question and left it to mark his visit. It's now thought that Baldassare Peruzzi, architect of the villa, must have made the drawing ... This tale gives a sense of the intense rivalry in 16th-century Rome between all these outstanding artists.

The villa of Agostino Chigi "the magnificent" was of proverbial beauty, but this did not last long. The building was occupied and damaged during the sack of Rome, then sold in 1581 by Chigi's bankrupt heirs to the Farnese family, who named it after themselves. But the gardens were later abandoned and the loggia overlooking the river was in ruins. The new owners eventually lost interest, as did the Bourbons of Naples who inherited the villa. The newly appointed Spanish ambassador bought it in 1870 and renovated a few rooms, but the hardest blow was dealt by the new Italian state: forty per cent of the land between the villa and the Tiber was requisitioned for river development projects. When the state finally acquired the villa in 1927, this architectural gem was in an appalling state of neglect and seemed unlikely to survive. Now spectacularly renovated, it is one of Rome's last surviving examples of a private Renaissance palace.

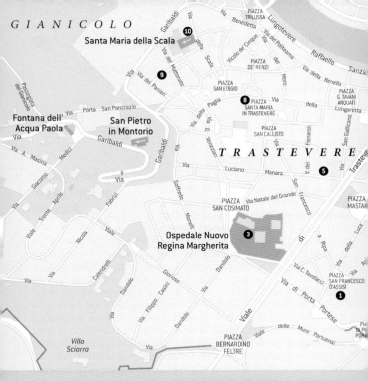

TRASTEVERE

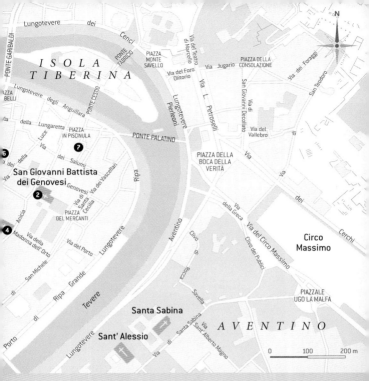

THE MECHANISM OF THE RELIQUARY OF SAINT FRANCIS' CELL

①

San Francesco d'Assisi a Ripa Grande
Piazza San Francesco d'Assisi
• Tel: 06 5819020
• Open 9am-12pm and 4:30pm-7:30pm

> *Relics hidden in a precious artefact*

Saint Francis of Assisi and his disciples were lodged in a cell annexed to this church, which belonged to Benedictine monks before Pope Gregory IX asked them, in 1229, to hand it and the adjacent hospice over to the Order of Friars Minor (the Franciscans), who renamed it San Francesco d'Assisi a Ripa Grande.

It is not widely known that this cell, later converted into a chapel, holds a curious Baroque masterpiece: an amazing altar was carved from the roots of a walnut tree between 1698 and 1708 by the Franciscan brother Bernardino da Jesi, and later embellished with traditional paintings.

In the middle of the wood panelling is a magnificent 13th-century altarpiece featuring a portrait of Saint Francis attributed to the school of Margheritone d'Arezzo. The altarpiece is flanked by two 14th-century paintings depicting Saint Anthony of Padua and Saint Louis of Toulouse, while the side panels feature the Virgin and the Angel of the Annunciation, late 17th-century works by an artist of the school of Carlo Maratta. It was Cardinal Ranuccio Pallavicini who commissioned this rare artefact for the church, to which he also bequeathed his impressive collection of relics. The altarpiece in fact incorporates an ingenious mechanism: the

relics are kept inside the altar, in precious silver coffers. When the mechanism is activated, all the visible parts pivot to reveal the treasures inside, thus transforming the altar into a sumptuous reliquary.

Next to the altar, in a niche closed by a grille, a stone on which Saint Francis is said to have laid his head has also been preserved.

THE CLOISTER OF SAN GIOVANNI BATTISTA ❷ DEI GENOVESI

12 Via Anicia
• Open Tuesdays and Thursdays, 2pm-4pm in winter and 3pm-5pm in summer

A little-known 15th-century marvel

A mong the maze of buildings in the Trastevere district is the headquarters of the brotherhood of Saint John the Baptist, where one of the most beautiful cloisters in Rome is hidden from the street. Access is via the church through a little door in the left-hand wall.

You will find yourself in a haven of peace and silence, immediately entranced by the beauty of the ground-floor archways buttressed onto octagonal columns and the architraves of the upper storey, as well as the contrast between their shade and the luxuriant green plants bathed in sunshine. In the centre of the garden stands a 14th-century travertine well, set off by two antique columns in Ionic style.

Fragments of antique marble are scattered here and there beneath the arcades. The church and most of the buildings were given so many facelifts between the 15th and 19th centuries that they have lost their original appearance, with the exception of the old hospice and the cloister, built in 1481 and attributed to Baccio Pontelli, designer of the Sistine Chapel.

An inscription on a funerary stele explains that inside the cloister there used to be a compound, demolished at the end of the 18th century, while another inscription on a column, in Latin this time, says that in this cloister the very first palm tree to be imported to Rome was planted by a friar from Savona in the late 16th century.

The cycle of frescoes attributed to Guido Signorini and Gerolamo Margotti date from the beginning of the 17th century, however. They were discovered in the 1970s under a thick coat of lime-washed plaster during the restoration of the site.

The brotherhood was founded in 1533, although the church dedicated to Saint John the Baptist (patron saint of the city of Genoa) and its hospice (founded by Pope Sixtus IV and paid for by the Genoese ambassador to help sailors) already existed.

WHY IS JOHN THE BAPTIST THE PATRON SAINT OF GENOA?
Around the year 1100, on the way back to Genoa from the Crusades, Genoese sailors stopped off along the coast of Lycia (now south-western Turkey) and found the ashes of Saint John the Baptist in a convent, not far from the town of Myra (modern Demre). Following this episode, the town adopted the saint as its patron.

THE CLOISTERS OF THE NUOVO REGINA MARGHERITA HOSPITAL

Piazza San Cosimato
• Tram: 8

Hidden cloisters

The former monastery of Santi Cosma e Damiano in Mica Aurea, so named because it was built on the golden-coloured sand of the slopes of Janiculum Hill, later became known as San Cosimato. Today, it is part of the Nuovo Regina Margherita hospital complex, opened in 1970.

Apart from hospital staff, patients and their families, and passers-by, few people know that the hospital grounds contain two spectacular cloisters. The first is medieval, dating back to the beginning of the 12th century, and the other Renaissance, built during restoration work commissioned by Pope Sixtus IV.

The first cloister, which was one of the biggest in medieval Rome, is the most impressive. With arcades on all four sides, small twin columns supporting the narrow brick arches, the cloister is filled with fragments of ancient inscriptions. Columns and sarcophagi are scattered over the lawn and among the trees in the garden.

A few steps lead to the second cloister, square-shaped and smaller than the first. It is embellished with arcades of octagonal pilasters in travertine topped by lovely capitals carved with plant motifs. The interior garden features a water tank dating back to the mid-19th century.

San Cosimato, with its complex architectural history divided between two medieval periods and the Renaissance, was for centuries one of the richest monasteries in Rome.

The monastery, founded in the first half of the 10th century by Benedictine monks, was not completed until the 13th century. The Franciscan Order of Poor Clare nuns took over the convent in 1234 and had it enlarged. This was followed by work carried out under Pope Sixtus IV for the 1475 Jubilee, during which a new church, a belfry and the second cloister were constructed.

After the unification of Italy and the introduction of legislation suppressing religious corporations, the Italian state ceded San Cosimato convent to the City of Rome. It was granted to a charitable organisation and then converted into a hospice.

THE FORTY-HOUR DEVICE ❹

Church of Santa Maria dell'Orto
10 Via Anicia
• Open daily, 9am-12pm
• Tram: 8, station Trastevere/Piazza Mastai

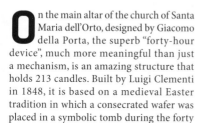

Forty hours, the time that Jesus spent in the tomb

On the main altar of the church of Santa Maria dell'Orto, designed by Giacomo della Porta, the superb "forty-hour device", much more meaningful than just a mechanism, is an amazing structure that holds 213 candles. Built by Luigi Clementi in 1848, it is based on a medieval Easter tradition in which a consecrated wafer was placed in a symbolic tomb during the forty hours that Jesus would have spent in the tomb between Good Friday (his death) and Easter Sunday (his resurrection).

In the 16th century this ritual was replaced by periods of forty hours of continuous prayer. The faithful went from church to church to pray and the altars were often adorned with a temporary structure (known as the *apparato*) housing the communion host.

At the end of the 16th century, in order to distract people from the temptations of carnival festivals, the Roman clerics established the custom of celebrating the forty hours over nine days in February, in the churches of San Lorenzo in Damaso and the Gesù, which led Pietro da Cortona to construct a superb forty-hour device in 1632 for San Lorenzo in Damaso. Most of the time, these devices were built using materials that were easy to work with, like the wooden structures on which stucco or papier mâché decorations could be added. The one in Santa Maria dell'Orto is very finely worked, so well that it has evolved from a temporary to a permanent structure, the last of its kind to survive in Rome.

It is still used today during the Mass of the Last Supper on Holy (Maundy) Thursday: all the candles of the main altar are lit at the same time. On this occasion the church remains open until midnight so that the faithful can gather around this spectacle, as leaving the candles lit for forty hours is no longer feasible for technical reasons.

The device itself can be seen in the church during the fifty days following Easter, after which it is removed.

ANATOMY THEATRE OF SAN GALLICANO HOSPITAL

5

Sede Storica Istituto San Gallicano
25 Via San Gallicano
• Open Saturdays, 10am-4pm

> *A room for dissecting corpses*

Within the constantly busy precincts of the Santa Maria e San Gallicano hospital can be found its former anatomy theatre. Here, in this room decorated with stucco bas-reliefs, dissections of human bodies used to be carried out. On the floor, below the light flooding from the pierced vault, a large marble slab marks the location of the table on which the corpses lay. The room is now headquarters to the institute's scientific management.

Pope Leo XII had this anatomy theatre built in 1826 to celebrate the centenary of the Institute of Santa Maria and San Gallicano. The architect Giacomo Palazzi was commissioned to design this oval room at the centre of which opens a round vault surrounded by allegories of medicine. Around the sides, stucco medallions depict eighteen illustrious Roman doctors, from Celsus, known as the Latin Hippocrates (1st century AD) to the great anatomist Gabriele Fallopio (1523-1562) who described certain essential aspects of the reproductive and auditory systems, and Lancisi (1654-1720) who established the correlation between mosquitoes and malaria.

The main beauty of this room lies in the stucco bas-reliefs sculpted by Ignazio del Sarti, representing the legend of Asclepius as recounted in Ovid's *Metamorphoses* (see below).

WAS ASCLEPIUS, GOD OF MEDICINE, BEHIND THE CREATION OF TIBER ISLAND?

According to Ovid's account in *Metamorphoses*, when a great plague decimated the population of Rome, the Romans went to consult the oracle at Delphi. The prophetess replied that they needed the help of her son, the god of medicine, rather than Apollo. So the Roman Senate sent a delegation to fetch Asclepius by ship from Epidaurus. He told them that he would appear as a serpent and that they would need to recognise him in this form. The Romans prayed to the god and a great serpent appeared, which they allowed on board. The serpent dispelled the perils of the voyage and the ship sailed safely back up the Tiber. On arriving at Rome, the serpent wrapped itself around the trunk of a tree. At this very spot the river divided into two channels, creating an island. The serpent then slithered down from the tree and healed Rome's citizens.

There are also well-preserved anatomy theatres in London, Barcelona, Pistoia (Tuscany), Padua and Bologna. See *Secret London – an unusual guide*, *Secret Tuscany*, and *Secret Barcelona* from the same publisher.

THE *EXCUBITORIUM* ❻

Via della Settima Coorte
• Visits on request by telephoning the Fine Arts department of
the Municipality of Rome (*Sovrintendenza Capitolina*) at 06 0608,
alternatively through cultural associations such as *Roma Sotterranea*
(www.romasotterranea.it)
• Tram: 3, 8

*Firemen
from ancient
Rome*

D uring excavation work in the mid-19th
century, some rooms from the Roman
period were discovered about 8 metres
beneath the current street level. The building
was identified as housing a detachment from
the 7th cohort of the city's guards, or firemen,
thanks to the large amount of graffiti present on the walls. The guard corps was
composed of seven cohorts, each with 1,000 to 1,200 men. Each cohort had
to protect two of the 14 districts into which the city was subdivided, and had
their barracks in one district and a detachment (*excubitorium*) in the other.

Unfortunately, the area was abandoned after the excavation work, with
serious consequences for the preservation of the structure and the graffiti of
the ancient firemen. A splendid floor mosaic was also destroyed during the
Second World War. Only a century later was the monument finally roofed over,
while maintenance and restoration work was finished 20 years later.

It seems that these firemen's quarters were installed within a private
residence towards the end of the 2nd century AD. By going down a modern
staircase, you enter a large hall where there is a peculiar hexagonal basin with
concave sides. On the far wall there is a door leading into a *lararium* (chapel)
dedicated to the protector of the guards, *genio excubitori,* in which only the
remains of paintings on the walls of the *edicola* (wall shrine) and on the lintel
are preserved. In other rooms, pieces of terracotta floors have been found with
bricks in an *opus spicatum* or herringbone design as well as a buried *dolium*
(large ceramic jar) in which wine, oil and grain were usually kept.

In the drawings and photographs that document the room's large black
and white floor mosaic that is now gone, two Tritons are visible, one holding a
lighted torch and the other an extinguished torch.

Of all these important relics that had survived until the time of the
excavations, unfortunately hardly anything remains, except for the fresco with
a cherub and seahorses on a door lintel. The most serious loss is that of almost
one hundred pieces of the firemen's graffiti, which fortunately were transcribed
after their discovery. This unique evidence regarding the organisation of the
firemen and their life in these quarters was written on the plastered walls
between AD 215 and AD 245 by the firemen themselves. The graffiti included
greetings to the emperors, expressed their fatigue and their thanks to the gods
and the *genio excubitori*, and mentioned the name and number of the cohort
and the names and ranks of the guards.

THE CHURCH BELL OF SAN BENEDETTO IN PISCINULA

❼

40 Piazza in Piscinula
• Open 7:30am-12pm and 5pm-7pm
• Tram: 8

The smallest bell in Rome

San Benedetto in Piscinula is a small and beautiful 13th-century church. Known as "San Benedettino" by Trastevere residents, it was built on the ruins of the Domus Aniciorum – the house of the Anicii, an old Roman family to which Saint Benedict is said to have belonged, and whose cell is annexed to the church.

Besides the saint's cell, the charming little Romanesque belfry is the real curiosity of this church. Its bell, 45 cm in diameter, is said to be

the smallest and oldest in Rome. The inscription "1069" engraved in the bronze, indicating the year it was made, has survived centuries of wear and is still legible. The inside of the church is very irregular and, as is often the case in Rome, contains a hotchpotch of works dating back to different periods. The columns go back to the Roman period, and the floor tiles to medieval times. The remains of frescoes depicting scenes from the Old Testament on the right wall, with the Last Judgement opposite, are from the 12th century.

NEARBY

THE FORGOTTEN MOSAICS OF SANTA MARIA IN TRASTEVERE CHURCH ⑧

Sacristy of Santa Maria in Trastevere
Piazza Santa Maria in Trastevere
• Tel: 06 5814802
• Open 7:30am-1pm and 4pm-7pm
• Vestry: open on request
• Tram: 8

Santa Maria in Trastevere is one of the most beautiful basilicas in Rome, with its 12th-century bell tower (one of the tallest in the city), its Roman columns salvaged from other monuments, and its precious mosaics.

Almost all Romans have admired at some time the extraordinary medieval mosaic featuring the enthroned Virgin and Child.

However, few people know that the oldest mosaics, dating back to the 1st century AD, are the two smallest and most discreet. These magnificent mosaics are set into the walls to the right of the sacristy vestry, and they depict water birds and fishing scenes.

The exterior mosaics of the church curve inwards to prevent rain damage.

VICOLO DEI PANIERI ⑨

• Tram: 8 – Piazza Giuseppe Gioacchino Belli stop

The place where Garibaldi's Uruguayan "Moor" died

On 30 June 1849, Andrea Aguyar died on Vicolo dei Panieri (which was known at the time as Vicolo del Canestraro). He was struck on the head by a fragment from a grenade thrown by French soldiers, who were in Rome in order to restore the Papal States, which had been temporarily suppressed by the short-lived Roman Republic (9 February–4 July 1849) of Mazzini and Garibaldi. Born in Montevideo of African parents, Aguyar was actively involved in the war for the liberation of Uruguay, during which he joined the legion of Giuseppe Garibaldi, whose faithful follower he became. His imposing appearance, skin colour and great courage in combat made Aguyar a hero in the eyes of his comrades-in-arms. One of them, the Dutch painter Jan Koelman, described him as an "ebony-coloured Hercules, riding a stallion as black as the face of its master, which glistened in the sunlight". Garibaldi's Moor had an unusual way of fighting: he would capture his enemies with a lasso or even face them with a trident-shaped lance.

In 1849 Aguyar and Garibaldi arrived in Rome, accompanied by a large number of volunteers from all over the world, determined to defend the revolutionary ideals proclaimed by the Roman Republic. Nevertheless,

after a one-month siege (2 June–3 July), the French troops were victorious, causing many casualties among the Garibaldians. The lifeless body of Aguyar was transported from Vicolo dei Panieri to the Church of Santa Maria della Scala, which had been transformed into a hospital for the occasion. A famous painting by the Garibaldian Eleuterio Pagliano (National Gallery of Modern Art) depicts Aguyar's corpse close to that of Luciano Manara, commander of the Bersaglieri, who also died on the same day.

In 2012 the City of Rome dedicated the great stairway situated between Via Saffi and Via Poerio to Andrea Aguyar. His remains are to be found in the Mausoleum Ossuary Garibaldi, on the Janiculum Hill, and the grenade fragment that killed him is preserved at the Garibaldi Museum on the Capitoline Hill. It is possible that the current Vicolo del Moro, near Piazza Trilussa, in the Trastevere area, derives its name from Garibaldi's Moor.

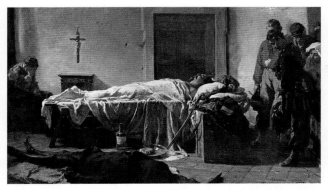

MUSSOLINI'S BUNKERS AT VILLA TORLONIA ⓫

Villa Torlonia
70 Via Nomentana
• Tel: 06 0608
• Visits on reservation only: Sovraintendenza Comunale (town planning services)

> ## *Three secret bunkers for Il Duce*

Villa Torlonia, the residence of Benito Mussolini from 1925 to 1943, dates from the 19th century. It is fitted with three bunkers, the construction of which first required the modification of a double cellar under the Fucino Basin (former lake bed where the villa is sited), fixing armour-plated doors, anti-gas filters, a bathroom and electricity. Even though it was only a short distance from Casino Nobile (the building where Mussolini and his family lived), this bunker was not a secure shelter in emergencies, because you had to cross open ground to reach it.

So it was decided to build a new shelter in the basement of Casino Nobile, where the villa kitchens were located. The ceiling was reinforced with a concrete framework and the living space fitted with two entrances and with sleeping compartments, which themselves had double gas-proof doors with peepholes.

This second solution was unlikely to have satisfied Il Duce, because a third bunker was built, a veritable air-raid shelter, linked by a tunnel to the basements of the villa. Consisting of two semi-circular galleries each about 10 metres long, laid out in the form of a cross with a reinforced concrete framework some 4 metres thick, it had two emergency exits that led directly into the park. This third shelter was never completed and the doors were not even fitted: on 25 July 1943, Mussolini was dismissed from office by the Fascist Grand Council, which had him arrested and replaced by General Badoglio.

HIDDEN SEPULCHRES

In one of the two sleeping compartments of the second bunker, recent archaeological excavations have unearthed a series of sepulchres dating from the 2nd century AD. One of the walls has three columbarium niches containing funerary urns, and a number of bodies have been found buried lying in a prone position, a customary fate for those presumed guilty of an infamous act.

THE ETRUSCAN TOMB OF VILLA TORLONIA

70 Via Nomentana
- Tel: 06 0608
- Enquiries to Sovraintendenza Comunale (town planning services)

A fake Etruscan tomb

I n 2004, during reconstruction work at the Casino Nobile of Villa Torlonia, a forgotten room was rediscovered: an underground circular space 6 metres in diameter with a lowered cupola, built in the manner of an Etruscan tomb, the shape and decoration of which are reminiscent of Etruscan and Corinthian pottery.

This discovery confirmed once again the eclecticism and unusual taste of the Torlonia family, one of the last great Roman patrons of the arts who organised digs in the 1840s, bringing to light a number of Etruscan tombs in their estates of Cerveteri and Vulci. This room was probably designed by the architect Giovan Battista Caretti. It does in fact appear in some of his drawings, but it was thought never to have been built. The wall incorporates twenty niches that would have held vases and, just above, a red band with spiralling plant motifs, within which is reproduced the silhouette of a crowned female form dressed in a peplos and holding a mirror, perhaps the embodiment of Prudence. The cupola, the three superimposed orders of which are separated by bands of floral decoration, is painted with wolves and boars, dogs and hares, deer, birds and panthers. These black and ochre figures stand out against a cream-coloured background. In the centre an oculus, now closed, would have illuminated the room.

A corridor, which led directly from the basement of the villa to this room, was partitioned off when an anti-aircraft shelter was built (see Mussolini's bunkers, pages 363 and 373), while a second corridor leading to the theatre was blocked by a rockfall. Questions remain as to the function of this room: secret passage, unexpected place to surprise guests, or even, bearing in mind the Masonic sympathies of Prince Alessandro Torlonia, site of secret meetings between "brothers".

MUSEO DI STORIA DELLA MEDICINA

34a Viale dell'Università
• Tel: 06 49914445
• E-mail: museo.stomed@uniroma1.it • www.histmed.it
• Open Monday to Friday 9:30am-1:30pm and Tuesday and Thursday
2:30pm-5pm
• Guided tours on reservation
• Metro: Policlinico or Castro Pretorio

*A trip
back in time*

Part of the Università degli Studi di Roma "La Sapienza", the remarkable though little-known Museum of the History of Medicine brings together charming reconstructions of historical settings with the educational interest of a modern museum. Most of the collections were amassed in 1938 by Adalberto Pazzini, founder of the museum and former professor at La Sapienza.

On the first floor, visitors will find a modern section with exhibitions on the history of medicine, from prehistoric times to today's technology. The antiquities section presents Egyptian, Greek and Roman medicine with educational aids such as plaster casts and reproductions of surgical instruments. The most interesting display concerns Etruscan medicine: you discover, for example, that the Etruscans had efficient techniques for replacing rotten teeth, but with animal rather than human teeth as it was forbidden to plunder the dead. You can also see the bronze reproduction of a sheep's liver dating from the 3rd to 2nd centuries BC, subdivided into zones corresponding to parts of the heavens. Animal organs were, in fact, used by haruspices (seers) to foretell the future. The medieval section throws light on monastic medicine and the re-establishment of scientific medicine in the West based on the Arab tradition. In the modern section, the accent is on the Italian contribution to medicine from the late Middle Ages to the Renaissance. In 1316, it was the Italian physician and anatomist Mondino De' Luzzi who carried out the first dissection at a University of Bologna public lecture. The reconstructions in the basement offer a double trip back in time. There is an alchemist's laboratory,

a Renaissance medical lecture hall, a 17th-century apothecary's shop, and more. Pazzini also collected pottery jars from Italian and French pharmacies of the 17th and 18th centuries.

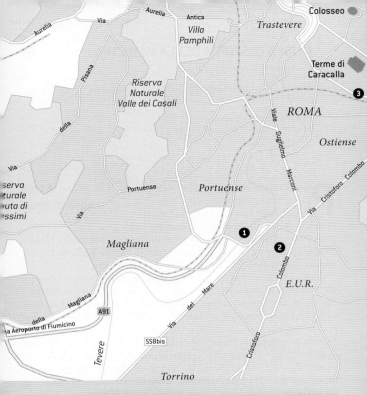

OUTSIDE THE CENTRE SOUTH

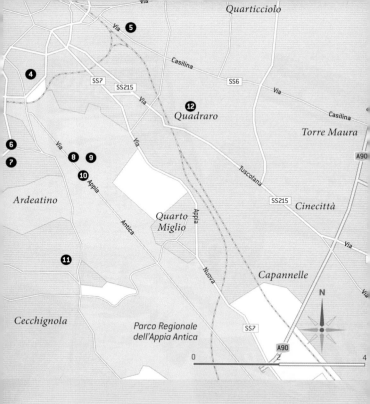

ALFONSO TOZZI'S COLLECTION

27 Via Pescaglia
• Tel: 06 55285165
• Opening times: prior reservation required
• Bus: 780, 781

27,000 razor blades

Alfonso Tozzi is a nice, friendly man, who instantly transmits his enthusiasm for his collection, a passion for which he has dedicated thirty years of his life, helped and encouraged by his wife.

The subject of his private collection of 27,000 razor blades with their illustrated wrappers, is not only curious and extraordinary, but also has an unimaginable historic, cultural and aesthetic value, which will surprise anyone, even those not interested in collecting, and even less so in razor blades.

With the discretion necessary on entering a private residence, collectors and those who are simply curious can make an appointment by telephone and be received in the Tozzi home to admire this exceptional collection. Sitting comfortably on a sofa in front of the albums in which thousands of paper wrappers are tidily classified in alphabetical order, one discovers that starting from the idea of a razor blade, the conversation can touch on an incredible variety of topics.

Prehistoric men began to shave with rudimentary obsidian blades, later replaced by flint and bronze blades. Razors continued to evolve, both in terms of the materials used to make them and in their shape, until in 1903 King Camp Gillette had the great idea of making a small steel blade, which was both robust and extremely thin, and could be fixed to a support and thrown away after use. In 1904, the Gillette Safety Razor Co. sold almost twelve and a half million blades.

From 1921, the year in which Gillette's exclusive patent ended, other blade manufacturers multiplied, staking everything, or almost everything, on the packaging, from the originality of the name to the graphic appearance of the product. They never imagined that forty years after this type of packaging disappeared, collectors the world over would reconstitute the tastes and daily life of the first sixty years of the 20th century in a fascinating way, thanks to these small coloured paper wrappers.

The colours, the styles, the themes are infinite; the slogans are funny and often disconcerting. You can thus discover razor blades inspired by sport, or by war and cannons. There are also blades inspired by 1930s cinema, by fascism, by animals, the city, the mountains, boats, aviation and so on.

AIR-RAID SHELTER IN THE EUR DISTRICT

8 Piazzale K. Adenauer
• The bunker is open for events, exhibitions or guided tours; please visit
www.eurspa.it

*Mussolini's
bunker ...*

The EUR district lies on the south side of Rome, along the intended route of the subway planned during the Fascist period to link the central government buildings on the Capitoline hill with the seashore. The entire zone was to be the site of the 1942 World's Fair (Esposizione Universale di Roma, hence the acronym EUR, or E42), which was cancelled because of the Second World War.

The construction of some of the buildings was begun in 1938, but many were left unfinished until after 1951, following radical changes to the initial project. The zone was then relaunched to host a number of competitions during the 1960 Olympics.

When the administrative centre of Palazzo degli Uffici was built, an air-raid shelter was added in the sub-basement which, according to the designers, could hold as many as 300 people. The pre-war international political climate was so tense that such a structure did seem necessary.

A gap some two metres wide isolates the bunker from the rest of

the building. The entire construction consisted of reinforced concrete in order to deaden the shockwaves from bombardments.

Even though it has never been used, this bunker is fitted with gas-proof double doors with peepholes, as well as ventilation and air-filtration systems. It is equipped with remarkable electrical installations powered by two specially adapted bicycles. There were also lavatories and a kitchen. Some of the original notices with instructions for the occupants can still be seen.

You can also visit another air-raid shelter in Villa Torlonia, which was the private residence of Benito Mussolini from 1925. Two underground bunkers – one gas-proof and the other bomb-proof – were also added in the basement (see page 363).

FRESCO AT VILLA OSIO

55 Via di Porta Ardeatina
• Visits: 8am-5pm from October to April, 8am-8pm from May to September and, after hours, depending on teaching and concert sessions of the "Casa del Jazz"
• Bus: 714 (from south, Porta Ardeatina; from north, Marco Polo)

> ### A jazz club in a mobster's former residence

Villa Osio consists of three buildings standing in a park of about 2.5 hectares where you can still walk around and "discover" fragments, cippi (boundary stones) and sarcophagi from the Roman period. It was built between 1937 and 1940 by the architect Cesare Pascoletti, collaborator of the famous Marcello Piacentini, who – following the fashion of the day – was inspired by the simple, elegant forms of ancient Roman tradition. The villa is named after its owner, Arturo Osio, one of the founders of Banca Nazionale del Lavoro.

The property is a short distance from the Servian Wall, near the magnificent stretch with Antonio da Sangallo the Younger's bastion. There used to be a 17th-century country house on the site, which was demolished to make way for the villa.

Since 2005, the 150-seat auditorium and vast outdoor spaces host world-

renowned jazz musicians, but the house conceals little-known details and anecdotes.

In what was the dining room, there is a view of Piazza Navona (over 8 metres long and 2.80 metres high) by Amerigo Bartoli Natinguerra, who also painted a number of other works inside several of the bank's buildings, Osio himself being one of the owners. Strangely, Natinguerra never completed the fresco, which explains the unfinished sky and some missing buildings in the background.

In the rear portico, now used as a ticket office, is a magnificent mosaic floor with black and white tiles and marine motifs typical of the imperial repertoire of ancient Rome.

The villa was then acquired by the Vatican before being sold in 1980 to Enrico Nicoletti, considered one of the most prominent members of the notorious and dreaded Banda della Magliana, the largest criminal organisation ever to operate in the Eternal City. A number of modifications were made to the buildings during this period, both inside and outside. Nicoletti, like the aristocrats of old, even had the faces of himself and his family painted over those of certain characters in the Piazza Navona scene in the former dining room.

When the villa was confiscated and handed over to the Rome municipality in 2001, it underwent a comprehensive historical and architectural restoration. At the entrance, a stone commemorates the 639 mafia victims between 1893 and 2005.

THE THREE COLUMBARIA OF VIGNA CODINI ❹
AND THE TOMB OF POMPONIUS HYLAS

Columbaria of Vigna Codini: 14 Via di Porta Latina, on private property
Tomb of Pomponius Hylas: 10 Via di Porta Latina, in Scipion park
Visits: • Columbaria of Vigna Codini: contact any of the numerous cultural associations (e.g. *Roma Sotterranea*, www.romasotterranea.it).
• Tomb of Pomponius Hylas: on request by telephoning the Cultural Heritage department of the Municipality of Rome (*Sovraintendenza Comunale ai Beni Culturali*) at 06 0608; alternatively through cultural associations such as *Roma Sotterranea* (www.romasotterranea.it)

> ## *Some of the most fascinating tombs in Rome*

On leaving Rome by the Porta Latina, after a short distance you will notice a gateway on the left leading to private villas. In this intimate environment and in the adjoining public park some of the city's most fascinating tombs can be found.

The columbaria of Vigna Codini are imposing funerary monuments, each of which once held hundreds of tombs. The cinerary urns of members of corporations or associations were laid to rest there. Each niche could hold several urns and was marked with a plaque bearing the name and sometimes even the sculpted portrait of the deceased. The first columbarium indicated, intended for the freed slaves of the emperors Tiberius and Claudius, is the most majestic: in the centre of a rectangular space of around 40 m² an enormous pillar supports the lattice vaults. Dozens of niches have been carved within this pillar.

The second columbarium, some 7 metres deep and rectangular in plan, includes the tombs of members of a college of musicians and those of a flower merchants' guild. In certain places, you can still see sections of wall paintings in particularly bright colours.

Designed in a U-shape, the third columbarium was occupied by the tombs of slaves of the Julian-Claudian dynasty. The vault is richly decorated and there is a small adjoining chamber (called the *ustrinum*) where bodies were cremated, a rather unusual arrangement for a building which, like the preceding two, was intended to receive the bodies of the lower classes.

The tomb of Pomponius Hylas, reached through the adjoining public gardens, belonged to a wealthy family that could afford its own underground sepulchre. It dates from the first half of the 1st century AD. Built along the same lines as a small columbarium, it is richly decorated with bas-reliefs and polychrome stucco-work, as well as paintings and mosaics. This tomb, although rather cramped, is almost intact (with the exception of a few missing motifs) and all the more disconcerting because it gives the impression of having remained unchanged for over two millennia.

MUSEO DELLA MEMORIA GIOCOSA

24-26 Via Vincenzo Coronelli
• Tel: 06 21700782
• Open Tuesday to Friday, 10:30am-12pm and 3pm-6pm
• Saturday and Sunday: on appointment only
• Admission: Free
• Bus: 105, 157, 553, 545
• Tram: 5, 14, 19

Toys in their thousands

The Museum of Childhood Memories (Museo della Memoria Giocosa) opened in 1979 thanks to the collection that Lisa and Franco Palmieri inherited from Fritz Billig, an Austrian who took refuge in New York following the arrival of Nazism. He managed to take his childhood toys with him, which included wind-up toys and cars by Lehman and Tippco, Jewish companies requisitioned by Hitler's Germany.

Children from all over Europe, regardless of their culture, race or religion, played with these toys. For Billig, they became the symbol of an ideal world where everyone would be equal. This notion encouraged him to continue collecting toys for the rest of his life. Today his collection is exhibited in this museum, a space of about 300 m² in the Pigneto-Prenestino-Labicano district.

The collection comprises European, American and Asian toys and games made between 1920 and 1960. The museum also has a 60-seat theatre, Albero delle Favole (The Story Tree), where children's shows are organised. There is also a bar, a thematic library, catalogues, posters, brochures and objects linked to the world of toys as well as a very interesting collection of illustrative and advertising material on cars.

This remarkable museum, the only one of its kind in Italy, also contains a large-scale model railway layout dating from 1937.

THE CISTERN OF VIA CRISTOFORO COLOMBO ❻

Via Cristoforo Colombo, level with No. 142 (Ostiense)
• Visits on request, by telephoning the Cultural Heritage department of
the Municipality of Rome (*Sovraintendenza Comunale ai Beni Culturali*)
at 06 0608; alternatively through cultural associations such as *Roma
Sotterranea* (www.romasotterranea.it)

*The remains
of an ancient
water tank*

The two circular buildings adjoining Via Cristoforo Colombo at the junction of Circonvallazione Ostiense and Piazza dei Navigatori are actually the remains of a water tank.

A farmhouse concealed their presence until it was demolished at the end of the 1930s to make way for the construction of the former Via Imperiale, a highway that linked the city to the coast.

The larger of the two buildings dates back to the first half of the 2nd century AD and was intended to supply agricultural needs in the area. It measures some 15 metres in diameter and apparently was used as a cistern, as borne out by the traces of cement on the walls and a system of pipes that could empty the cistern for maintenance, although it has not yet been established how water was brought in or where it came from. Inside are two concentric rings of corridors, the first ring consisting of ten barrel-vaulted sections separated by archways, while the second forms a single circular room. From there, a corridor leads to a central chamber that is 3 metres in diameter. All these chambers are in very poor condition, the structure having been converted and redeveloped more than once.

The second building, of more recent date, could not have held water due to the thinness of its walls, but we still do not know what it was used for.

Although this neighbourhood was a suburb (*suburbio*) on the outskirts of the city, it would have been well connected to the heart of Rome by the Appian Way only a few hundred metres away, at least, that is, until the construction of the Aurelian Wall (AD 271-275).

MUSEO DELLE AUTO DELLA POLIZIA DI STATO ❼

20 Via dell' Arcadia
- Tel: 06 5141861
- museoautopolizia@interno.it
- Open Monday to Friday 9:30am-2pm, afternoons by appointment
- Admission: €3; concessions: €1.50
- Bus: 714 – Colombo or Georgofili

A Ferrari at the service of the law

Nowadays, the fastest car belonging to the Italian police is a Lamborghini Gallardo, which can reach speeds of up to 325 km/h and has a defibrillator and a refrigerated container for transporting organs. But the police have used other superfast cars in the past too: one of them is the "star exhibit" in the State Police Car Museum.

The Ferrari 250 GTE (Gran Turismo Evoluzione) was designed in 1962 by the famous Pininfarina of Turin in a bid to capture the US auto market. With a 12-cylinder engine of 3,000 cc, supplying 235 horsepower, the four-seater could do over 230 km/h. In the early 1960s the police authorities decided that if they acquired a Ferrari it might help to challenge the image and excessive power of the Roman underworld, which at the time, aboard "souped-up" cars, was running rings round the prestigious but already outdated Alfa Romeo 1900 (which is also found in the museum).

To drive the Ferrari, four officers were chosen from police headquarters in Rome and sent to the Maranello factory on a special training course in fast cars. One of them was the famous Brigadier Armando Spatafora, hero of countless car chases in the glory days of the Dolce Vita.

The vehicles on display at the museum, which are all in working order, cover a period of over eighty years. You can see a jeep, motorcycles, vans, helmets, boots, headgear and other items from the state police kit.

It is a strange experience to open the doors of vehicles that have carried some of the major figures in the history of Italy, such as the 1939 Lancia Artena in which Benito Mussolini was driven around, or the beautiful De Tomaso 892 Deauville, used in the late 1970s by Alessandro Pertini, then President of the Republic.

Other models (the FIAT 500 and 600, the FIAT AR 55 Campagnola and the Alfa Romeo Giulietta 1300) evoke the great car designers of the 1960s.

The more technological section of the museum consists of several multimedia consoles at which visitors can experience the "operations room" – nothing if not exhilarating.

THE *SALVATOR MUNDI* BY BERNINI

Basilica of San Sebastiano fuori le mura
136 Via Appia Antica
- Tel: 06 78 87 035
- Open daily 8am - 7pm
- Bus: 218; or 5 km on foot from Circo Massimo

Bernini's last masterpiece found!

The basilica of San Sebastiano fuori le mura (Saint Sebastian outside the walls) flanks the celebrated Appian Way, the *regina viarum* ("queen of roads"). In 2001, Bernini's last masterpiece, still largely unknown to the general public, was found in the adjoining convent.

To reach the basilica, you can avoid the traffic by following the route of the catacombs of Saint Calixtus, departing from the church known as *Domine Quo Vadis* and emerging near the basilica. Strangely enough, you will pass sheep grazing along the roadside.

A church was first built here in the 4th century on the site of the catacombs of Saint Sebastian. It was rebuilt by Pope Nicholas I (858-867), but we owe the present edifice to Cardinal Scipion Borghese (1576-1633) who had it built at the beginning of the 17th century. The façade dates from the 18th century.

In August 2001, through a series of coincidences, art historians identified a statue by Bernini in a small niche at the entrance to the convent of Saint Sebastian. The work, which had been sought for a long time, and allegedly found several times since 1972, had disappeared at the end of the 17th century.

The bust now stands beside the Relics Chapel. The finesse of the marble sculpture, and the gesture of the hand raised in blessing, is proof enough that we are in the presence of work by the great master of Baroque sculpture, Gian Lorenzo Bernini (1598-1680). The *Salvator Mundi* is a marble bust of Christ that is considered to be his last masterpiece, sculpted in 1679. Bernini's son, Pier Filippo, wrote in his 1680 biography of his father that the latter had "worked in marble until his 81st year, which he finished with a Saviour out of his devotion".

In the Relics Chapel is a stone bearing the imprint of the foot of Christ at the moment when he appeared to Saint Peter. Tradition has it that, fleeing Rome to avoid persecution, Peter met the risen Jesus along the Appian Way and asked him: "*Quo vadis, Domine?*" ("Where are you going, Lord?"). Jesus answered: "*Eo Romam iterum crucifigi.*" ("I am going to Rome to be crucified again.") This meeting convinced Peter to retrace his steps and face martyrdom in Rome.

The Relics Chapel also contains one of the arrows that struck Saint Sebastian during his martyrdom. Directly opposite is a beautiful sculpture of the saint by Antonio Giorgetti, one of Bernini's pupils.

JEWISH CATACOMBS OF VIGNA RANDANINI

4 Via Appia Pignatelli, in the grounds of a private residence (Appia Antica)
• Visits on request, through the cultural association *Roma Sotterranea*
(www.romasotterranea.it).

Discovered around 1859, the Jewish catacombs of Vigna Randanini, on the Appia Pignatelli road, date from the 3rd century AD and are the only catacombs of their kind in Rome that can be visited. Not all these galleries, extending over a surface of almost 720 m² at a depth of some 10 metres, are accessible.

The only Jewish catacombs in Rome open to the public

A small building on the surface houses an entry to the catacombs. It is thought that during the original construction phase (first half of the 2nd century AD), they consisted simply of a square chamber characterised by two exedras and a niche. The second phase (3rd-4th centuries) was notable for the general reorganization of the whole structure, which nevertheless spared the two exedras. It was probably during this phase that the black and white mosaic paving that can still be seen today was installed.

On entering the galleries, it is immediately clear that most of the tombs are in the form of niches, arches, or small funerary chambers.

In a section further away from the entrance are a great number of kokhim (hollowed-out tombs typical of Jewish culture, of which there are no other examples in Rome). Three of the funerary chambers are decorated with paintings: the first consists of frescoes with simple geometric motifs, coloured red on a white background; the second, preceded by a vestibule rendered in white, is embellished in the four corners with date palms.

But it is in the galleries on the lower level where the rooms with the most interesting frescoes are to be found, including a double chamber with geometrical decorations and divisions. The various images are shown inside a honeycomb of cells. The central ceiling motif of the first chamber is a Winged Victory surrounded by peacocks, birds and baskets of fruit, in the act of crowning a naked young man. In the second chamber, the central figure of the vault is an allegory of Fortune with a horn of abundance in her hand. The border is decorated with fish and ducks interspersed with baskets of fruit. The four seasons are represented in the corners of the chamber.

The rear wall, today badly damaged, depicted a man standing between two horses.

The catacombs were also covered with a number of Latin and Greek inscriptions, most of which are now illegible.

GEODETIC BASELINE ON THE APPIAN WAY 🔟

Via Appia Antica
• Links: Archeobus tourist line

A to B

On the Appian Way near the mausoleum of Cecilia Metella, daughter of a Roman consul, a small manhole in the roadway covers a travertine slab 84 × 84 cm and 33 cm thick, with a piece of metal embedded at its centre. The following inscription is engraved in the stone: "Base Termin. A 1855". As indicated by a plaque next to it, this piece of metal is benchmark "A" of a geodetic baseline.

Five hundred metres away on the left is a high sepulchre known as Torre di Capo di Bove. Here, a second more explicit inscription recalls: "In the year 1855, following in the footsteps of R. G. Boscovich, P. A. Secchi rigorously measured a geodetic baseline on the Appian Way and, establishing in the year 1870 at its two terminals this trig point and another at Frattocchie, he created this new baseline which made it possible to verify the Italian geodetic network commissioned in the year 1871 by the military to measure the European degree."

The questions of the Earth's shape and the mapping of territory were being widely debated in academic circles: starting from a few geodetic baselines, that is to say easily measurable distances between benchmarks "A" and "B", the principles of trigonometry could be used to survey large areas using a geodesic coordinate system of triangles.

In 1751, the Jesuit priest Boscovich was the first to measure the geodetic baseline of the Appian Way, and to revise the censal (taxpayers) and geographical map of the Papal States. Father Angelo Secchi (1818-1878) was director of the Astronomical Observatory at the Roman College from 1850 until his death. While involved in archaeological excavations along the *regina viarum* (queen of roads), he was asked in 1854 by the archaeologist and architect Luigi Canina to measure the road and the distances between the old milestones in order to accurately calculate the relationship between the Roman mile and the metric measurement. As benchmark "B" calculated by Boscovich had been lost, Secchi took the opportunity to make his own measurements for a new geodetic baseline. There were over one hundred figures to transcribe every 4 metres. As little help was available, the work lasted from November 1854 to April 1855. The baseline measures 12,043.14 metres precisely.

Afterwards the "A" and "B" benchmarks were deliberately buried by Secchi, who feared that they would be stolen by "shepherds and peasants". Marker "A" was rediscovered in 1999 and marker "B" in 2012, after a long search.

GEODESY AND TRIANGULATION: A DISCIPLINE THAT LED TO THE METRE

Triangulation is a technique based on the laws of trigonometry, which state that if one side and two angles of a triangle are known, the other two sides and angles can be readily calculated.

Six hundred years before the Christian era, the Greek philosopher Thales had already used this technique to estimate the distance between a ship at sea and the coast. To obtain a rough measurement, he positioned two observers on the shore, separated by a known distance.

He asked each of them to measure the angle between the straight line linking him to the boat and the straight line linking him to the other observer.

This technique, which was repeated several times, was used by French scientists Delambre and Méchain from 1792 to 1798 to measure the arc of the meridian between Dunkirk and Barcelona (about 1,147 km).

MUSEUM OF PERIOD COACHES

693 Via Millevoi
• Tel: 06 51958112
• Open Tuesday to Friday 10am-1pm and 3:30pm-7pm,
Saturday and Sunday 9:30am-1:30pm and 3:30pm-7:30pm
• Admission: €5.16; Concessions: €3.62
• Bus: 766

I n this recently opened museum, an
exceptional collection of period carriages
and characteristic coaches is exhibited.

*Vehicles
of yesteryear*

They have been acquired over a period of forty years by their passionate owner.
The collection is made up of 293 models, half of which are exhibited. Most
of them have been restored and are in perfect working order. These splendid
coaches occupy an exhibition space of 3,000 m², offering a striking overall view
assembled here, but they also constitute a precious cultural heritage, as each
one of them testifies to a historic and social reality. Apart from the coaches, over
one hundred pieces including saddles and trappings are also exhibited. The
museum is in the Ardeatina area, close to the catacombs of San Callistus and to
the Archaeological Park of Appia Antica. The exhibition is managed by a cultural
non-profit-making association. Among the exhibits are the hackney coach that
belonged to Anna Magnani, which she used to move around the city during
the war, Ben Hur's chariot, the pram given to Princess Sissi of Austria-Hungary
when she was small and the horse-drawn carriage used by John Wayne in *The
Quiet Man*. There are also carriages from the 18th and 19th centuries, firemen's
coaches, American stagecoaches, mail wagons and seven monumental carriages
decorated with frescoes of the 19th century belonging to the city of Rome.

NEARBY

MAUSOLEO DI MONTE DEL GRANO
Piazza dei Tribuni (Via Tuscolana - Quadraro)
• Visits on request, by contacting cultural associations such as *Roma
Sotterranea* (www.romasotterranea.it)

The large buildings of the working-class district of Quadraro screen
an imposing tomb, the third largest in Rome, surpassed only by the
mausoleums of Hadrian and Augustus. This mausoleum was nicknamed
"Monte del Grano" because of its shape, reminiscent of an upturned ear
of wheat, after the blocks of travertine that had originally covered it had
been removed for other uses. The construction, 12 metres high, with a
circumference of 140 metres, now looks like a small overgrown hill. Access
is by a 20-metre corridor opening onto a circular enclosure with brick-lined
walls, about 10 metres in diameter. In the past, this enclosure was divided
into two floors and two shafts provided light and ventilation. In 1582 a large
sarcophagus, now in the Capitoline Museums, was found inside, which was
thought to feature the Emperor Severus Alexander (AD 222-235). In fact,
the markings on some of the bricks show that the structure had been built
well before then, during the reign of the Emperor Hadrian (around AD 150).
In any case, such an important monument could certainly only have been
intended for a leading representative of the imperial family or for a senator.

ALPHABETICAL INDEX

ALPHABETICAL INDEX

ALPHABETICAL INDEX

NOTES

The Farmacia di Santa Maria della Scala, which was opened by Carmelites who arrived in Rome in the late 16th century, became famous among convent pharmacies thanks to the various specialities invented there to fight the plague and other serious diseases. The pharmacy managed to keep a free dispensary open to the public until the 1950s and stayed open until 1978.

The upper floor of this old pharmacy has been preserved, above a more modern working establishment, virtually intact, as it was in the 18th century, and offers visitors a unique experience.

One of the monks working in the pharmacy, Brother Basil, became so well-known for his herbal remedies and especially for his famous Acqua Antipestilenziale (Anti-Plague Water), which cured various types of ailments, that kings, cardinals and popes consulted him. In 1726 he began to teach chemistry, botany and pharmacy to his disciples. The eulogistic inscriptions on two paintings featuring this well-loved monk, who died in

1804 after almost sixty years of professional activity, sum up his life. His famous essays have been carefully preserved as precious artefacts.

Ghezzi's 18th-century painting, which is kept in the vestry, perfectly conveys the idea of the beauty and importance of the pharmacy at the time. It features Brother Basil teaching his disciples, surrounded by stills and mortars, shelves overflowing with heavy tomes, and cupboards with jars filled with salts and herbs.

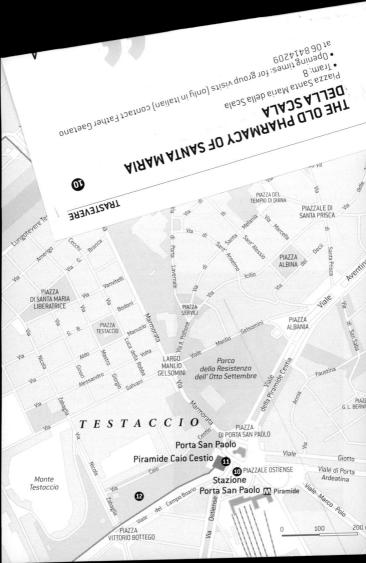

⑩

THE OLD PHARMACY OF SANTA MARIA
DELLA SCALA

Piazza Santa Maria della Scala

• Tram: 8
• Opening times: for group visits (only in Italian) contact Father Gaetano
at 06 8414209

TRASTEVERE

PIAZZA DEL
TEMPIO DI DIANA

PIAZZALE DI
SANTA PRISCA

Lungotevere Te...

Amerigo

Cecchi

Branca

Via

di Porta Lavernale

Via

di

Santa

Melania

Via Marcella

di

Sant' Anselmo

Sant' Alessio

Icilio

PIAZZA
ALBINA

Decii

Santa Prisca

del

Aventin...

PIAZZA
DI SANTA MARIA
LIBERATRICE

Vanvitelli

Via

G.

B.

Bodoni

PIAZZA
SERVILI

Viale

di San Saba

Via

PIAZZA
TESTACCIO

Manuzio

Via

Luca della Robia

Marmorata

Via A. Pellone

Manlio

Gelsomini

PIAZZA
ALBANIA

Via

Nicola

Aldo

Mastro

Volta

Giorgio

LARGO
MANLIO
GELSOMINI

Viale

Parco
della Resistenza
dell' Otto Settembre

Viale della Piramide Cestia

Faustina

PIAZZ...
G. L. BERNI...

Via

Ginori

Alessandro

Galvani

Marmorata

Annia

Via

Zabaglia

TESTACCIO

Cestio

PIAZZA
DI PORTA SAN PAOLO

Monte
Testaccio

Nicola

Caio

Porta San Paolo
Piramide Caio Cestio ⑪

⑩ PIAZZALE OSTIENSE

Viale

Giotto

Viale di Porta
Ardeatina

Via

Zabaglia

⑫

Viale del Campo Boario

Stazione
Porta San Paolo Ⓜ Piramide

Via Ostiense

Viale Marco Polo

PIAZZA
VITTORIO BOTTEGO

0   100   200 ...

AVENTINO - TESTACCIO

THE FIGURES MISSING FROM THE ARCH OF THE MONEYCHANGERS ❶

Arco degli Argentarii
Via del Velabro

> **Fratricide between the sons of Septimius Severus**

J ust beside the ancient church of San Giorgio al Velabro stands an arch known as the Arco degli Argentarii (Arch of the Moneychangers), for it was the moneychangers of Rome who together with the meat merchants dedicated this monumental gateway to the emperor Septimius Severus.

The arch was not simply ornamental but probably served as one of the main points of access to the Forum Boarium, the ancient cattle market. Rich decoration with plant motifs covers almost the entire surface of the pillars and architrave. You can still read the original inscription, with the dedication dating from AD 204 to Septimius Severus, his wife Julia Domna and his son Bassianus, better known as Caracalla. The nickname came from a floor-length cloak that he had made fashionable. The inner faces of the pillars show Caracalla carrying out a religious sacrifice, on the left, and the imperial family, on the right.

If you look more closely you will see among these images empty spaces where other figures have been deliberately obliterated.

After the death of Septimius Severus and according to his wishes, his two sons Caracalla and Geta governed together for almost a year, until Geta was assassinated by his brother, in their mother's arms, according to Aelius Spartianus's account in his *History of Augustus*. Caracalla accused Geta of attempting to poison him and the senate was obliged to believe this story, declaring Geta henceforth a public enemy and sentencing him to *damnatio memoriae*, a sanction that meant his image would be destroyed and his name deleted from all inscriptions.

This enabled Caracalla to erase the name and portrait of his murdered brother, who had certainly been shown alongside his parents, as well as those of his wife Plautilla and his father-in-law, the praetorian prefect Plautianus (commander of the imperial guard).

NEARBY

THE HOLES IN THE ARCH OF THE MONEYCHANGERS ❷
Another notable feature of the back of the arch is a number of holes, drilled in the Middle Ages. They were made by fortune-seekers who believed the story that a great treasure was hidden inside.

TRACES OF JUDAISM IN THE ROSETO COMUNALE

❸

Via di Valle Murcia
• Open 8am-4:30pm from 9 to 20 May, and 8am-7:30pm from 22 May to 19 June
• Admission: Free

A menorah-shaped public garden

Visitors to the Roseto Comunale (Municipal Rose Garden) have probably never noticed that the widest section of the garden is laid out in the shape of a menorah, the seven-branched candelabrum used in the rituals of Judaism. Moreover, plaques shaped like the Tablets of the Law are fixed near both entrances.

This constant reminder of the Jewish religion is rooted in the history of the occupation of the site. For three centuries, from 1645 until 1934, Rome's Jewish community used these uncultivated lands on the Aventine Hill as a cemetery. The cemetery of Verano (which was exclusively for Roman Catholics) was opened in 1836, but it was not until the unification of Italy in 1870 that the Jews were allowed to use it. In 1934, Via di Valle Murcia was completed and the early tombs had to be transferred to the Jewish section of Verano. Over the centuries the area had reverted to a green space, but not until 1950 was it finally landscaped. With the approval of the Jewish community, the local authority decided to plant a rose garden there, while preserving the memory of the former Aventine cemetery. The tall cypresses at the end of the garden are the very ones that grew among the graves.

WINNING BLOOMS

Every year, in late spring and early summer, the eastern slopes of the Aventine Hill overlooking the Circus Maximus are covered with thousands of roses, creating a superb, though short-lived, natural spectacle. Towards the end of May a famous international rose competition takes place, the *Premio Roma*. The oval in the centre of the garden hosts the award-winning blooms from previous years. You can still admire an example of the first winning variety from 1933.

AN AMERICAN BEHIND ROME'S ROSE

Garden Countess Mary Gayley Senni was behind the idea of creating a Municipal Rose Garden. She was passionate about roses and grew a wide range of varieties in the garden of her property outside Rome. She donated her collection to the city in 1924 but was extremely dissatisfied with the use made of it. Her persistence resulted in the creation of a rose garden in 1932 on the Colle Oppio (Oppian Hill) near the Colosseum, modelled on those in other capital cities. This garden, which was destroyed during the war, was then moved to the Aventine Hill. As representative of the American Rose Society, Mary Gayley Senni was involved in running the new garden until 1954.

THE ORANGE TREE OF SANTA SABINA CLOISTER ❹

Basilica di Santa Sabina
1 Piazza Pietro d'Illiria
• Open 6:30am-1pm and 3:30pm-7pm

> *The legend
> of Saint
> Dominic's
> orange tree*

anta Sabina basilica, on the Aventine Hill, dates from the 5th century. It is one of the oldest churches in Rome, although it has frequently undergone major conversions since it was built. In the atrium, by a small oval window opening onto the courtyard of the neighbouring convent, an orange tree can be glimpsed growing in the very spot where, according to Dominican traditions, Saint Dominic planted it around 1220.

A number of anecdotes concerning this orange tree, more or less apocryphal, have endured down the ages. One notable claim is that Saint Dominic brought it back from Spain and planted it at the north-west corner of the former four-arched portico (no longer standing) where he liked to sleep. Until then, oranges had never been known to grow in Italy.

For centuries, this tree was described as miraculous, a new plant perennially springing from the dessicated trunk. Saint Francis de Sales (1567-1622) mentioned it in a letter to Saint Jane Frances de Chantal, in which he demonstrated how the tree had become a focus of the cult of Saint Dominic.

Its oranges are said to have been used to make garlands and mementoes for popes and cardinals. And the story goes that the preserved oranges that Catherine of Sienna offered to Urban VI in 1379 came from this miraculous tree.

In 1936, the ground was levelled where the tree grew. During the work, a coin dating from the 14th century was found among its roots.

NAPOLEON ON A 5TH-CENTURY DOOR!

Carved in the 5th century AD, the famous wooden panels covering the church door depict scenes from the Old and New Testaments. Curiously enough, a portrait of Napoleon can be seen there, shown as the pharaoh pursuing the Jews at the crossing of the Red Sea.

In fact, in the first half of the 19th century, a sculptor restoring the door had taken it upon himself to depict Napoleon as a persecutor of God's chosen people.

The reality was somewhat different, however, concerning Napoleon and the Jews: he was the first European monarch to liberate them from their ghettos, such as the one in Venice, and to grant them certain rights.

THE DEVIL'S STONE

⑤

Basilica di Santa Sabina
1 Piazza Pietro d'Illiria
• Open 6:30am-1pm and 3:30pm-7pm
• Metro: B – Circo Massimo

A magical black stone?

I f you have never been close to an object cast by the Devil, just go into the basilica of Santa Sabina by the main entrance and walk round to the left: at the corner, on top of a beautiful twisted column, you will see a black stone thought to have magical powers. It is in fact a well-preserved basalt counterweight dating from Roman times.

In 1586, Pope Sixtus V (1585-1590) commissioned the architect Domenico Fontana to restore the church. During the renovations – to which there were many objections – the architect had a marble slab commemorating the removal of the mortal remains of the martyrs Alexander, Evence and Theodule lifted from the floor. Unfortunately the slab fell and shattered into a thousand pieces, which were later collected and reassembled at the centre of what is now the Schola Cantorum. However, popular legend turned the story on its head to say that the marble slab was destroyed by a terrible black stone – *lapis diaboli* – launched by the Devil himself to strike St Dominic while he was deep in prayer over the martyrs' tomb.

The basilica of Santa Sabina was founded under the papacy of Celestine I (422-432) by Bishop Peter of Illyria. Excavations under the building have unearthed ancient structures from various periods. Materials plundered from nearby Roman ruins were used in the construction of the church, such as the 24 columns separating the three naves which come from the temple of Juno. In the 9th century, Pope Eugenius II (824-827) had the Schola Cantorum built and commissioned a silver ciborium to be placed there, which was unfortunately stolen by lansquenet mercenaries during the 1527 sack of Rome.

In 1219, Pope Honorius III donated Santa Sabina to the Spanish founder of the Dominican order, Domingo de Guzmán (Saint Dominic).

THE OLDEST KNOWN CRUCIFIXION SCENE

The front doors of the church, made of cypress wood, date back to its founding in the 5th century. They feature scenes from the Old and New Testaments, including the oldest known representation of the Crucifixion of Christ.

For centuries the basilica has been the first station of Lent where, on Ash Wednesday (the first day of penance and fasting), the pontifs give their homily, 44 days before Easter.

THE HIDING PLACE OF SAINT ALEXIUS

Church of Santi Boniface e Alessio
23 Piazza Sant'Alessio
• Open 8:30am-12:30pm and 3:30pm-6:30pm

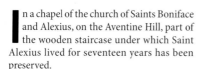

I n a chapel of the church of Saints Boniface and Alexius, on the Aventine Hill, part of the wooden staircase under which Saint Alexius lived for seventeen years has been preserved.

The saint who lived under the stairs

Before the 10th century, there is no record of Saint Alexius in the West, but from then on his celebrity became such that he inspired frescoes (a fine example of which is conserved in the Lower Basilica of San Clemente), poems and pieces of music which have fascinating histories.

Alexius was miraculously born to noble but barren parents in Rome. Although raised in the lap of luxury, he fled to Odessa in the East, where he lived on charity for several years as an ascetic. When his reputation for sanctity grew to be a burden, Alexius decided to leave and sail to Tarsa, but the direction of the wind, or perhaps destiny, took him instead to Ostia. He headed for Rome and presented himself at his father's house. His father welcomed him without recognising him; thinking that he was a beggar, he offered shelter beneath the staircase. Alexius lived there for 17 years and wrote his life story on a roll of paper. Only when he died did his family discover his true identity, revealed in the scroll that he still clutched in his hand.

The church dates back to the 4th century, when Pope Honorius III ordered the reconstruction of a building dedicated to Saint Boniface already erected on the Aventine. In 1217, it was also dedicated to Saint Alexius.

The plan of the church, which owes its current appearance to restorations of the 16th, 17th and 19th centuries, is a replica of the Roman building with three naves, where you can still see the belltower and crypt (which has a fresco painted between the 13th and 14th centuries, the only example of its kind in Rome) from whence came the fragment of staircase preserved in the chapel of Sant'Alessio.

Antonio Bergondi, apprentice sculptor to Bernini, executed a marble statue for this chapel, representing the saint as a pilgrim on his deathbed.

In the church there is also a well that, it is said, formerly stood within the house of Alexius' father, as well as the 3rd-century icon of the Assumption of Mary, which legend has it the saint brought back from the East.

GARDENS OF THE KNIGHTS OF MALTA PRIORY   ❼

Piazza dei Cavalieri di Malta
• Visits by reservation, except on Sundays: 06 67581234
(groups: minimum 10 people)
• Metro: B – Circo Massimo

> *The ancient garden of the Templars*

The origins of the priory date back to the 10th century, when as Santa Maria Aventina it formed part of a Benedictine abbey dedicated to Saint Basil of Cappadocia. In the 12th century the abbey passed into the hands of the Templars and, at the beginning of the 14th century, to the Knights of Rhodes – later known as the Knights of Malta. Today, you can overcome the frustration born of peering through the priory keyhole (see below), as group visits can be booked to tour the priory and its grounds. Access is by a magnificent although relatively small garden, whose exoticism gives it a heady air of romance. In one corner of the garden a well built by the Templars still survives, the only vestige of their passing. You can also visit the church of Santa Maria del Priorato, built in the 16th century. It is the only architectural work – apart from the piazza – carried out by Piranesi himself. The single-nave interior has been entirely covered in white stucco to his design, and the façade offers a typical example of Piranesian style.

NEARBY   ❽

THE ORDER OF MALTA'S KEYHOLE

The Piazza dei Cavalieri di Malta (Square of the Knights of Malta) is encircled

by palm and cypress trees and flamboyant walls, rich in steles and obelisks, designed by Giovanni Battista Piranesi. The monumental entrance to the priory, headquarters of the Knights of Malta, seems to conceal a mysterious and unapproachable world but even the outside has a surprise in store.

By placing your eye to the keyhole of the main entrance, the dome of St Peter's Basilica can be seen, framed by an avenue of luxuriant greenery within the walled gardens. The Grand Prior Giovan Battista Rezzonico commissioned Piranesi to design the site, property of the Sovereign Order of Malta.

**THE ORDER OF MALTA: THE ONLY PRIVATE INSTITUTION IN THE WORLD
WITH THE ATTRIBUTES OF A SOVEREIGN STATE – EXTRATERRITORIALITY,
EMBASSIES ...**

The Sovereign Military and Hospitaller Order of St John of Jerusalem, of
Rhodes, and of Malta, more commonly known down the ages as Knights
Hospitaller, Order of the Knights of Rhodes, and Order of Malta, is one of the
most ancient Roman Catholic religious orders whose current mission is to
defend the faith and assist the poor and needy.

Founded in Jerusalem around 1050 by merchants of the former republic
of Amalfi to care for pilgrims in the Holy Land, this monastic community
dedicated to John the Baptist was recognised as a religious order by Pope
Paschal II in 1113.

The Hospitallers rapidly became militarised after the taking of Jerusalem
during the First Crusade of 1099, second only to the Templars as a fighting
force in the Holy Land. After the fall of Jerusalem and Saint Jean d'Acre
in 1291, the Order retreated to Cyprus from 1291 to 1309. As the knights'
rivalry with the King of Cyprus was creating difficulties, they conquered
the island of Rhodes, then under Byzantine rule, and made it their new
headquarters in 1310, ruling there until 1523. The island situation led
them to acquire a fleet that became the scourge of Muslim shipping.
Eventually vanquished by the Turks, the knights sailed to Civitavecchia and
then Viterbo, in Italy, before travelling to Nice and in 1530 finally settling
in Malta, given to them by the Holy Roman Emperor Charles V who had
understood how useful they could be against any Ottoman advances. But
Napoleon drove them out when he occupied the island in 1798, and they
were finally welcomed in Rome by the pope in 1834.

Before the loss of Malta, most members of the order were monks who had
taken the three vows of poverty, chastity and obedience. Even today some
members are monks, but most of the knights and dames that now make
up the Order are lay members (there are 11,000 of them). The military
function has not been exercised since 1798.

Although, in the past, the knights of the Order had to come from chivalrous
and noble Christian families, current members need only distinguish
themselves by their faith, morality and the virtues sought within the
Church and the Order itself. Although volunteers are always welcome, you
can only become a member by invitation.

The Order maintains diplomatic relations with 100 countries through
its embassies. It has a very special status, making it the only private
institution that is treated almost like a country in itself. Activities are
financed by donations from members and other private parties.

Its headquarters are at two sites in Rome, which have been granted
extraterritoriality. These are Palazzo di Malta at 68 Via dei Condotti, where
the grand master resides and meets with government bodies, and Villa
Malta on the Aventine Hill, which houses the Grand Priory of Rome, the
Embassy of the Order to the Holy See and the Embassy of the Order to the
Italian Republic.

THE MALTESE CROSS

Founded in 11th-century Jerusalem by merchants from Amalfi (near Naples), the Sovereign Order of the Knights Hospitaller of St John of Jerusalem (the future Knights of Malta) first took the symbol of Amalfi's port (without its blue background) to be theirs. Then, in 1130, Raymond de Puy converted the charitable brotherhood into a military Order and won the right to use a white cross from Pope Innocent II; the colour was chosen to avoid confusion with the Templars' red cross. Shortly after the Turks drove them off the island of Rhodes in 1523, the Order settled on Malta. At that point, the island's red flag, inherited from the period of Norman occupation, became the background to the white cross, thus creating the Maltese Cross.

THE MEANING OF THE EIGHT POINTS IN THE MALTESE CROSS

The eight points in the Maltese Cross signify various things:
- the eight sides of the Dome of the Rock at Jerusalem.
- the eight nationalities of the original knights of the Order of St John of Jerusalem (the future Order of Malta) or the eight principles they undertook to live by: spirituality, simplicity, humility, compassion, justice, pity, sincerity and patience.
- the eight virtues which a knight of the Order of Malta was expected to possess: loyalty, pity, frankness, courage, honour, contempt of death, solidarity with the sick and poor, respect for the Catholic Church.
- the Eight Beatitudes which Christ listed in his Sermon on the Mount (St Matthew's Gospel, Chapter 5):
Blessed are the poor in spirit: for theirs is the kingdom of heaven. (Verse 3)
Blessed are the meek: for they shall possess the land. (Verse 4)
Blessed are they who mourn: for they shall be comforted. (Verse 5)
Blessed are they that hunger and thirst after justice: for they shall have their fill. (Verse 6)
Blessed are the merciful: for they shall obtain mercy. (Verse 7)
Blessed are the clean of heart: for they shall see God. (Verse 8)
Blessed are the peacemakers: for they shall be called the children of God. (Verse 9)
Blessed are they that suffer persecution for justice' sake, for theirs is the kingdom of heaven. (Verse 10)

The National Institute of Roman Studies was founded in 1925 as a private initiative by Carlo Galazzi Paluzzi, a great lover of Roman history. Public interest soon grew and since 1951 the institute has been seen as a cultural and scientific centre for the research and dissemination of anything that furthers the knowledge of Rome, from antiquity to the present day. To this end it organises congresses, conferences and visits, maintains a well-endowed library and publishes the journal *Studi romani* (Roman Studies). It also runs the *Certamen Capitolinum* Latin prose and poetry competition, whose programme, incidentally, is published in Latin.

ISTITUTO NAZIONALE DI STUDI ROMANI

2 Piazza dei Cavalieri di Malta
• Tel: 06 5743442
• Admission: Free

**A haven
of peace**

The priory in Piazza dei Cavalieri di Malta, a Piranesi masterpiece, is well known as the Rome headquarters of the Knights of Malta. No. 2, the National Institute of Roman Studies, is also a small haven of peace that should not be missed. It is housed in one of Rome's major monastic centres from the High Middle Ages, the monastery of Saints Boniface and Alexius, thought to have been built around the 7th century on the ruins of an imposing Roman sanctuary.

The present building dates mainly from the 17th and 18th centuries, with restructuring work by the architect Giovanni Battista Nolli. At the entrance is a large square courtyard with archaeological remains. The heart of the former monastery is the 16th-century cloister, built by reusing antique columns of marble and granite, topped with capitals, each one different from the others. An entire wing of the building overlooks the Tiber, and a loggia leads to a vast panoramic garden. From there, you can go in and admire the few remaining — though very interesting — decorations. The ceiling of the Sala di Presidenza (Hall of the Presidency), the former library, has a fresco dating from 1754 entitled *Allegory of the Progress of the Sciences and the Arts*, covering the main themes dear to the Enlightenment. The rest of the main floor was occupied by Charles IV of Spain who, driven from his country by Napoleon's troops, took refuge in Rome and decided to settle here. The apartments are adorned with marble floors and Pompeian-style frescoes.

GIOVANNI BATTISTA NOLLI: ARCHITECT CARTOGRAPHER

History teems with stories of polymath scientists or artists. Giovanni Battista Nolli (1692-1756) is a prime example. He was trained as a surveyor but became interested in astronomy and mathematics. On joining the court of the Albani and Corsini families, he rubbed shoulders with scholars and scientists and decided to fill a gap by drawing up the first modern map of Rome. With the support of Pope Benedict XIV, the help of his son and the collaboration of Piranesi and Giuseppe Vasi, he obtained permission to enter all the city's private properties, including the monasteries, to survey their records. His new map, the *Nuova Topografia*, was published in 1744. He was also a practising architect (see above).

PARK OF THE MUSEO FERROVIARIO DI PORTA SAN PAOLO

11 Piazzale Ostiense
• Open Monday-Thursday 9am-4pm, Fri 9am-1pm
• Admission: Free
• Metro: B – Piramide

"No Spitting"

I n a former freight yard next to the elegant Roma-Lido railway station, which was designed by the famous architect Marcello Piacentini and opened in 1924, a park-museum tells the story of rail transport in the capital and its suburbs.

There in the open air, among the palms and lavender bushes, are witnesses to the first public rail network between Rome and Ostia Lido, the Castelli Romani (towns in the hills south of Rome), Viterbo and Frosinone: locomotives, tramcars and first- or second-class carriages, freight cars, all beautifully restored. The oldest is a Breda locomotive of 1915, registered 01, which ran on the Rome-Fiuggi-Frosinone line. For enthusiasts, the highlight of the exhibition is carriage 404 of the STEFER (Società Tranvie E Ferrovie Elettriche Romane), the first in the world made of two articulated sections joined by the so-called *giostra Urbinati* (literally "Urbinati carousel"), an invention patented by engineer Mario Urbinati in 1941. This tram remained in service on the Termini-Cinecittà line until the opening of metro line A in 1980.

The exhibition continues inside, where you can see tramcars, transmission equipment, old ticket books, employment contracts of former railwaymen and "No Spitting" notices.

THE MORTUARY CHAMBER OF PIRAMIDE DI CAIO CESTIO   ⓫

Piazza di Porta San Paolo (Ostiense)
• For reservations contact Pierreci
• Tel: 06 39967700 (Mon-Sat 9am-1:30pm and 2:30pm-5pm)

You can go inside the pyramid ...

The Pyramid of Gaius Cestius, which today forms part of the Aurelian Wall near the Porta San Paolo, is one of Rome's best-known and most unusual "minor" monuments.

The Roman taste for obelisks, sphinxes and sculptures from Egypt dates back to the 1st century BC. Temples dedicated to Isis and Serapis sprang up in the four corners of the empire and certain patricians even had the idea of erecting their own pyramid as a final resting place. Historical documents testify to the existence of at least three funerary pyramids in Rome.

Few people know, however, that the mortuary chamber of the Pyramid of Cestius, decorated with sumptuous frescoes, is open to the public.

Access to the monument is via a modern gallery. The interior consists of a single chamber measuring 4 by 6 metres, with a very austere barrel vault. A long gallery rises to the left. It was probably excavated in the Middle Ages by the first visitors to the tomb, hunting for treasure. At the time, the pyramid was partially buried, and the entrance was at a higher point than the original level.

The portrait of the deceased, Gaius Cestius, would have been displayed on the rear wall, or perhaps in the centre of the vaulting, but the looters must have taken it, leaving large holes in its place. Abundant graffiti also bear witness to the number of curious visitors, not to mention scholars such as Antonio Bosio, who entered the tomb at the beginning of the 17th century. Bosio was the first to scientifically analyse the city's forgotten underground structures, in particular the catacombs.

Among the many testimonies left by visitors is a drawing by one "Giorgio Bafaia Florentino".

The most striking feature, however, is the decoration of the main body (*cella*) of the monument. Some of the figures in the fresco painting stand out clearly from a white background, all executed with great finesse. Priestesses, amphoras and candelabras can be identified, as well as four superb Winged Victories on the vaulting – magnificent frescoes carried out in the purest Pompeian style.

THE PROTESTANT CEMETERY

6 Via Caio Cestio
• Tel: 06 5741900
• Open 9am-4pm from 1 October to 31 March, and 9am-5:30pm from
1 April to 30 September
• Tram: 3; Metro: B – Piramide

Beside the Cestia Pyramid (the great imitation of the ancient Egyptian pyramids), built as a mausoleum by Caio Cestio, rises an old cemetery protected by pine and cypress trees and by ancient Roman walls. A hidden corner of tranquility, it is one of the most romantic places in the city.

"Here Lies One Whose Name is Writ in Water."

This cemetery, in which about four thousand people of every race and creed are buried, has many names: the English Cemetery, due to the fact that the majority of the deceased are of English nationality, the Artists and Poets' Cemetery, not just because of the very large number of artists and poets buried there, but also because of the fact that so many artists and poets have loved it and sung its praises, and finally, probably the most correct name is that of Protestant Cemetery.

What surprises most while strolling along its paths, however, is the magic atmosphere that predominates, the distinctive appeal, the feeling of calm and serenity that make you think that perhaps, in such a place eternal sleep is not so bad.

The cemetery is divided in two by a wall and a ditch. The more recent part has an impressive number of graves, scattered among the trees and covered with flowers planted everywhere, amongst which that of the great English poet Percy Bysshe Shelley, for example, who drowned at the age of thirty on Viareggio beach, and those of August Von Goethe, Johann Wolfgang's natural son, the famous poet Carlo Emilio Gadda and Antonio Gramsci. The older part of the cemetery is different, yet nonetheless still striking, its few graves almost disappearing under the grass of the first piece of land given to the pope in 1722 to bury the Protestants inside the city walls (a practice that was not allowed until then). The grave of another very young English poet is also here: John Keats, who was misunderstood while alive, asked to have the following inscription put on his headstone: "Here Lies One Whose Name is Writ in Water."

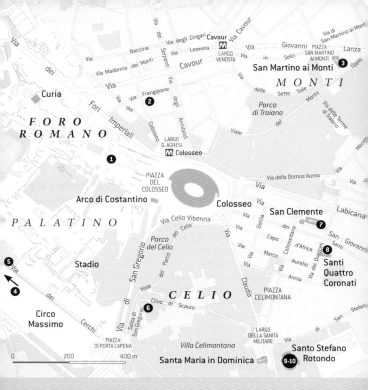

LATERAN - COLOSSEUM - FORUM - CELIO

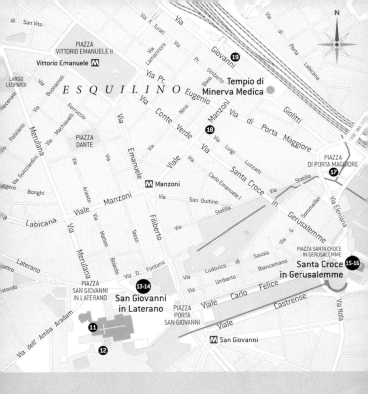

IN QVESTE
PIETRE POSE
LE GINOCHIA S·PIETRO
QVANDO I DEMONII PORT·
SIMON MAGO
PER ARIA

THE MARKS OF SAINT PETER'S KNEES

Church of Santa Francesca Romana
Piazza Santa Francesca Romana
• Tel: 06 6795528
• Open 9:30am-12pm and 4pm-7pm

*Prayer
to interrupt
the levitation
of a sorceror*

Two stone slabs, worn down in the centre, are ensconced in the right wall of the transept of the church dedicated to Saint Frances of Rome (previously to Santa Maria Nuova), as you can see by ascending the two flights of stairs by the side of the crypt.

Tradition holds that these are the imprints left by Saint Peter's knees (or Saint Peter's and Saint Paul's, according to some sources) while praying to God to intervene against Simon Magus, who had levitated himself in the space above the Forum to show his superiority over the two Apostles. The prayer proved effective as the heretic fell to the ground and died on the spot.

Documents bearing witness to the life of Simon Magus have rarely been officially recognised, as the texts do not always agree and are largely derived from apocryphal sources, but according to the most popular version Simon was a magician or sorcerer from a small village in Samaria. On hearing Christian teaching, he requested baptism, although that did not stop him trying to bribe Saint Peter – who took it very badly – in order to acquire the privilege of transmitting the Holy Spirit by the laying on of hands.

It was precisely this legendary attempt by Simon Magus to commercialise spiritual gifts that gave rise to the term *simony*.

BLESSING MOTORISTS

Every year on 9 March a vast number of the faithful gather in their cars in Via dei Fori Imperiali and Piazza del Colosseo, trying their best to park as near to the church as possible to receive the solemn blessing bestowed in the name of Saint Frances of Rome.

This rich and noble lady lived in Rome until her death in 1440. She owed her fame to her generosity, having devoted her life to helping the poor and the sick. In 1425 she founded the Oblate Congregation of Tor de' Specchi (see page 153). She was declared a saint in 1608 and made patron saint of motorists in 1925.

Apparently motorists requested the protection of Saint Frances of Rome because a guardian angel had accompanied her throughout her "route" in life.

ENRICO STURANI'S PRIVATE COLLECTION ❷

14 Via del Cardello
• Tel: 06 486970
• Visits by reservation only
• Metro: B – Cavour or Colosseo

**140,000
postcards**

Enrico Sturani, the owner of a unique and fascinating collection, warmly welcomes curious visitors, thus allowing them to discover the little-known world of postcards. Along with numerous geography schoolbooks, this cultured man with an original personality has an exceptional collection of postcards in his unkempt apartment just a stone's throw from the Colosseum. This incredibly varied repertory of about 140,000 cards allows visitors to step back in time and go on an imaginary trip to the four corners of the world. All you have to do is ask and from the hundreds of cards that fill the shelves of every room, he will take out sometimes extraordinarily beautiful postcards dating from the beginning of the 20th century right up to recent times. Many of these cards come from France, New Zealand and other far away places.

It is almost impossible to find a subject, a year over the last century or a place that has escaped this passionate collector. From war cards to porn cards, from political cards to "lovers" cards, from those with animals to ones with chubby babies, both surreal and futuristic ones, everything becomes unexpectedly interesting especially with Mr Sturani's explanations, and the cards are a unique way of understanding the mentality, culture, tastes and psychology of people over the past hundred years.

TITULUS EQUITII BELOW THE BASILICA OF SAN MARTINO AI MONTI ❸

28 Via Monte Oppio
• Visits on request, by contacting the cultural association *Roma Sotterranea* (www.romasotterranea.it)

> **One of the most interesting constructions of early Christian Rome**

O n the slopes of Colle Oppio, the basilica of San Martino ai Monti (Saint Martin of the Mountains) has one of the most interesting constructions of early Christian Rome preserved in its crypt.

Since excavations were carried out in 1637, a series of chambers has been discovered whose original use is disputed because of the numerous transformations they have undergone over the centuries.

On the outside, along Via Equizia, the change in level between apse and façade is offset by a massive wall composed of blocks of volcanic tufa, perhaps quarried from the ramparts known as the Mura Serviane (Servian Wall).

Once inside the church, you cross the central nave to a staircase leading down into a Baroque crypt beneath the main altar. From there, through a door to the left, is another stairway that gives access to a large rectangular brick-built hall, 14 by 17 metres, divided into three naves by six pillars. The original cladding is still there, with lattice vaults reinforced by concrete joists. This construction, which dates back to the 3rd century AD, used to be part of the neighbouring Baths of Trajan. Afterwards it was probably used for commercial purposes such as a covered market or a warehouse. Some scholars, however, believe it may have been a rich man's house (*domus*). From the late 3rd century, it is thought that it was used as a meeting place by the early Christians.

It was Pope Sylvester I (AD 314-335) who founded the basilica on this property, donated by one Equitius, hence the name *Titulus Equitii*, converting it to the requirements of the Christian rite at communal meetings.

It soon became a site of major importance for the Christian Church: the Synods of AD 499 and AD 595 were both held here.

The church above was built in the 9th century, and the crypts were restored and embellished at the same time. Certain sections of painting that can still be seen on the vaulting are from this period: scenes of saints surrounded by the Virgin and Jesus, whose postures and strikingly coloured clothing are typical of Byzantine art.

Fragments of mosaic are also visible on the black-and-white paving, which along with the ornamental motifs of some of the frescoes, seems to date from the early 3rd century, at the time when the site was still in commercial use.

A second flight of steps leads to other underground chambers, unfortunately completely buried.

THE MITHRAIC SANCTUARY OF CIRCO MASSIMO

16 Piazza della Bocca della Verità
• Visits on request, by telephoning the Cultural Heritage department of the Municipality of Rome (*Sovraintendenza Comunale ai Beni Culturali*) at 06 0608; alternatively through cultural associations such as *Roma Sotterranea* (www.romasotterranea.it)

> **One of the largest Mithraic sanctuaries in Rome**

I n the early 1930s, during restoration work on the building facing the north-west of the Circo Massimo (Circus Maximus), at a depth of 14 metres below the present road level, the remains of a vast brick building from the 2nd century AD were discovered. Its location suggested a public building related to the neighbouring circus. This hypothesis is confirmed by the presence of a majestic flight of steps, a later addition leading to an upper storey.

In the 3rd century AD, certain ground-floor rooms were converted to house one of the largest Mithraic sanctuaries known in Rome (see page 275). Access is by a secondary entrance and a passage to the right, from which opens a service chamber.

A wide brick archway separates this chamber from the sanctuary proper, the sides of which are fitted with raised stone benches for use by worshippers. On the rear wall, a semi-circular niche probably held a statue

of the god. The floor is paved with blocks of salvaged marble while in the centre of the sanctuary stands a circular alabaster stone remarkable for its size. The scene is completed by an incredible white marble relief showing Mithras in the act of slaying a bull, surrounded by his two torch-bearers (*dadofori*) Cautes and Cautopates, the Sun, the Moon, a raven, a scorpion, a dog and a serpent.

OTHER MITHRAIC SANCTUARIES IN ROME

The sanctuary of Santa Prisca has some important paintings, a splendid effigy of the Sun god in *opus sectile* (composed of fragments of marble), and in a niche in the rear wall, the image of Mithras, unusually depicted naked, slaying the bull. An additional bonus is a reclining image of the god Saturn made with fragments of amphorae covered with stucco.

The sanctuary of San Clemente is located on the lowest level of the crypt of the church of the same name. The chamber is small in size and equipped with a central altar carved on all four sides. The vault, decorated with stucco stars, is pierced with eleven apertures: the largest, circular ones probably represent the seven planets of the solar system that were known at the time and which were associated with the seven grades of initiation, while four smaller rectangular openings feature the four seasons. At the back of the chamber, a niche houses a small statue of Mithras springing from the rock at his birth.

The sanctuary of the Palazzo Barberini park is unique because it features 10 small paintings illustrating key episodes in the life of Mithras. These pictures frame a large painting of the tauroctony and the 12 signs of the zodiac.

The sanctuary of the Baths of Caracalla is the largest known in Rome. Roofed by large barrel vaults, the main chamber measures 23 by 10 metres. In the centre is a pit where an underground passage ends. This was thought to have been the *fossa sanguinis* of the sanctuary – the place where the initiate would lie prostrate during the ceremony in order to be doused with blood from the bull sacrificed in the hall overhead. This hypothesis seems dubious, however, given the practical difficulties of sacrificing such a large animal in these cramped and difficult to access caverns. This Mithraic sanctuary has retained its paving of white mosaic with a border of black tiles.

The sanctuary of the cellar of the church of Santo Stefano Rotondo is still decorated with a few frescoes of the Sun and Moon.

The sanctuary of Via Giovanni Lanza measures less than 6 m². Probably a site for private use, it was miraculously intact when discovered. The relief ornamentation, altar, oil lamps and antique vases were even in their original places ...

Sanctuary of Santa Prisca: 13 Via di Santa Prisca
Information and reservations from Pierreci at 06 39967700. Open 2nd and 4th Sundays of the month at 4pm for individual visits and at 3pm and 5pm for groups.
Sanctuary of San Clemente: 95 Via Labicana. Open: 9am-12:30pm and 3pm-6:30pm. Open Sundays at 10am. October until March until 6pm. Admission: € 6.
The sanctuaries of the Palazzo Barberini park, Santo Stefano Rotondo, Baths of Caracalla and Via Giovanni Lanza can only be visited through a number of cultural associations such as *Roma Sotterranea* (www.romasotterranea.it).

MITHRAISM – A FASCINATING ANCIENT CULT FOR INITIATES

Mithraism is a religion centred on Mithras, a god of Persian origin.

Mithras was born naked, springing from the living rock armed with a knife, a flaming torch in his hand, and a Phrygian cap on his head. A pact was signed after Mithras defeated the Sun. He thereby received the Sun's radiant crown, which became his emblem. In his tireless struggle against evil, with the help of his dog he captured and killed a bull, symbol of the impetuous animal forces that must be overcome. Grain miraculously spilled from the bull's wound, while its blood became the grapevine. Its death thus allowed rebirth ... The evil spirit Ahriman, however, refused to admit defeat: he sent a scorpion and a serpent to attack Mithras, but to no avail. Mithras and the Sun then held a celebratory ritual meal known as an *agape*, a term still current today.

The cult of Mithras was usually celebrated in caves and grottoes, not because of any link with the powers of darkness, as some detractors would have it, but rather because the cave was a symbol of the cosmos, towards which believers tried to reach out during the ceremonies.

Mithras was flanked by two torchbearers: Cautes and Cautopates, with whom he formed a triad (or Trinity). The first carried a lighted torch which represented the day, while the second carried an extinguished torch, pointing downwards, symbol of the night.

The concept of the soul's journey across the cosmos is key to all this: the way consisted of seven steps, linked to the seven planets, the seven days of the week, the seven metals and the seven stages of the soul which had to be gradually left behind. The cult was clearly a means of advancing on this path and progressively freeing oneself from passion. The *agape* feast, based on bread and wine, of course recalls the Eucharist, and the sacrifice of the bull from which life sprang is a strange reminder of the crucifixion and resurrection ...

Mithraism spread to the West from the 1st century BC and was at its peak in the 3rd century AD, before being supplanted by Christianity.

CHRISTMAS OWES 25 DECEMBER TO THE WINTER SOLSTICE AND MITHRAISM ...

Contrary to widespread belief, no Christian scriptures actually claim that Jesus was born on the night of 24 to 25 December. The date of 25 December for Christ's birth was decreed in AD 354 by Pope Liberius to combat pagan Roman cults, and above all, Mithraism, which celebrated the birth of its god Mithras on 25 December to roughly coincide with the winter solstice (prior to the Gregorian reform of the calendar, the winter solstice was not fixed and did not always fall on 21 December — which incidentally was one reason for the reform).

The appropriation of this date by the Church also allowed some very beautiful symbolism to develop: at the time of year when the days were shortest and night reigned supreme, the birth of Christ was a powerful symbol of day breaking once again, chasing away the shadows and heralding the resurrection.

Previously, Christians celebrated the birth of Christ on 6 January, the day of the Adoration of the Magi. Only the Armenian Apostolic Church still celebrates Christmas on that date. Orthodox faiths continue to commemorate Christmas on 25 December, but according to the Julian calendar, which differs by several days from the reformed Gregorian version.

Note also that Jesus was probably not born in AD 1, but sometime between 6 BC and AD 6 ...

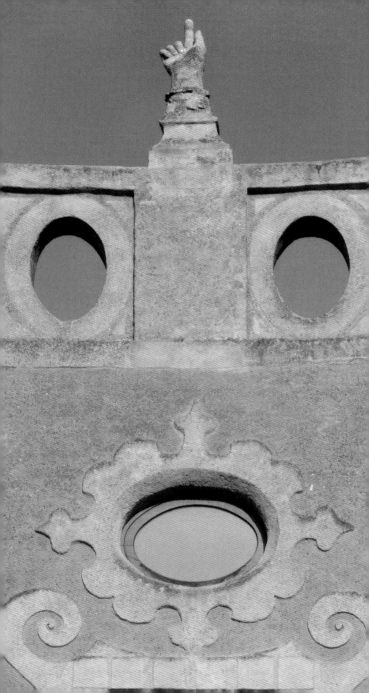

THE HAND ON VIA DEI CERCHI

87 Via dei Cerchi
• Metro: B – Circo Massimo

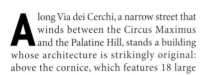

**The hand
of Cicero**

A long Via dei Cerchi, a narrow street that winds between the Circus Maximus and the Palatine Hill, stands a building whose architecture is strikingly original: above the cornice, which features 18 large oculi, a strange hand crowns the construction.

This hand is a plaster copy – on a smaller scale – of a Roman marble original that was found in the area and originally featured on the façade of the little church of the Madonna dei Cerchi, also known as Santa Maria de Manu, built in the 13th century and demolished in 1939. The thumb and forefinger of the hand point towards the sky. In ancient Rome, from the days of the Republic, this gesture had a precise meaning: it was how military commanders and emperors demanded silence before the *adlocutio*, a speech to rouse the troops before battle.

Popular tradition refers to this sculpture as the "hand of Cicero", although there is no reason to associate it with the famous Roman orator.

Inside the building, the windows are surrounded with decorative motifs, notably the fleur-de-lys, heraldic symbol of the Farnese family. The site is in fact at the foot of the Orti Farnesiani (Farnese gardens), which Cardinal Alessandro Farnese ordered to be planted from 1520. In this northern section of the Palatine Hill, the first private botanical gardens in Europe were created; they were inherited by the Bourbons of Naples and subsequently sold to Napoleon III, before the Italian government acquired them after unification in 1870.

The building must originally have been one of the farmhouses on the extensive Farnese estate, but it was embellished with this complex façade during renovations at the end of the 17th century. It is now part of the properties of the Olivetan Benedictine monks, who own the basilica of Sant'Anastasia, whose apse lies behind this building.

At the time of Sixtus V (1585-1590), the common people believed that the hand indicated the price of wine: 1 sou per *fojetta* (half a litre).

WHY IS THERE A TOWER WITHIN THE CIRCUS MAXIMUS?

The medieval Torre della Moletta (Tower of the Little Mill) was part of a fortified complex that belonged to the Frangipane family, a powerful Roman clan. It is so called because of a nearby water mill, powered by the Aqua Mariana channel that flowed right through the centre of the circus.

THE TABLE OF SANTA BARBARA ORATORY ❻

Piazza di San Gregorio
• Open Tuesdays, Thursdays and Sundays 9:30am-12:30pm

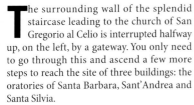

> *Here Saint Gregory fed twelve paupers – and an angel joined them as thirteenth guest*

The surrounding wall of the splendid staircase leading to the church of San Gregorio al Celio is interrupted halfway up, on the left, by a gateway. You only need to go through this and ascend a few more steps to reach the site of three buildings: the oratories of Santa Barbara, Sant'Andrea and Santa Silvia.

It is said that the Barbara oratory was the former residence of Pope Saint Gregory I (Gregory the Great, 590-604) and that the sovereign pontiff had installed therein a large marble table on which he offered a daily meal to twelve paupers. One day, a thirteenth guest was present at the table – an angel who had taken on the guise of a poor man – and Gregory decided to feed him too. It is tempting to see in this person the figure of the traitor Judas, the thirteenth at the Last Supper, and to interpret Gregory's invitation as a call to love and forgive even those who betray us. Hence began the tradition, which persisted until 1870, to bring together thirteen guests at a meal offered by the pope each Holy Thursday, symbolising the pardoning of the traitor. The popular superstition that it is wiser to avoid seating thirteen at table is no less active today.

This very old oratory includes the ruins of a 3rd-century Roman building. It was restored on the initiative of Cardinal Baronio between 1602 and 1603. A marble statue representing Saint Gregory the Great bestowing a blessing, the work of Nicolas Cordier, stands in a niche. The walls are decorated with a series of frescoes attributed to Antonio Viviani carried out in 1603 and 1604, with scenes from the life of the pontiff.

The most striking object, in the centre of the chamber, is of course the large table, the very one where the twelve paupers ate. This massive structure in white marble, supported by two large stone griffons with a central palm tree, dates from the 3rd century AD. An inscription recalling the miracle of the angel reads: *Bissenos hoc Gregorius pascebat egentes – Angelus et decimus tertius accubuit* (Here Saint Gregory fed 12 paupers – and an angel joined them as thirteenth guest).

ORIGIN OF THE WORD "GROTESQUE"

When Nero died in AD 68, his successors strived to eliminate the last traces of his extraordinary palace on the Esquiline, the famous Domus Aurea (Golden House).

The rooms, glittering with gold and precious stones and decorated with frescoes, marble sculptures and multi-coloured stucco, were looted and then buried up to the ceilings to serve as foundations for the imposing baths of Titus and Trajan. The lake in the valley below was drained and on its bed the Colosseum was erected.

The sumptuous frescoes of the Domus Aurea would thus remain hidden until their rediscovery in 1480, apparently quite by accident.

Legend has it that a young Roman fell into a crevice that had opened up on the Oppian Hill, to find himself in a kind of passageway with walls covered in painted figures. The news quickly spread and the prominent artists of the time, lovers of the arts of antiquity such as Pinturicchio, Ghirlandaio, Raphael, Giovanni da Udine, Filippino Lippi and Giulio Romano, were let down on ropes to look around what was thought at first to be caverns (grotte) and to copy the amazing decorations that covered every surface. For this reason, the decorations of the Domus Aurea and all those inspired by them over the following centuries (they were much in vogue throughout the 16th century) came to be known as *grottesche* (grotesques). Unfortunately those of the Domus Aurea have almost completely disappeared. Their rediscovery caused serious damage to the paintings and stuccos which, on exposure to the air and humidity, very quickly lost their colour.

The remains of the Domus Aurea were soon forgotten and excavations were only relaunched at the end of the 18th century after the discovery of the Pompeii frescoes.

This pictorial style did not meet with unanimous approval, however. It was often accused of being unseemly or ridiculous because of its brightly coloured fragile silhouettes painted in a calligraphic manner on a monochrome background devoid of perspective – rather monstrous hybrids with naturalistic effects in a geometric framework.

In time, these criticisms would give to the word "grotesque" a sense of the unusual and bizarre, extending to the caricatural or extravagant.

One of the artists who drew many grotesques was nicknamed "Morto" da Feltre because he had spent more time underground than on the surface, copying these strange ornamental motifs.

THE FIRST KNOWN GROTESQUE DECORATION OF THE RENAISSANCE

The church of Santa Maria del Popolo is home to a superb Pinturicchio painting, in the first chapel to the right of the main entrance. The painted decorations to each side of it are the first representation of grotesques following the discovery of the Domus Aurea.

VERBAL ABUSE IN BASILICA SAN CLEMENTE ❼

- Open 9am-12:30pm and 3pm-6:30pm. Sundays from 10am
- Metro Colosseo

**Sons
of whores,
pull harder!**

I n the Lower Basilica of San Clemente, the 11th-century frescoes showing Saint Clement celebrating Mass reveal a little-known episode in the life of the saint (bottom right of fresco).

The Roman prefect Sisinnius' wife Theodora, who had been converted to Christianity by Saint Clement, was beginning to spend a great deal of her time at church. Her husband, suspicious of her new faith, took her frequent absences as signs of infidelity and decided to follow her to find out what was going on, although she was simply attending Mass.

During the service, however, divine intervention struck down the jealous husband, rendering him deaf and blind. Theodora implored Saint Clement to heal her husband and the saint, praying to God, did so, but Sisinnius then got it into his head that the saint was a magician who had bewitched his wife in order to take advantage of her. So he ordered his servants to seize Clement and carry him away.

For the second time a miracle occurred: the servants, believing they had trussed up the saint, found that they had only managed to tie their ropes around a stout column. The fresco describes the exact moment when the exasperated Sisinnius, right, dressed in a toga, cries: "*Fili de le pute, traite!*" ["Pull harder, you sons of whores!"] – the terms of abuse are clearly visible on the fresco. One of the servants, Gosmari, repeats the order to another, Albertel: "*Albertel, traite*", who in turn asks a third fellow for help: "*Falite dereto co lo palo, Carvoncelle*" ["Carvoncelle, get behind with a lever"] – the inscription can still be seen bottom left.

Meanwhile, Clement, safely out of the way, comments on the scene in learned Latin: "*Duritiam cordis vestri saxa trahere meruisti*" ["You deserve to carry a great burden given the hardness of your hearts"].

THE LEGEND OF POPE JOAN

In an oratory at the junction of Via Santi Quattro and Via dei Querceti there is a painting in very poor condition that has often been interpreted as a memorial of the scandal of the legendary Pope Joan, who gave birth in the street. In fact it is simply a Virgin and Child.

The anti-papal satire of Pope Joan probably originated in popular culture during the 9th century and enjoyed great success in 13th and 14th-century court circles, although largely forgotten today.

It is said that on the death of Pope Leo IV, a young man from the German city of Mainz was elected pope under the title of John VIII and supposedly reigned from 853 to 855 (the pontificate of Leo IV in fact lasted until his death in 855, and Benedict III succeeded him a few weeks later). The young man in question was really a young girl who had just arrived in Rome disguised as a man, after studying in Athens. As she excelled in literary and scientific argument, she gained the respect of a number of academics. Still dressed in male attire, she quickly surrounded herself with followers and became so celebrated that she was made pope. Struggling with great difficulty against her natural desires, however, the young woman grew infatuated with a handsome cardinal, who at first was annoyed by the way she was looking at him. But his irritation melted as soon as he realised that the pope was really a young and beautiful Papessa. The two clerics wasted no time in becoming lovers and, uniquely in the history of the Church, the pope fell pregnant.

The story goes on to say that one day, on the processional route between the Lateran and Saint Peter's, the Papessa's waters broke and she gave birth in the middle of the road, near Saint Clement's church. The place is marked with a stone slab and the street, which no longer exists, came to be known as Vico della Papessa.

Pope Joan's name does not appear today on the list of holy pontiffs, in an attempt to eradicate the memory of this shameful incident. Moreover, the legend has it that thereafter it was stipulated that during a pope's consecration ceremony two cardinals must verify the sex of the new candidate by seating him on a seat with a hole in it, to check his attributes, and

that after verification they should declare: "*Habet duos testiculos et bene pendentes*" (he has two well-hung testicles). But this story was rather discredited by the existence of "commodes" manufactured long before the election of the Papessa. The Church officially denied the legend in 1570, but it is said that until then the Easter processions carefully avoided the Vico della Papessa.

In fact the papal processions never used that street.

GAME IN THE CLOISTER OF SANTI QUATTRO CORONATI BASILICA ❽

Santi Quattro Coronati Basilica
Via dei Santi Quattro Coronati
• Cloister opening hours: 10am-11:45am (9:30am-10:30am on public holidays) and 4pm-5:45pm
• Metro: Colosseo

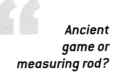

Ancient game or measuring rod?

The basilica of Santi Quattro Coronati, although little known by the public, is one of the most charming and romantic religious buildings in Rome. The cloister, founded in the 13th century, is a marvel of beauty, sweetness and light, accentuated by the second-floor gallery and the double columns supporting it.

Just at the entrance to the cloister, on a low wall set between two rows of columns, 15 parallel lines are carved into the stone, in the middle of which can be read signs that might be interpreted as Roman numerals. Some have seen this as a measuring rod or abacus from antiquity, others believe it was an ancient game resembling either snakes and ladders or dice, in which the number of points won depended on the distance from the two columns.

Almost opposite these lines on the other side of the cloister, there are more inscriptions, also subject to various interpretations. Two of these – the Nine Men's Morris and the esoteric symbol of the triple enclosure – have their supporters. The same inscription is found carved a second time on the wall of the cloister itself but has been almost obliterated.

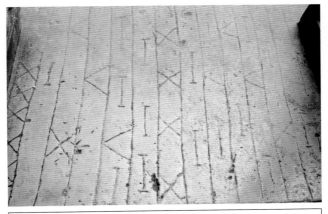

For more information on triple enclosures, see page 295.

X-RATED FRESCOES IN ST STEPHEN'S ⑨

Church of Santo Stefano Rotondo
7 Via di Santo Stefano Rotondo
• Open Monday-Sunday
• Winter: 9:30am-12:30pm and 2pm-5pm
• Summer: 9:30am-12:30pm and 3pm-6pm
• Metro: B – Colosseo; Bus: 3 – Colosseo

The
spectre of death
in a foreign land ...

In 1580, Pope Gregory XIII handed over the church of Santo Stefano al Celio to the Jesuits of the Collegium Germanicum et Hungaricum, where clergymen were trained for the evangelisation of northern and central Europe. After 1517, many inhabitants of these regions had joined Luther's Protestant Reformation. The Roman Catholic Church therefore decided – after the Council of Trent (1545-1563) – to save their souls by sending young Jesuits to proselytise among them.

To accustom young priests to the idea that they might die on this mission, the Jesuits of the Collegium Germanicum commissioned a series of murals for the walls of the circular nave. This resulted in 34 scenes of martyrdom

by famous painters of the time, including Niccolò Pomarancio and Antonio Tempesta. These terrifyingly graphic paintings can still be seen today. The artists were perhaps inspired by the writings of Antonio Gallonio, a priest of the same period – known for his biography of Saint Philip Neri – who in one of his works, illustrated by Tempesta himself, had described in great detail the martyrdom of early Christians.

The church of Santo Stefano Rotondo (Saint Stephen in the Round) on the Celian Hill, dating from the 5th century, seems to have taken its central plan from Eastern architecture. At the centre was a drum 22 metres high and 22 metres in diameter, lit by twenty-two windows and supported by twenty-two columns. Around this nucleus ran two circular naves, with ambulatories and other architectural features. At the time of Pope Theodore I (642-649), the relics of the martyrs Primus and Felicianus were placed in one of the original chapels. This, in addition to the beautiful mosaic in the apse depicting the two martyrs, is the only chapel to have survived the ravages of time. Over the centuries, the outer circular nave was destroyed, so that the inner nave has come to form the perimeter wall of the church.

NEARBY

MITHRAEUM UNDER THE CHURCH ❿

To arrange a visit, contact one of the many cultural associations, such as Roma Sotterranea (www.romasotterranea.it).

THE URN OF CLEMENT XII

⑪

Basilica di San Giovanni in Laterano
4 Piazza di San Giovanni in Laterano
• Open daily 7am-6:45pm
• Metro: A – San Giovanni

*Urn
missing
from
the Pantheon*

Go through the portico of the Pantheon and, in the large niche on the left, you will see two Latin inscriptions with the same text: "The great Pope Leo X, provident prince, ordered this elegant vessel in Numidian stone to be placed here and restored so that it would not fall into disuse, stained by neglect and dirt."

The term "vessel", as used in the Leo X epigraph, in fact referred to two urns of red porphyry.

During the pontificate of Eugenius IV (1431-1447), the area around the Pantheon (which was then known as the church of Santa Maria Rotonda) was cleared of a collection of lean-to huts and shops. Work carried out to level the square in front of the monument, where the ground was frequently impassable when the river was in flood, revealed two red porphyry urns and two basalt lions. The urns probably came from baths such as those of Agrippa, Nero or Severus Alexander, and the lions were perhaps from the temple of Isis and Serapis on the Campo Marzio (Field of Mars, 43 BC).

Pope Eugenius IV decided to place the artefacts in front of the portico of the Pantheon, but the recurrent flooding of the Tiber and the doubtful cleanliness of the area – which was also a marketplace – obliged Pope Leo X (1513-1521) to have the lions restored and raise the urns onto two bases on which were engraved the inscriptions you can see today in the left niche. In the late 16th century, one of the urns was lost and the other moved inside the portico, where it remained until 1730, when Pope Clement XII (1730-1740) seized on it for his funerary monument.

LEO · X · PONT · MAX · PROVIDENTISSIMVS ·
PRINCEPS · VAS · ELEGANTISSIMVM ~
EX · LAPIDE · NVMIDICO · NE · POLLVTVM ~
NEGLIGENTIE · SORDIBVS · OBSOLESCERET
IN · HVNC · MODVM · REPONI · EXORNARIQ
IVSSIT
BARTHOLOMEVS · VALLA
RAMVNDVS · CAPOFERREVS
AEDILES · FAC · CVR ~

Clement XII's urn can now be found inside the basilica of San Giovanni in Laterano (Saint John Lateran), in the nobiliary chapel of the Corsini family at the entrance to the left nave.

Since antiquity, porphyry has been considered an exceptional material. The Romans began to import it when Egypt was made a Roman province (30 BC). Its use has always been associated with the imperial family.

NINE MEN'S MORRIS OR ESOTERIC SYMBOL?

The same grid, composed of three interlocking squares with four horizontal lines that stop short of the central square, can be found carved in many places in Europe, and even in China and Sri Lanka. Although some see this as just a board game known as Nine Men's Morris, it has been pointed out that this inscription has been found carved on vertical walls or reproduced on a very small scale, which would prevent it from being used as the basis for a game. Thus the grid is also thought to be an esoteric symbol used in spiritual quests, representing the three gradations on an initiate's path from the temporal to the sacred final goal, passing through the three worlds of the physical, intellectual, and spiritual or divine. It could also represent Heavenly Jerusalem with its twelve doors (three on each side of the grid). Used by the Knights Templar to mark sacred geographical sites or places where there was a particular concentration of physical and spiritual energy, the grid is also sometimes found in circular form. The circle initially would have corresponded to the beginning of the road while the square signified the culmination of the quest, hence the expression "squaring the circle" to symbolise the successful resolution of a problem.

Nine Men's Morris, also known as Mills or Merrills in English, has been played since antiquity (in Rome, Greece and Egypt). Two players each have nine pieces ("men") and take turns placing them on one of the board's 24 intersections. The object of the game is to align three pieces belonging to the same player. Sometimes ordinary pebbles of different colours are used.

THE TRIPLE ENCLOSURES OF SAN GIOVANNI ⓬ IN LATERANO CLOISTER

Cloister of San Giovanni in Laterano
• Tel: 06 77207991
• Open daily 9am-6pm
• Admission: €3

*Just
a game,
or an esoteric
symbol?*

The superb cloister of San Giovanni in Laterano (Saint John Lateran), designed by Vassalletto in the 13th century, has three curious and discreet inscriptions within its grounds. Just to the right of the entrance is the first of these three markings, which some refer to as "triple enclosures". There are two other sets of these interlocking squares in the cloister, this time traced vertically on the outer walls of the cloister. Numerous interpretations of these inscriptions exist (see opposite).

There are four places in Rome where such a grid can be seen: the basilicas of Santi Quattro Coronati, San Giovanni in Laterano, San Paulo Fuori le Mura, and San Lorenzo Fuori le Mura.

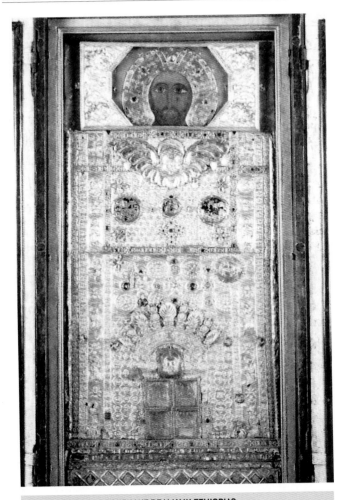

IS THE ARK OF THE COVENANT REALLY IN ETHIOPIA?

According to various sources, the Ark of the Covenant probably still exists. In *The Sign and the Seal: The Quest for the Lost Ark of the Covenant*, Graham Hancock recounts his search for the mythical Ark. After Jerusalem was invaded in the 6th century BC, the Ark is thought to have been taken across the Sinai Desert and along the Nile as far as Ethiopia, where it remains to this day, at Aksum. The almost magical influence of the Ark's presence might explain why Ethiopia is one of the few countries in the world that has never been totally colonised.

PRIVATE VISIT TO THE SANCTA SANCTORUM ⓫

Piazza San Giovanni in Laterano
• Tel: 06 7726641
• Open Saturdays with prior booking at 10:30am, 12:30pm, 3pm and 4pm

> *Yes,*
> *you can enter*
> *the Holy*
> *of Holies*

Contrary to common belief, the pope is not the only person authorized to enter the heart of the Sancta Sanctorum. On Saturdays anyone having pre-booked can visit this sanctuary, which is still held to be one of the most sacred in the Christian world, as borne out by the Latin inscription on the main fresco: "*Non est in toto sanctior orbe locus*" (There is no holier place in all the world).

In the former Temple of Solomon at Jerusalem, the term Sancta Sanctorum designated the most sacred part of the building, which housed the treasure of the temple as well as the mythical Ark of the Covenant containing the tablets of the Law of Moses, the rod of Aaron and the vial of manna from heaven (see opposite). Tradition dictated that only the High Priest had access to the Holy of Holies, once a year.

This sanctuary, now the pope's private chapel, was only accessible to a select few apart from the pontiff himself. Dedicated to Saint Lawrence, it was built by Pope Nicholas III in 1278. Many relics are preserved there, including a miraculous acheiropoietic image (not made by human hands) of Christ (see page 171). Tradition holds that it was painted by Saint Luke himself, with the help of an angel. In the Middle Ages, the image was carried in procession to ward off the plague and other diseases. To prevent deterioration the image was covered with a layer of gold fitted with an opening for the face and little doors for the hands, feet and flank, which were opened at Easter for the worship of the five wounds of Christ's Passion.

In the following centuries, the image of Christ was damaged and was replaced by the copy we see today.

THE RELIC OF CHRIST'S FORESKIN

Sancta Sanctorum
• Tel: 06 7726641
• Open Saturdays with prior booking at 10:30am, 12:30pm, 3pm and 4pm

> **Is the Holy Prepuce at the Lateran?**

According to Jewish tradition, Jesus was circumcised eight days after his birth. At a time when Christianity was fighting over the possession of holy relics, a great many far-fetched artefacts saw the light of day (see pages 168-169), including the foreskin of Christ. This is very likely to be one of the many faked relics and moreover one that is not recognised by the Church.

At Coulombs Abbey in France, a local belief attributes the holy relic with the power to make barren women fertile and give pregnant women an easy childbirth. This was why Catherine of Valois, the wife of King Henry V of England, had the relic brought to her in 1421 to ensure a successful birth.

In the Middle Ages, there were as many as 15 different Holy Prepuces in Europe, although the one in Rome was the most renowned. It was said to have been offered as a wedding gift by the Byzantine empress, Irene the Athenian, and placed in the Sancta Santorum of the Lateran by the pope.

Several examples having been destroyed during the French Revolution, three other places of the original 15 now claim the holy relic: Antwerp in Belgium, Conques and Vebret (Auvergne) in France.

MORE POWERFUL THAN THE HOLY FORESKIN, THE HOLY UMBILICAL CORD OF CHRIST!

At the height of the competition over holy relics (see pages 168-169), an improbable example was invented by unscrupulous merchants: the Holy Umbilicus, said to be the remains of Jesus' umbilical cord. This relic is preserved today at the church of San Giovanni in Laterano with another small fragment at Santa Maria del Popolo. Note that another Holy Umbilicus is thought to have existed at Châlons-en-Champagne, in France, until 1707, when the relic was destroyed by the bishop who judged it to be a fake. The town is said to have acquired the relic thanks to Charlemagne who himself received it from the Byzantine emperor. He was supposed to have given it to one of the popes, whose successor, probably the Frenchman Clement V, passed on a fragment to the bishop of Châlons.

THE INRI INSCRIPTION AT SANTA CROCE IN GERUSALEMME

⑮

Chapel of Relics and Sanctuary of the Cross
9A Piazza di Santa Croce in Gerusalemme
• Tel: 06 70 14 769 • www.basilicasantacroce.it
• Open daily 7am-1pm and 2pm-6:30pm

Where is the True Cross of Christ?

Among the main relics in the Basilica of Santa Croce in Gerusalemme (Holy Cross in Jerusalem) is that of the inscription on the cross on which Christ was crucified.

St John's Gospel is the only one that mentions this inscription. In his text, the words "Jesus of Nazareth the King of the Jews" are said to have been written in three languages: Hebrew, Greek and Latin. Note that, according to this same Gospel, the Jewish priests had asked Pilate that the inscription should instead read: "He said, I am King of the Jews", but Pilate refused. The tradition is that a fragment of the cross bearing this inscription was brought back from the Holy Land by Helena, mother of Constantine, the first Roman emperor to convert to Christianity and founder of Constantinople, the city named after him.

According to Saint Ambrose, Bishop of Milan (died 397), Helena discovered the True Cross of Christ in 325, distinguishing it from the two other crucifixes thanks to the famous inscription. She then brought the fragment back to Rome, for her palace at Sessoriano, within which the Basilica of Santa Croce in Gerusalemme was built. Later, similar relics cropped up elsewhere (see pages 168-169), until several crosses and inscriptions were competing with each other.

Another INRI inscription was reported in Jerusalem at the end of the 4th century, but this one had a different wording: *Hic est Rex Iudaeorum* (This is the King of the Jews). A third inscription came to light in Paris in the 13th century and a fourth was displayed in the cathedral of Toulouse. The inscription of Santa Croce in Gerusalemme was rediscovered in 1492, concealed behind a stone in the wall, in a lead box with the seal of Pope Lucius II (1144-1145). In 2001, two scientists, Francesco Bella and Carlo Azzi, analysed it by carbon-14 dating and found that it originated around 1020.

CAN THE TRUE CROSS BE TRACED BACK TO ADAM, SOLOMON AND THE QUEEN OF SHEBA?

According to the *Legenda aurea* (*Golden Legend*) by Jacobus de Voragine (1228-1298), Adam in his great age asked his son Seth to procure oil from the Archangel Michael to anoint him before he died. The archangel refused but instead gave him a small branch from the Tree of [Knowledge of] Good and Evil with the command to place it in Adam's mouth at the moment of his burial. This small branch would then grow from Adam's body into a great tree that would save him from his sins, ensuring his salvation.

Much later, when King Solomon was having the Temple of Jerusalem built, this tree was cut down to be used in the construction, but it so happened that the beam kept changing size and was either too short or too long for its intended use. The workmen got rid of it by casting it into the River Siloe to use as a footbridge.

The Queen of Sheba, who had journeyed to visit Solomon, had a premonition as soon as she stepped on the bridge: this beam of wood will one day be used for the crucifixion of Christ and the reign of the Jews will come to an end. In order to avoid this tragic fate, King Solomon had the beam taken away and buried. At the time of Jesus' trial, however, the beam sprang miraculously from the soil and was ultimately used for the cross on which he was crucified. In order to avoid crosses becoming cult objects, they were buried and forgotten until the Roman Emperor Constantine, while fighting his rival Maxentius, had a vision of an illuminated cross on which was inscribed: "*in hoc signo vinces*" ["In this sign, conquer"]. His army having won the decisive battle of the Milvian Bridge by following the sign of the cross, Constantine wished to recover the Cross of Christ and sent his mother Helena to Jerusalem to look for it.

After torturing a Jew who knew the burial site of the three crosses [Jesus and the two thieves] for seven days, Helena rediscovered them. A miraculous event then revealed which of the three was the True Cross: a young man who had just died was instantly revived when his lifeless body touched the wood of the Cross of Christ.

Part of the Cross was retained in Jerusalem while another fragment was taken to Constantinople, the new imperial capital.

MUSEO STORICO DEI GRANATIERI DI SARDEGNA

7 Piazza Santa Croce in Gerusalemme
- Tel: 06 7028287
- Open Monday-Friday 9am-12pm • Admission: Free
- Metro: A – San Giovanni; Tram: 3; Bus: 571 – S. Croce in Gerusalemme

Real daggers in the grand staircase

The bronze bust of King Umberto I disfigured by two pistol shots is perhaps the most unusual piece among the thousands of exhibits in the Historical Museum of the Grenadiers of Sardinia. Behind the basilica of Santa Croce in Gerusalemme (Holy Cross in Jerusalem) used to stand the Umberto I barracks, headquarters of the 2nd Regiment of Grenadiers, partially destroyed in 1943 by the Allied bombing of San Lorenzo railway station. The shots were fired almost at the end of the Second World War by some German soldiers who burst into the barracks the day after the armistice of 8 September 1943. They were sure they would find the reigning monarch Victor Emmanuel III, who had in fact fled Rome during the night. In their fury, they fired their pistols at the bust of his father, which then stood in the courtyard of the barracks.

The Grenadiers of Sardinia regiment was formed in 1659 in the Duchy of Savoy. Originally known as the "regiment of royal guards", they took the name Grenadiers when every company included six soldiers whose duty was to advance before the troops and throw devices filled with small grains of explosive powder (which became known as grenades) at the enemy. An exploding grenade still features on the regimental flag.

The museum, which opened in 1924, has 15 rooms tracing the history of the various events in which the Grenadiers took part: the Napoleonic campaigns in three Italian wars of independence, the colonial wars in Eritrea and Libya and the two World Wars.

In addition to the bronze bust of King Umberto scarred by pistol shots, the numerous exhibits include flags, weapons, uniforms and personal items, many of which were donated by former Grenadiers or their families. Also on display are a vast number of documents, photographs and large plans of major battlefields.

On the way up the grand staircase, note also that the iron banisters incorporate real daggers in their sheaths.

In the white-painted grand reception room on the first floor, just below the ceiling and along the walls, medallions feature all the members of the House of Savoy dynasty, from the first counts to the kings of Sardinia and Italy.

The tour ends with a visit to the memorial, a very moving experience. On the circular porphyry walls over 8,500 names are engraved in gold letters: those of Grenadiers fallen in all the wars of the 20th century. In the centre of the dome, on the skylight that faintly illuminates the room, is written: "Beyond the boundaries of life."

THE BAKER'S TOMB

Piazza Maggiore

> **An imperial tomb for a simple baker**

Virtually an imperial monument, the monument to Marco Virgilio Eurisace is just the tomb of an ordinary baker. It was rediscovered in the late 19th century when Pope Gregory XVI demolished the defensive towers that Honorius had built beside the Porta Maggiore in 1838, in order to restore the site to the aspect it enjoyed in the Aurelian era. Constructed from concrete and travertine in 30 BC, the monument curiously resembles the patrician tombs of the Appian Way.

As the inscription points out: *Est hoc monimentum Marcei Vergilei Eurysacis pistoris, redemptoris, apparet* (This is the tomb of Marcus Vergilius Eurysaces, baker, contractor, provisioning breadmaker). The man, who was a subordinate (*apparitore*) to a high-ranking figure, was probably an emancipated slave who worked for the state.

On the tomb are a number of symbols of the baker's trade. The tomb itself is shaped like the vessel in which he would have kneaded the bread. It is decorated with numerous bas-reliefs representing the utensils used to make bread, as well as the production process itself: weighing the wheat, sifting the flour, preparing the dough, placing the bread in the oven …

The urn in which the ashes of his wife Atinia are preserved, now in the Museo delle Terme in Rome, was made in the form of a dough trough. Finally, the bas-relief depicting two spouses at the Capitoline Museums probably comes from another, now ruined, section of this monument.

The Museo della Civiltà Romana (Museum of Roman Civilisation), in the EUR district, holds a miniature reproduction of the tomb.

The Porta Maggiore was so named to indicate to pilgrims the route that led to the church of Santa Maria Maggiore.

HYPOGEUM OF THE AURELII

Ipogeo degli Aurelii
2 Via Luzzati
• Visits by appointment: Pontificia Commissione di Archaeologia Sacra
(tel: 06 4465610)

> **Where Prometheus, Hercules and Circe rub shoulders with Adam and Christ ...**

At the corner of Via Manzoni and Via Luzzati is a wonderful funerary catacomb built for the Aurelii family in the 3rd century AD. The hypogeum, which was discovered in 1919 during the construction of a garage, now consists mainly of one large and two smaller rooms dug into the tuff at a lower level. An old gate opens onto an alley between two villas and from there you enter a vestibule and then follow the steps down to the hypogeum.

The grandiose paintings that decorate the space are among the most remarkable of the 3rd century, and also raise problems of interpretation which are far from being resolved. It is difficult to associate them with any one iconographic school; their eclecticism is typical of the multi-religious climate of the time, when new religions from the East coexisted with more classical Greco-Roman ideologies.

Frescoes depicting the Twelve Apostles, the four Evangelists and Christ the Good Shepherd are found next to banqueting and triumphal scenes (which can perhaps be interpreted as the triumphal entry of souls to the heavenly Jerusalem), urban scenes, mythological animals, philosophers, and so on. Another cycle follows the Homeric tradition, with Ulysses returning from Ithaca and finding Penelope at her loom, or Ulysses and the sorceress Circe. Others are even more enigmatic: recognisable are Prometheus creating man and Heracles in the Garden of Eden or, according to another interpretation, the creation of Adam and the expulsion from Paradise.

The final room is even more ambiguous. There is a figure pointing at the Cross – an extremely unusual representation for that time – as well as figures of men and veiled women, probably initiates. The central medallion has an initiation or exorcism scene, suggesting the presence here of a religious brotherhood.

Seen in this light, the Hypogeum of the Aurelii is a striking example of a community which, without fully embracing Christianity, interpreted it by the multi-faith and aesthetic criteria of 3rd-century Rome.

THE DUST OF THE PILLAR OF SANTA BIBIANA ⓘ

Church of Santa Bibiana
154 Via G. Giolitti
• Open 7:30am-11am and 4:30pm-7:30pm
• Tram: 5 or 14; Metro A or B – Termini

> *A potion made from the blood of a martyr*

Located just a short distance from the Termini train station and squeezed between the tracks of old and new railway lines, this small church goes unnoticed due to its unfortunate position, hidden by the train pylons, by its own enclosure, and by trees. To find the entrance, you have to cross the old tracks and a street that is difficult for pedestrians to access.

It is, in fact, an old basilica dedicated to Bibiana, a legendary 4th-century martyr. It was built in the 5th century at the behest of Pope Simplicius over the remains of thousands of martyrs. Reconstructed for the first time by Pope Honorius III in 1224, it was reconstructed a second time by Pope Urban VIII in 1626, with numerous interventions by Bernini, who gave it a new façade with an atrium and a loggia that were later closed. Bernini redesigned the apse, adding two chapels to the lateral naves at the back, where the altar paintings depicting Defrosa di Pietro da Cortona and Demetria di Agostino Ciampelli (Bibiana's mother and sister respectively, both martyrs) can be seen. He also renovated the main chapel, inserting a statue of Bibiana in a niche.

Under the main altar, a precious alabaster jar contains the remains of Bibiana, Demetria and Defrosa.

The trunk of the pillar to which Bibiana was tied and flogged to death is kept in the left-hand nave. It is worn down by the hands of all those who for centuries have scraped up the dust. By dissolving this dust in water from the well in the nearby kitchen garden, and mixing it with the grass growing on the spot where the martyr's blood flowed, believers try to obtain a potion with miraculous powers.

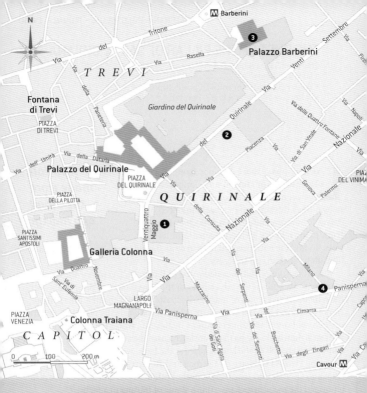

QUIRINALE -TERMINI - MONTI - ESQUILINO

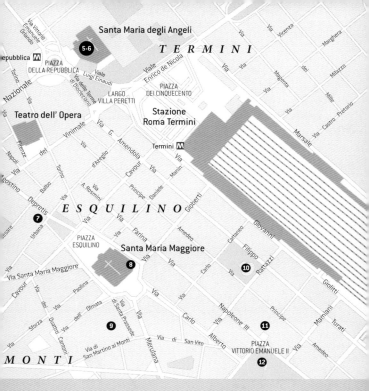

PALLAVICINI

PALLAVICINI

CASINO DELL'AURORA

Palazzo Pallavicini-Rospigliosi
43 Via XXIV Maggio
• Tel: 06 83467000
• Open first day of the month, 10am-12pm and 3pm-5pm
• Admission: Free
• Private visits: Every day, group of 20 people minimum (€15 per person on weekdays and €20 per person on public holidays)
• Specialised foreign language guides available on request

> **See the dawn once a month**

In the grounds of the extraordinary Palazzo Pallavicini-Rospigliosi, the Casino dell'Aurora (Dawn Pavilion) is open to the public free of charge on the first day of every month. The palace, built in 1610 over the ruins of the Baths of Constantine, was the former home of the powerful Cardinal Mazarin (Giulio Mazzarino). The *casino* (pavilion), designed at the same time as the hanging garden and the semicircular fountain on the opposite side, was built by the Flemish cabinet-maker Giovanni Vasanzio (the Italian name of Jan Van Santen), who became the assistant of the celebrated architect Flaminio Ponzio upon arriving in Rome. The building's two levels are only visible on the outside from Via XXIV Maggio, because on the other side, which faces the garden, the lower level is buried due to the difference in height between street and garden. The building, which on both levels consists of a central hall flanked by two smaller rooms, has the typical "C" form of hunting lodges and suburban villas built from the end of the 15th century, and the garden side corresponds to the second floor of the building reserved for banquets and formal ceremonies. On the ceiling of the central hall is the fresco masterpiece that gives the pavilion its name: *Aurora* by Guido Reni, painted 1613-1614, and one of the most copied works in the history of art over the past four centuries. The central hall is filled with 17th-century marble busts of Roman emperors and famous Greek statues, such as *Artemis the Huntress* and the *Rospigliosi Athena*.

PRIVATE VISIT: THE SIDE ROOMS OF CASINO DELL'AURORA

By booking (Madame Capaccioli at 06 83467000), not only can you visit the pavilion in peace but also gain access to two side rooms that are closed during the monthly public tours.

The ceilings are frescoed with Giovanni Baglione's *Renaldo and Armida* and Passignano's *Battle of Armida*. There are also two paintings by Guido Reni, *Christ Crucified* and *Andromeda Freed by Perseus*, as well as *The Death of Julian the Apostate* and *The Conversion of Saul* by Luca Giordano.

PAVILION OF THE MUSES

Exceptionally it may also be possible to visit the Pavilion of the Muses, which forms part of the same palace complex. Some very fine frescoes can be seen there by Orazio Gentileschi and Agostino Tassi. Reservation again through Madame Capaccioli at 06 83467000.

THE STATUE OF STANISLAS KOSTKA

Church of San Andrea al Quirinale
29 Via del Quirinale
• Tel: 06 4744872
• Open Monday to Friday 8:30am-12pm and 3:30pm-7pm, and Saturday and Sunday 9am-12pm and 4pm-7pm

> *A marvellous statue embedded in a picture frame*

Most visitors to San Andrea al Quirinale, who restrict themselves to the main church precinct, will not suspect they are missing the best part: at the back of the church a passage to the right leads into a corridor where postcards and other souvenirs are sold.

From there you can enter the two most interesting places in the building, but you need to know about them because they are usually closed. You only have to ask, however, and the door to the superb sacristy will be opened.

This room, with a beautiful richly frescoed ceiling, can be admired with the help of the lamps that will be lit for you, but we recommend investing 50 centimes in some extra lighting to see it better. For the modest sum of €1, you can also ask to see the rooms housing the relics of Saint Stanislas Kostka on the first floor of the building (home of the Jesuit seminary). Born in Poland in 1550 and dead by the age of 18 in 1568, Stanislas Kostka entered the Jesuits novitiate in Rome when he was 16, after studying in Vienna. Against the wishes of his father, he had run away from home in 1567 and crossed the whole of Germany on foot. In the second room is a quite extraordinary and neglected sculpture by Pierre Legros the Younger, dating from 1702 to 1703. In spectacular detail, it shows the saint lying on his deathbed in a superb blend of polychrome marble that captures the smallest folds in the draperies. The black marble tunic he is wearing is incredible enough: more like a 19th-century dandy's coat than a religious habit, it means that the saint had not yet been ordained as a priest.

You will also notice the curious detail that a section from the painting behind the marble bed has been cut out. This work by Tommaso Minardi depicting the Holy Virgin, Saint Barbara, Sainte Cecilia and Saint Agnes welcoming the saint, was hung after the Legros sculpture was in place. As the statue touched the wall, a section of the frame had to be removed to fit in the painting, which is of little interest in itself.

DIVINE WISDOM FRESCO ❸

Galleria Nazionale d'Arte Antica - Palazzo Barberini
13 Via delle Quattro Fontane
• http://galleriabarberini.beniculturali.it
• Open Tuesday to Sunday 8:30am-7pm
• Metro: A – Barberini

> **Mirroring the theology of Tommaso Campanella**

The *Allegory of Divine Wisdom* in the beautiful Palazzo Barberini was commissioned by Taddeo Barberini (1603-1647), nephew of Pope Urban VIII, from the Italian painter Andrea Sacchi (1599-1661), who masterfully carried out the task between 1629 and 1631-33.

Sacchi was a friend and disciple of the philosopher and theologian Tommaso Campanella (1568-1639), a follower of the Gnostic ideas of his time and a supporter of Church reform, which condemned him to many years in prison for heresy and conspiracy. Campanella entered the Dominican Order in his youth. However, in both thought and action, he was a Christian who

believed that the pope – as the spiritual leader of Christendom – could establish a state with perfect social justice among countries while ruling from the Vatican, a state where religion and politics were reconciled in perfect harmony: a true papal theocracy. He even wrote a utopian treatise entitled *La città del sole* (The City of the Sun).

According to Campanella, Pope Urban VIII had all the cultural and moral qualities of a truly supreme pontiff. Campanella became an intimate adviser and friend of the Vatican curia and when, in 1634, the Inquisition again tried to arrest him, the pope personally arranged his flight to Paris. Previously, Campanella had immortalised Urban VIII Barberini and affirmed his divine mission on Earth, once risen to papal power, through Sacchi's *Divine Wisdom* fresco: it represents the famous City of the Sun that Campanella yearned for.

In a 1633 treatise Campanella had already described his ideal of the universal emperor of a Catholic monarchy, *Monarchia messiae,* an evocative title that reflected the ideas previously expressed in *City of God* by another Neoplatonic, Saint Augustine.

In Campanella's opinion, the reign of Urban VIII was the realisation on Earth of the City of the Sun. In the fresco, Divine Wisdom is surrounded by the virtues essential to this realisation: Nobility wearing the crown of Ariane, Eternity and the serpent biting its tail forming the circle of infinity, Justice with the scales, Courage with the key of Hercules, Gentleness with a lyre, Divinity with the triangle, Charity with an ear of wheat, Holiness with the cross and the burning altar, Purity with the swan, Insight with the eagle and Beauty with the hair of Berenice.

In the sky appear two winged figures: a man astride a winged lion, an allegory of God's love; and, opposite, Cupid holding an arrow and pointing to a hare that symbolises the fear of God.

Finally, at the feet of Divine Wisdom and in alignment, a huge globe appears to rotate in orbit around the throne. It suggests that Andrea Sacchi knew the heliocentric theory supported by Galileo, but instigated by Copernicus.

HERMETIC FRESCO

Note also in the *Divine Wisdom* fresco the small stars positioned near the painted virtues. They represent the sky on the night of 5 to 6 August 1623, when Urban VIII Barberini was elected pope. Thus, in perfect correspondence with the Hermetic theories of the time (see page 214), this painting was not just decorative but served as a talisman. It was supposed to reproduce and disseminate the conjunctions of the stars favourable to Urban VIII, thus protecting him from the negative influences of Mars and Saturn at the time of solar and lunar eclipses. Urban VIII was a discreet but dedicated believer in astrology and Campanella had even studied the planets that influenced the pope in his work *Campanellae Astrologicorum Libri VI*, under the title *De siderali fato vitando*.

MUSEO DI PATOLOGIA DEL LIBRO ❹

76 Via Milano
• Tel: 06 48291 – 48291304 – 48291235
• E-mail: icplform@tin.it
• Open by appointment
• Admission: Free

The little-known Museum of Book Pathology was set up in 1938 on the initiative of the Museo dell'Istituto Centrale di Patologia del Libro (Central Institute for Book Pathology). Since then, it has assiduously built up a collection

> **Books may suffer, but they will be well looked after**

illustrating how books are manufactured and how they eventually deteriorate.

The museum has now been completely refurbished on a new site. A particular attempt has been made to promote a collection of one-of-a-kind objects via a tour laid out in three sections. The first section is devoted to the production materials and techniques of both ancient and modern books. The second covers the various ways in which books can be damaged, and the third their conservation and restoration.

Thanks to the experience acquired by the museum staff and the collaboration of the Institute's laboratories, it has been possible to make new teaching aids available to the public that actively encourage visitor participation, making the tour much more interesting for adults as well as for children.

The average length of the museum visit is around 45 minutes. Audio guides in Italian or English are available for all age groups. A series of panels provide a short introduction to each section, while a video illustrates the work of the Institute. There is also an educational workshop entirely devoted to younger children.

THE SUNDIAL OF SANTA MARIA DEGLI ANGELI CHURCH ❺

Piazza delle Repubblica
• Open Saturdays, 7:30am-6:30pm, and Sundays, 8:30am-7:30pm
• Metro: B – Repubblica

> *A testimonial to momentous reform*

Santa Maria degli Angeli (Our Lady of the Angels) is a majestic basilica built within the Baths of Diocletian according to designs by Michelangelo, with later additions by Vanvitelli.

On the floor of the basilica in front of Diaz's tomb, one can admire a very beautiful sundial measuring 45 metres long, also called the *Linea Clementina* (Clementine Line) since it was inaugurated by Pope Clement XI on 6 October 1702.

This beautiful bronze and marble inlay had become rather worn after centuries of being tread upon by churchgoers, but restoration work in 2000 rendered it all its former beauty.

Its creation dates back to 1700, when, in order to check the accuracy of the Gregorian reform of the calendar, Pope Clement XI asked the mathematician and astronomer Francesco Bianchini to build a monumental sundial that would indicate the spring equinox and therefore help to determine the exact date of Easter Sunday.

According to the rules set out by the Fathers of the Church at the Council of Nicaea in 325, Easter was to be celebrated on the first Sunday after the first full moon following the spring equinox. Therefore it was extremely important to avoid mistakes that would have inevitably moved the dates of all the other movable religious holidays.

Alongside the sundial is another old marble inlay representing the signs of the Zodiac. These were based on Maratta's drawings, using the images of Bayer's *Uranometria Nova*.

To the right of the line, the signs of summer and autumn constellations appear; to the left, those of spring and winter. Every day of the year at midday, the rays of the sun, entering the building through the centre of the heraldic coat of arms of Pope Clement XI, touch a different point of the line, advancing from Cancer during the summer solstice to Capricorn during the winter solstice, and then back through the rest of the signs to Cancer.

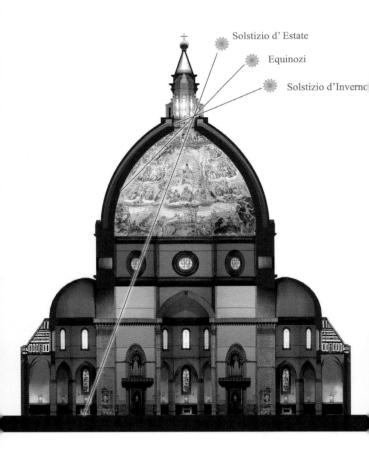

Solstizio d' Estate

Equinozi

Solstizio d'Inverno

HOW DOES A MERIDIAN WORK?

Instead of using the shadow of a gnomon, meridians use a small hole placed at a certain height, through which the sun's light falls onto a meridian line (i.e. one aligned exactly north-south). The fact that the sun's rays perform the function of the shadow in a traditional sundial means that the opening is sometimes referred to as a "gnomonic opening".

The higher the opening, the more efficient the meridian, hence the interest in using cathedrals (see page 325 "Why where meridians installed in cathedrals?"); the circumference of the hole had to be no more than one thousandth of the height above the ground. Obviously, the opening had to be installed on the south side of the building in order to let in the rays of the sun, which lies to the south in the northern hemisphere. The meridian line should run from the point which stands perpendicularly below the axis of the opening, not always easy to determine using the instruments available to scientists in the past. The length of the line depends on the height of the opening; in some cases, where the building was not long enough to trace the entire meridian line across the floor (as was the case at Saint-Sulpice in Paris), an obelisk was added at its end, so that the movement of the sun's rays could then be measured up the vertical. In summer, when the sun is highest in the sky, the sun's rays fall onto the meridian line closer to the south wall (where that line begins) than they do in winter, when the sun is lower over the horizon and the rays tend to strike towards the far end of the meridian line.

The main principle behind the working of the meridian is that at noon, solar time, the sun is at its apex and, by definition, its rays fall straight along a line running exactly north-south. So, the exact moment when those rays strike the meridian line, which does run north-south, indicates the solar noon.

Furthermore, the exact place on the meridian line where the rays fall makes it possible to determine the day of the year: the point right at the beginning of the line is reached solely on the day of the summer solstice, while the exact end of the line is reached on the day of the winter solstice. Experience and observation meant that the meridian line could be calibrated to identify different days of the year.

Once this was done, the line could be used to establish the date of various movable feasts, such as Easter – one of the great scientific and religious uses of meridians. Similarly, the different periods corresponding with the signs of the Zodiac could be established, which explains why such signs are indicated along the length of a number of meridian lines.

WHY WAS 4 OCTOBER FOLLOWED IMMEDIATELY BY 15 OCTOBER IN THE YEAR 1582?
THE MEASUREMENT OF TIME AND THE ORIGIN OF THE MERIDIANS

The entire problem of the measurement of time and the establishment of calendars arises from the fact that the Earth does not take an exact number of days to orbit the sun: one orbit in fact takes neither 365 nor 366 days but rather 365 days, 5 hours, 48 minutes and 45 seconds.

At the time of Julius Caesar, Sosigenes of Alexandria calculated this orbit as 365 days and 6 hours. In order to make up for this difference of an extra 6 hours, he came up with the idea of an extra day every four years: thus the Julian calendar – and the leap year – came into being.

In AD 325, the Council of Nicaea established the temporal power of the Church (it had been called by Constantine, the first Roman emperor to embrace Christianity). The Church's liturgical year contained fixed feasts such as Christmas, but also movable feasts such as Easter. The latter was of essential importance as it commemorated the death and resurrection of Christ, and so the Church decided that it should fall on the first Sunday following the full moon after the spring equinox. That year, the equinox fell on 21 March, which was thus established as its permanent date.

However, over the years, observation of the heavens showed that the equinox (which corresponds with a certain known position of the stars) no longer fell on 21 March ... The 11 minute and 15 second difference between the real and assumed time of the Earth's orbit around the sun was resulting in an increasing gap between the actual equinox and 21 March.

By the 16th century, that gap had increased to ten full days and so Pope Gregory XIII decided to intervene. Quite simply, ten days would be removed from the calendar in 1582, and it would pass directly from 4 October to 15 October. It was also decided, on the basis of complex calculations (carried out most notably by the Calabrian astronomer Luigi Giglio), that the first year of each century (ending in 00) would not actually be a leap year, even though divisible by four. The exceptions would fall every 400 years, which would mean that in 400 years there would be a total of just 97 (rather than 100) leap years. This came closest to making up the shortfall resulting from difference between the real and assumed time of orbit. Thus 1700, 1800 and 1900 would not be leap years, but 2000 would ...

In order to establish the full credibility of this new calendar – and convince the various Protestant nations that continued to use the Julian calendar – Rome initiated the installation of large meridians within its churches. A wonderful scientific epic had begun ...

The technical name for a leap year is a bissextile year. The term comes from the fact that the additional day was once placed between 24 and 25 February. In Latin, 24 February was the sixth (*sextus*) day before the calends of March, hence the name *bis sextus*, to indicate a supplementary sixth day. The *calends* were the first day of each month in the Roman calendar.

THE MERIDIAN OF SANTA MARIA DEL FIORE: THE HIGHEST MERIDIAN IN THE WORLD

From the 15th to the 18th centuries almost 70 meridians were installed in churches in France and Italy. Only nine, however, have a gnomonic opening that is more than 10 metres above floor level – that height being crucial to the accuracy of the instrument:

S. Maria del Fiore (Florence)	90.11 m
S. Petronio (Bologna)	27.07 m
St-Sulpice (Paris)	26.00 m
Monastery of San Nicolo l'Arena (Catania, Sicily)	23.92 m
Cathedral (Milan)	23.82 m
S. Maria degli Angeli (Rome)	20.34 m
S. Giorgio (Modica, Sicily)	14.18 m
Museo Nazionale (Naples)	14.00 m
Cathedral (Palermo)	11.78 m

WHY WERE MERIDIANS INSTALLED IN CATHEDRALS?

To make their measurements more precise, astronomers required enclosed spaces where the point admitting light was as high as possible from the ground: the longer the beam of light, the more accurately they could establish that it was meeting the floor along an exactly perpendicular plane. Cathedrals were soon recognised as the ideal location for such scientific instruments as meridians. Furthermore, the Church had a vested interest as well, because meridians could be used to establish the exact date of Easter.

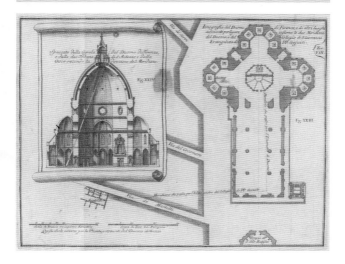

THE BOREAL MERIDIAN OF SANTA MARIA DEGLI ANGELI CHURCH ❻

Piazza delle Repubblica
• Open on Saturdays 7:30am-6:30pm and on Sundays 8:30am-7:30pm
• Metro: B – Repubblica

> **The only meridian in the world for tracking the pole star**

Although the solar meridian of Santa Maria degli Angeli is relatively well known, the extraordinary boreal meridian also found in the transept of this church is much less so. Oriented north, in contrast to the sundial which is oriented south, this boreal meridian is the only known example of its kind.

It is intended to track on the church floor the movement around the North

Pole of the pole star (Polaris), which can be seen through a hole located high up (27.20 m) on the right wing of the church. Near the beginning of the solar meridian 17 magnificent ellipses correspond to the various trajectories of the star. This boreal meridian is an extraordinary and rare instrument that makes it possible to measure the effect of the precession of the equinoxes (see below).

Other than its astronomical function, Bianchini's meridian also marks the midnight hour, corresponding to the beginning of the ecclesiastical day (see also preceding double-page spread).

WHERE DOES THE WORD "BOREAL" COME FROM?
In Greek mythology, Boreas was the son of Eos and Astraeus and personified the north wind. The adjective boreal, by extension, denotes the north or northern regions.

Further detail on the operation of the two meridians of Santa Maria degli Angeli church can be found in the remarkable book *Il cielo in Basilica* (Italian only, Agami publishers).

ANACHRONISTIC CHARACTERS
IN THE SANTA PUDENZIANA MOSAIC

Church of Santa Pudenziana
160 Via Urbana
• Open daily 8:30am-12pm and 3pm-6pm
• Bus and metro: Termini

Surprisingly, the faces of some figures in the ancient mosaic of Santa Pudenziana church are identical to those of famous people of the 16th century, immortalised by great artists.

Farnese and Caetani faces in place of those of Christ and the apostles?

The face of the second apostle next to Jesus thus bears a disturbing resemblance to Titian's portrait of Pope Paul III (Alessandro Farnese, 1468-1549), while the face of the fourth apostle is very like that of Giulia Farnese – Paul III's sister – shown as the "Lady and the Unicorn" in several Roman frescoes (Carracci gallery in Palazzo Farnese, Perseus room in Castel Sant'Angelo).

Coincidence? Surely not. The explanation lies in the kinship between Cardinal Enrico Caetani and the Farnese family – Alessandro Farnese's mother was Giovannella Caetani. The relationship between the two families was always very close, to the point that Paul III personally attended the wedding of his cousin, Camillo Caetani, grandfather of the Cardinal Caetani who restored the church in 1585.

The ancient church of Santa Pudenziana (late 4th century) stands beside an old Roman road – *vicus Patricius* – now known as Via Urbana. The church was built on the site of a *domus ecclesiae* known in the 2nd century as Titulus Pudentis. Over the years, the name Pudente was corrupted to Pudenziana and thus at the end of the 4th century the place was already known as Titulus Pudentianae. Popes Siricius and Innocent I (early 5th century) converted parts of the *domus* into a church. The mosaic of the apsidal arch (dating from 412) is the oldest one known among all Rome's Christian buildings.

In 1588, Cardinal Enrico Caetani – incumbent of Santa Pudenziana – entrusted the architect Francesco Capriani with the renovation of the church and restoration of the mosaic. Over the centuries, the tesserae that made up the six figures on the right (viewed from a low angle) had all but disappeared. The 16th-century restorer therefore replaced them with "engraved rendering". Over the following centuries the mosaic was restored several times: in 1831, during the renovation works of Vincenzo Camuccini, the 16th-century plaster additions were removed and replaced with new tesserae, which nevertheless respected the "Farnese likenesses".

CROSS COMMEMORATING THE ABJURATION OF KING HENRY IV OF FRANCE   ⑧

Piazza Santa Maria Maggiore

> *A cannon and Henry IV's conversion to Catholicism*

Directly in front of the basilica of Santa Maria Maggiore, in the parking lot, a red granite column about 3.5 metres high commemorates an important event in the history of France and one of the most noteworthy in the Wars of Religion: the abjuration of Henry IV. From the column's Corinthian capital there arises a grey marble cross decorated with fleurs-de-lys, supporting two bronze figures, Christ on the Cross and the Virgin of the Immaculate Conception.

The present location of the monument is certainly no tribute to the king, although it once stood in front of the nearby church of Sant'Antonio Abate all'Esquilino (Saint Anthony Abbot at the Esquiline) belonging to the French clergy. It was moved in 1880 on the opening of Via Carlo Alberto.

In 1595, Pope Clement VIII Aldobrandini granted King Henry IV, after his conversion to Roman Catholicism, solemn absolution from the sin of heresy, an event celebrated with great pomp at Saint Peter's. The curate of Saint Anthony's, Charles Anisson, immediately decided to raise this monument *ad memoriam absolutionis Henrici IV*, a dedication that lends itself to diverse interpretations. The column actually looks like the barrel of a cannon surmounted by a cross and bears the inscription *in hoc signo vinces* (by this sign you will conquer). Does this mean that only weapons can ensure the victory of Christianity? There is little doubt that the curate would have meant that the redeeming cross always prevails.

This was the precedent for the later, unsuccessful, clamour for the erection of a similar monument in honour of Louis XIV, who had "the far greater merit of destroying heresy" by revoking the Edict of Nantes in 1685, thus depriving French Protestants of their religious and civil liberties.

A STATUE TO RESTORE THE FRENCH KING'S IMAGE IN ROME

Rome retains another trace of the first Bourbon king of France, at the basilica of San Giovanni in Laterano (Saint John Lateran) under the portico of the right transept: a life-size bronze sculpture by Lorraine sculptor Nicolas Cordier, erected by the Lateran canonists in recognition of Henry IV's very generous donation to the Abbey of Clairac in France. This project was strongly supported by the king's ambassador in Rome, as indeed it had a political aspect: with this sculpture "at the door of the principal church of Christendom", the aim was to lessen the impact of the other column commemorating the submission of the monarch to the Holy See, and restore the prestige of a king whose images were still being burned only fifteen years earlier.

A MASS ON 13 DECEMBER IN HONOUR OF FRANCE

To thank the French king for his donation (see opposite), the Lateran chapter awarded him the title of canonist.

The President of the French Republic, as successor to the kings of France, has inherited the title.

The Lateran chapter holds a mass every 13 December, the anniversary of Henri IV's birth. This *pro felici ac prospero statu Galliae* ceremony is unusual in many respects: we do not know of any other solemn masses in favour of other nations held in the capital of Christianity. Another peculiarity is that the mass is said "for the happiness and prosperity" of a republic that proudly considers itself to be "secular". The mass, which is celebrated by the papal curate in the presence of representatives of the French authorities and the local French community, is still held today.

THE SQUARE HALO OF SANTA PRASSEDE BASILICA

❾

Santa Prassede Basilica
9 Via di Santa Prassede / Via di San Martino ai Monte
• Tel: 06 4882456
• Open daily 7:30am-12pm and 4pm-6:30pm
• Metro: Cavour or Vittorio Emanuele

> *Square halos were for subjects alive at the time a mosaic was created*

Santa Prassede Basilica, famous for its mosaic cycles made by Byzantine artists in the 9th century, was erected by command of Pope Paschal I (817-824) in honour of Saint Praxedes, the sister of Saint Pudentiana and daughter of Saint Pudens, with whom Saint Peter is said to have stayed. She is also mentioned in the Epistles of Paul. The celebrated mosaic in the apse depicts Saints Praxedes and Pudentiana ascending to heaven. To the right of Jesus, Praxedes stands between Saint Zeno and Pope Paschal I, who is presenting Christ with a model of the church he had had built. You will notice that his head is encircled by a very unusual halo: square and blue, instead of the traditional round golden halo (see below). Similarly, Paschal's mother Theodora, who is buried in the Saint Zeno chapel, is shown above the door on the left, inside the chapel, also wearing a square blue halo.

This type of halo can also be seen in the mosaics of the church of Santa Cecilia in Trastevere, again surrounding the head of Paschal I, who was the force behind the rebuilding of this church too. Outside the Basilica of Saint John Lateran, the apse mosaic of the remains of Leo III's papal dining hall (*Triclinium Leoninum*) also depicts the pope (795-816) with a square halo.

WHY SQUARE HALOS?

Until the 4th century, only Christ wore a halo, the symbol of those who lived as saints and who had been admitted to heaven. From the 9th century, the halo would nevertheless be accepted for all the saints. These were plain round haloes, the circle being a symbol of perfection and eternity, and golden in colour, symbol of divine light. Haloes are often interpreted as representations of the heavenly space (the aura, in more modern terms) that surrounds the saints. It is focused on the head, supposed to be the noblest part of the human body, the seat of the soul.

The square halo that surrounds certain figures in mosaics signifies that the person was alive at the time the mosaic was made. It represents the earth and the four points of the compass. Blue, the colour of the sky, is the most spiritual, the purest and closest to the divine. It symbolises self-detachment and the flight of the soul towards God and thus indicates an intermediate stage on the path to God and the colour gold.

FISH FARM NEAR STAZIONE TERMINI

Casa dell'Architettura – ex Acquario romano
Piazza Manfredo Fanti
• Open from 9:30am-5pm except during events
• For further details, call 06 97604580
• Metro: A or B – Termini

The troubled history of an unusual dream

This building in the Esquilino district, a new development in the heart of the Kingdom of Italy's fledgling capital, was originally the idea of Pietro Carganico, a Lombard entrepreneur who had arrived in Rome in 1881. His plan was to create a fish farm-cum-pisiculture centre, aquarium and outlet for the "wholesale supply of fish for food".

This unusual and elegant building of classical design, with an imposing pronaos (porch) shaped like a Greek arch, took only two years to build on ground conceded by the Municipality of Rome. Completed at the end of 1885, it was opened in 1887.

The cylindrical hall with mezzanine was filled with 22 aquariums aligned along the walls, and decorated with stucco, cast-iron columns, paintings on marine themes and polychrome mosaic flooring (unfortunately now covered over, with the exception of a tiny section at the entrance), all below a large iron-framed glass canopy.

Carganico's ambitions were thwarted long before work began, however: by a series of legal manoeuvres he was sidelined, and after many vicissitudes the building became the property of the municipality.

Until 1899 it was indeed used as an aquarium, before a disturbed period began in which the various spaces were given over to alternative uses: a venue for festivals and fairs, skating rink, circus, cinema and gymnasium. In 1908, the building was turned into a small-time theatre for variety shows and revues. The 1930s saw various proposals for converting the building into public baths or a regional bus station, or even demolishing it. In the meantime the building was used to store scenery for the Teatro dell'Opera di Roma (Rome Opera House) and as the municipal electoral offices.

In 1984, major renovation works began, which when completed six years later saw the building's original splendour restored. The "recovered" space is now home to Rome's Casa dell'Architettura (House of Architecture) and once again hosts cultural events.

Although nothing remains of the fish-farming constructions (which included an outside lake and pools in the basements), nor the 22 aquariums, the beauty of the building, with its numerous nods to the maritime way of life – a reminder of Pietro Carganico's dream – can still be appreciated.

BLESSING OF THE ANIMALS AT SANT'EUSEBIO

⓫

Sant'Eusebio church
Piazza Vittorio Emanuele II
• Tram: 5, 14
• Metro: A – Vittorio Emanuele

Bless your pet, horse or cow ...

Every year on 17 January, people have their animals blessed in front of this church. This used to happen in front of the church on Via Carlo Alberto dedicated to Saint Anthony the abbot, protector of animals, but the function was transferred to the front of Sant'Eusebio church because of traffic problems.

Although today this centuries-old tradition only concerns pets, in the past it was a rite concerning all animals, including horses, cows and other farmyard animals. Farmers having their animals blessed had to bring an offering in kind to the church, whereas nobles were asked for money, donations of various other types and large candles which were said to protect

the animals from all harm. In fact, the number of nobles asking for private services for their animals excessively increased the amounts of money linked to the blessing, so other parishes tried to organise similar ceremonies in their churches.

The phenomenon grew to such an extent that it finally forced the cardinal vicar in 1831 to threaten to suspend *a divinis* any priests who carried out blessings on animals without permission.

MARQUIS PALOMBARA'S PORTA ALCHEMICA ⑫

Piazza Vittorio Emanuele II
• Tram: 5, 14
• Metro: A – Vittorio Emanuele

A hermetic door?

T he Porta Alchemica (Alchemical Door, also known as the Magic Portal, Hermetic Door or Gate of Heaven) is an esoteric monument covered with astrological and alchemical symbols interspersed with Latin and Hebrew phrases with equally occult meanings.

Constructed in 1680, according to the date inscribed there, the Alchemical Door is the only survivor of the five gates of the Villa Palombara built by Massimiliano Palombara, marquis of Pietraforte (1614-1680). The villa was demolished in the late 19th century to enlarge the railway station. In 1873, this door was dismantled only to be reinstalled nearby in 1888, in the gardens of what is now Piazza Vittorio, on an old wall of the church of Saint Eusebius. Two statues of the Egyptian god Bes, taken from the Quirinal Palace, were then added (one on each side). This minor god of ancient Egypt protected the home from evil spirits and was therefore the patron of sleep, fertility and marriage. These attributes, together with his traditional grotesque image, liken him to the god of gnomes known by ancient students of Hermetism as Gob or Gobi.

Above the door, the medallion in which the orb (globe surmounted by a cross) is superimposed on the six-pointed star, commonly known as the "Star of David", represents the perfect balance in the harmony between Heaven (upright triangle) and Earth (inverted triangle).

In the centre of the first circle is another, smaller, circle, shaped like a stylised rose which in association with the cross recalls the esoteric Rosicrucian movement.

Around the two circles are the Latin phrases: *Centrum in trigono centri* (The centre is in the triangle of the centre) and *Tria sunt mirabilia Deus et Homo Mater et Virgo trinus and unus* (There are three marvels: God and man, mother and virgin, triune and one). These two phrases refer to the Third Person of the Trinity, the Holy Spirit, whose name is repeated on the lintel above (Ruach Elohim in Hebrew), next to the astrological signs of Saturn (left) and Jupiter. These are also configured as symbols of the constellations of Capricorn and Sagittarius, that is the manifestation of God in matter (Saturn) and the recognition by God of matter (Sagittarius). This is why Sagittarius is traditionally considered the "superior aspect" of Capricorn, as borne out by the Latin legend below the Hebrew inscription on the lintel: *Horti magici ingressum hespericus custodit draco et sine alcide colchicas delicias non gustasset iason* (A dragon guards the entrance to the magic garden of the Hesperides [Saturn] and, without Hercules [Hermes or Mercury], Jason would not have tasted the delights of Colchis [Jupiter]).

On the left door jamb are engraved symbols of Mars and Mercury, each with a Latin heading. The fact that the warlike Mars is in juxtaposition with Mercury means that the temperance of the latter balances and calms the impetuosity of the former, traditionally regarded as the planet of war. From the alchemical point of view, this means that iron (Mars) is moulded by the malleable quicksilver (Mercury). Hence the Latin inscription above the sign of Mars: *Quando in tua domo nigri corvi parturient albas columbas tunc vocaberis sapiens* (When in your house [Mars] black crows [base matter] give birth to white doves [refined matter], then will you be called wise).

Above the sign of Mercury is written: *Qui scit comburere aqua et lavare igne facit de terra caelum et de caelo terram pretiosam* (He who can burn with water and wash with fire makes a heaven of earth and a precious earth of heaven), an obvious reference to the "arrangement" or balance mentioned.

Engraved on the right door jamb are the symbols of Venus and the Moon, as depicted in the sixth house of the Zodiac by graphically inverting the symbol of Mercury. The sixth house is indeed that of Mercury: the feminine aspect is there in exaltation, represented by Venus (heavenly mother) on the Moon (mother of the world). Above the sign of Venus, the Latin epigraph reads: *Diameter spherae thau circuli crux orbis non orbis prosunt* (The diameter of the sphere, the tau in the circle, and the cross of the globe bring no joy to the blind), meaning those blind to spiritual understanding, non-believers in the sacred science. Above the Kabbalistic symbol of the Moon is written *Si feceris volare terram super caput tuum eius pennis aquas torrentium convertes in petram* (If you make the earth fly upside down, with its wings you may convert torrential waters to stone), referring to the action of the spirit of God incarnate in man trying to transform himself and, therefore, to transform nature. This is known as the work of the Holy Spirit.

At the base of the Alchemical Door, in the centre, is the sign of sulphur, terminated by the strongly initiatory emblem of the conjunction of Jupiter–Saturn: Rosicrucian initiates considered this to be a sign of the universal realisation of the presence of Christ on Earth, when Jupiter (spirit) and Saturn (matter) combine in perfect balance, where the spirit (indicated by the alchemical material sulphur) leads the immediate actions. This is the Rosicrucian enlightenment, equivalent to obtaining the Philosopher's Stone. Alongside, the double Latin epigraph illustrating this symbol refers to the same effect: *Est opus occultum veri sophi aperire terram ut germinet salutem pro populo* (It is an occult work of true wisdom to open the earth, so that it may generate salvation for the people) and *Filius noster mortuus vivit rex ab igne redit et coniugio gaudet occulto* (Our dead son lives, returns from the fire a king [of the world], and enjoys occult conjugation [of the spirit with matter, of Jupiter with Saturn]).

Senator Massimiliano Palombara was an alchemy adept as well as a member of the Rosicrucian brotherhood. The medallion over the door, the only vestige from his palace, is the same as the one on the cover of the alchemical text *Aureum Saeculum Redivivum* (The Golden Age Reborn) by Henricus Madatanus (pseudonym of Adrian von Mynsicht, 1603-1638), also a Rosicrucian. The cover of the original edition of this book published in 1621 is quite different from that of the posthumous edition of 1677 that had inspired Palombara.

According to a legend recorded in 1802 by the Italian bibliophile Francesco Girolamo Cancellieri, Marquis Palombara had lodged a passing Rosicrucian pilgrim, not recognised by non-believers, in his palace for the night. Some say that the pilgrim was the alchemist Francesco Giustiniani Bono, who gave his disciple a powder to manufacture gold together with a mysterious manuscript filled with esoteric symbols that contained the secret of the Philosopher's Stone. These symbols may well be those inscribed around the door, the threshold of which was incidently crossed the next morning by the mysterious sage, who disappeared for ever.

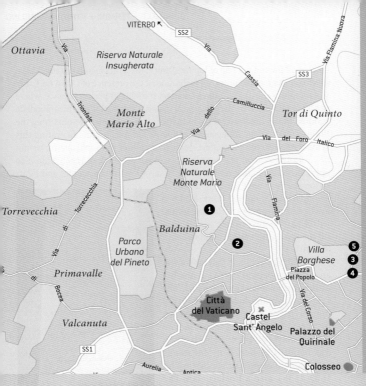

OUTSIDE THE CENTRE NORTH

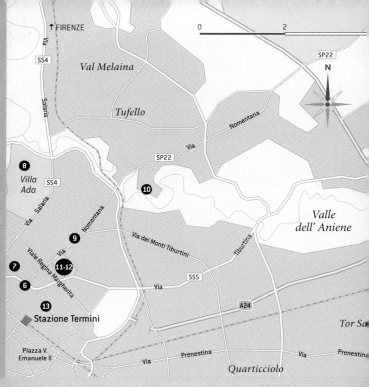

VILLA MADAMA ❶

Via di Villa Madama
• Tel: 06 36914284
• E-mail: cerimoniale.segreteria@esteri.it
• Visits on request to Ministry of Foreign Affairs at least 15 days in advance

> *A former papal residence where you can book a visit*

Built from 1518 for the Florentine Cardinal Giulio de' Medici, cousin of Pope Leo X, Villa Madama occupies a prime location north of the Vatican on Monte Mario. The initial project was entrusted to Raphael. After the artist's untimely death in 1520, the work was entrusted to the architect Antonio da Sangallo the Younger, his collaborator on Saint Peter's basilica. Building work started again around 1524-1525, shortly after Giulio de' Medici was elected Pope (1523), taking the name Clement VII. But the villa remained unfinished and, as a papal property, it was not spared by Charles V's lansquenets in the sack of Rome (1527). Pillaged and burned, abandoned to decay for several centuries, the building was finally restored and completed by the architect Pio Piacentini from 1913.

The decoration of the villa takes its inspiration from Ovid's *Metamorphoses* and is the work of a group of outstanding artists: Giulio Romano, Baldassare Peruzzi and Giovan Francesco Penni for the painting and decorations, Baccio Bandinelli for the sculpture and Giovanni da Udine for the stucco work. The most grandiose space is undoubtedly the loggia, which opens onto three large arcades, elegantly decorated by Giovanni da Udine and his team with stucco and grotesques inspired by Nero's villa, the Domus Aurea, discovered a few years previously. An aperture on the lower wall features the Cyclops Polyphemus by Giulio Romano.

In the gardens, which were originally planned to equal those of antiquity and run down to the Tiber, stands the curious elephant fountain, the work of Giovanni da Udine. It commemorates Hanno (Annone in Italian), the pet white elephant given to Leo X by the Ambassador of Portugal.

The villa is named after "Madama" Margaret of Austria, wife of Alessandro de' Medici, who also gave her name to Palazzo Madama, seat of the Italian Senate. It has been state property since 1941 and is now the official residence, hosting foreign heads of state received by the President of the Council and the Minister of Foreign Affairs.

VIGAMUS – VIDEO-GAME-MUSEUM

4 Via Sabotino
• www.vigamus.com/en/
• Open 10am-8pm Tuesday to Sunday
• Admission: €8; concessions: €5
• Metro: A – Lepanto (700 metres)

> *Play*
> *"Space Invaders"*
> *for free ...*

W hen did the first video game come out? Some people say as far back as 1958, the year of the first prototype game called *Tennis for Two*. Then came the Royden Sanders brand of target shooting in the 1960s, Atari ping-pong in the early 1970s and the legendary Commodore 64 of the 1980s.

So the history of video games goes back over fifty years, and since the end of 2012, thanks to a team of young enthusiasts (all aged between 20 and 30), it also has a unique museum in Italy, VIGAMUS (acronym for Video-Game-Museum).

There you can discover the evolution of an artform that, while still young, is already studded with memorable characters, bizarre anecdotes and enthralling tales of great commercial successes.

The museum has 63 explanatory panels and over 150 exhibits, ranging from consoles with interchangeable cartridges to more modern versions, from portable video games to arcade games – the famous slot machines – such as the legendary Space Invaders, which you can try for free.

Also on display are several unique objects, such as the master disks and

some original storyboards from *Doom*, the original "first-person shooter" game.

An interactive console gives access to a vast digital archive of magazines about video games. The museum also organises exhibitions on today's most popular games, as well as temporary exhibitions, seminars and conferences. VIGAMUS is proof that culture can also be transmitted through the history of what is, if not one of the most important revolutions of the 20th century, certainly one of the most entertaining.

THE CANNON BALL IN THE AURELIAN WALL ❸

Via Po

> ## Souvenir of the taking of Rome

In the section of the Aurelian Wall beyond Porta Pinciana, the tower overlooking Via Po holds a startling reminder of the 1870 battle that seems to pass unnoticed. A cannonball is quite simply and spectacularly embedded in the wall.

The nearby Porta Pia is renowned for the fighting of 20 September 1870, the day when the destruction of a section of the ramparts next to the gate marked the end of papal temporal rule.

The Italian artillery, seeking to claim Rome for the Kingdom of Italy and thus add the ultimate missing piece to unite the country after the long and bloody war of independence, succeeded, after several hours of fire, in forcing the pope's supporters to retreat. Breaching the ramparts at the place that has passed into posterity as Breccia di Porta Pia, the Italian soldiers entered the city, cheered on by the jubilant residents.

It was Emperor Aurelian who had the walls that bear his name constructed between AD 270 and AD 273, to defend the capital of the empire against barbarian attack. Some 19 kilometres long, the walls have been restored several times, both in antiquity and in more recent times, and are still in good repair today over almost two-thirds of their original circuit.

GUIDO RENI'S PAINTING OF SAINT MICHAEL THE ARCHANGEL ❹

Church of Santa Maria della Concezione dei Cappuccini
27 Via Veneto
• www.cappucciniviaveneto.it
• Open every day except Thursday, 9am-12pm and 3pm-6pm

I n the church of Santa Maria della Concezione dei Cappuccini (Our Lady of the Conception of the Capuchins) on Via Veneto, the first altar to the right holds a fine painting by Guido Reni, depicting the Archangel Michael casting down a devil. This work was, however, not to everybody's taste: Cardinal Giovanni Battista Pamphili, the future Pope Innocent X, complained bitterly about the incredible likeness between the devil's features and his own. Reni changed nothing in his painting, for the cardinal had not shown himself to be particularly virtuous. Among other exploits, he is said to have been the lover of his sister-in-law Olimpia, who obtained from him the concession of running the Roman brothels, as the audio guide to the museum of Palazzo Doria Pamphili explains.

> *A devil with the features of a future pope!*

IPOGEO DI VIA LIVENZA

Via Livenza
• Visits on request, by telephoning the Cultural Heritage department of the Municipality of Rome (*Sovraintendenza Comunale ai Beni Culturali*) at 06 0608; alternatively through cultural associations such as *Roma Sotterranea* (www.romasotterranea.it).

> *A 4th-century AD hypogeum above a garage*

I n 1923, during construction work on a private residence between Via Livenza and Via Po, about 250 metres from the Aurelian Wall, an underground structure dating from the second half of the 4th century AD was discovered but then partially destroyed. The preserved section contains a number of elements of great interest.

Access is by a door located along an access ramp to a private garage. Nine metres below, at the foot of the stairway, is an irregularly shaped chamber. One of the walls is particularly remarkable: an arch outlined by marble parapets encloses a deep rectangular bath, lined with waterproof concrete, at the bottom of which can be seen brick paving. Four steep and uneven steps lead to this bath, fitted with a system for supplying water. It cascaded down a terracotta pipe before flowing out through an opening with a valve connected to a drainage channel carved from the rock.

This hypogeum is lavishly decorated. In the centre of the rear wall above the bath there is a niche, the upper part of which is shaped like a fountain: the water runs down over a vase with two little birds perched on its rim. Just beside this niche, on the left, is a representation of Diana crowned with laurel leaves. The goddess is extracting an arrow from her quiver with her right hand, while holding the bow in her left. Two deer in flight can be seen. To the right of the niche is a nymph caressing the muzzle of a fawn. The side walls are tessellated with fused glass mosaics. Maritime scenes complete with *putti* add the finishing touches to this rich decorative art.

The monument is located in the heart of the Salario necropolis. Although almost all the structures excavated in the area are funerary monuments, the function of this one remains a mystery. Its basilical form, and especially the presence of the bath, suggests that it may originally have been a Christian baptismal hall.

Recently, other researchers have suggested that the hypogeum was a hideaway for practising magic, or perhaps a temple linked to a water cult, unless it was simply a nymphaeum or a fountain built to protect a natural underground spring.

BARBER'S SYMBOLS AT PORTA PIA 6

Piazzale di Porta Pia

> *An allusion to the humble origins of Pope Pius IV?*

The façade of Porta Pia, which looks onto Via XX Settembre, features (above the papal coat of arms) a brilliant white sculpture composed of three bas-reliefs, repeated a little lower down to the right and left of the door. At first glance it just looks like a decorative element, even if the meaning is hard to fathom. What these stylised motifs actually represent is a shaving dish complete with soap and surrounded by a fringed towel.

This is probably a nod by the artist to the humble origins of Pope Pius IV, who commissioned the gate. The Pope came from the Medici family of Milan rather than their prestigious Florentine namesake, and one of his ancestors seems to have been a barber, whose professional symbols are indeed the dish, soap and towel represented here.

The pontiff apparently did not hold this against the artist and perhaps even took a certain pride in it.

Porta Pia was built on the orders of Pope Pius IV to a design by Michelangelo. It replaced the nearby Porta Nomentana of Roman origin that was ill-adapted to the ongoing urban development.

You only have to glance at it to see its dramatic appeal, which distinguishes it from the other city gates. It forms part of a larger scenographic scheme: to create a long straight perspective leading from the Quirinal through the new opening in the wall and then rejoining Via Nomentana, which in those days led out into the Roman countryside.

A VISIT TO VILLA ALBANI

7

92 Via Salaria
• Apply by fax (06 68199934) or e-mail amministrazione@srdps.191.it

An (almost) inaccessible treasure

Most Romans believe that the fabulous Villa Albani is closed to the public, but in fact it can be visited by appointment.

This villa is one of Rome's largest and most important late Baroque buildings. Designed as a suburban residence for pleasure and leisure, it was filled with works of art and held festivals and concerts, all within a large park extending over 10 hectares – from Via Salaria to Viale Regina Margherita, the third-largest green space in the city. It also has a splendid Italian garden dotted with fountains.

The villa was built over a period of twenty years from 1747, under the direction of architect Carlo Marchionni, and was designed as the residence of Cardinal Alessandro Albani, nephew of Pope Clement XI. It was then inherited by the Castelbarco and Chigi families before being bought in 1866 by Prince Alessandro Torlonia, banker and art lover, who had carried out excavations at Villa Massenzio and Villa Quintili.

The main building consists of a ground floor flanked by two wings with arcades and a *piano nobile* (first-floor salon). Part of the Museo Torlonia (Torlonia Museum), the largest private collection of ancient sculptures – statues, bas-reliefs, sarcophagi and busts – is housed here. The villa also has a large art gallery, which has been inaccessible to the public for centuries but houses works by Perugino, Guercino, Van Dyck, Tintoretto, Giulio Romano and many other painters. There are also precious Etruscan frescoes

from the François Tomb at Vulci. Inside is the wonderful Parnassus salon, with its ceiling fresco by the neoclassical painter Anton Raphael Mengs. In an adjoining room the famous relief depicting Antinoüs, originally from Hadrian's Villa, stands in the hearth.

In one of these rooms, on the afternoon of 20 September 1870, a few hours after the nearby Porta Pia had been breached, leading to the fall of Rome, the Papal States signed the surrender of the city. The villa effectively became the headquarters of the Italian army. At the opposite end of the garden is a belvedere known as the "Caffehaus". There are other minor buildings in the park, including a small temple that served as an aviary and fake ruins built with authentic archaeological fragments.

For years there has been talk of the villa (which still belongs to the Torlonia family) being expropriated so that it can be enjoyed by the people of Rome, but this does not seem likely to happen any time soon.

BUNKER AT VILLA ADA SAVOIA ⑧

Villa Ada park, Panama entrance, at No. 55
• Guided tours organised by the Roma Sotterranea association on Saturdays, Sundays and some public holidays; other days by reservation only for groups of 10 or more
• www.bunkervillaada.it
• visit@bunkervillaada.it
• Admission: € 12, children under 8 free
• Bus: 168 - Panama or Lima; Tram: 3, 19 then bus 53, 360 - Liegi or Ungheria

Royal House of Savoy's air-raid shelter, accessible by car

In the "wildest" part of Villa Ada, the wooded parkland site of the royal family's residence until 1943, is an access road with a brick archway built into the hillside. The roadway leads to a gallery where few people had the courage to venture until a few years ago. For seventy years this place had been abandoned, frequented largely by vandals and vagrants and said to have been the scene of black masses and satanic rites. Several inscriptions exalting Satan earned it the nickname of "Devil's Bunker".

Since 2016, and following careful restoration, this air-raid shelter (built by Victor Emmanuel III in 1940–1941 for himself and his family) has regained its original appearance: the large metal armoured doors all work now, and just try opening and closing the main door with its two heavy weights, each of 1,200 kilos. The original brick-vaulted construction is shaped like a lifebuoy, and it includes a vast garage space – the bunker needed to be accessible by car as it was too far from the royal residence to travel on foot after a bomber alert.

In addition, there is a two-room shelter furnished in the style of the time with a bathroom annex, also carefully restored, and a bedroom equipped with two pedal-power electric fans (only one remains, resembling a bicycle). They would have allowed enough air to circulate should the electricity be cut off.

Last but not least, the bunker is equipped with a splendid spiral staircase in travertine, 13 m high, which served as an emergency exit. If you climb the slope outside, you can see the protective shield constructed from large slabs of reinforced concrete buttressed by small brick pillars. If the shelter had been hit by a bomb, this shield would have collapsed, cushioning the effects of the blast.

Nowadays the bunker has zero environmental impact: LED lighting is supplied by solar panels.

MUSEO DELLE FORZE ALLEATE

6 Via Tolmino
• Tel: 06 85358888 • www.ww2museumrome.eu/4/
• Visits by appointment only, Monday to Friday 9am-12pm and 4pm-8pm;
Saturday and Sunday 10am-1pm and 4pm-8pm
• Admission: Free

> **A small but fascinating museum**

In the Trieste district is a 1930s building which in June 1944, during the final stages of the Second World War, was a logistics base for the Allied Forces during the Liberation of Rome.

At the rear, in an outbuilding, Salvatore Rizzacasa has collected thousands of objects relating to the Allies. He started with some belonging to his own family and has then sourced others throughout Europe over the past decade to create this Museum of the Allied Forces.

You cannot miss the model of the famous Douglas C-47 Skytrain, suspended from the ceiling – this was the means of transport used by the Allied air forces on all fronts. This one is "Fifi Kate", which participated in the Normandy landings.

Besides the many uniforms and weapons, many of the items on display are rare: the first truly portable Motorola walkie-talkie, a precursor of the mobile phone; and a dinghy used by pilots of the Royal Air Force as a lifeboat and equipped with a telescopic aluminium pole, red sail, a hand pump to inflate it and hand flippers.

Not to mention everyday objects: tins of food, condensed and powdered milk, biscuits, packets of tobacco, cigarettes and matches.

Salvatore Rizzacasa will also show you magnetic metal buttons sewn to trouser flies (pile them up to act as an emergency compass), and pound

notes in different formats, forged by the Germans in astronomical quantities to undermine the British economy and so well made that the Bank of England did not hesitate to exchange vast quantities of them.

But the place of honour goes to a Willy's MB Jeep of 1943, in perfect working order, which, complete with trailer, landed in Sicily. It travelled all the way up to Trento, where it was given to the fire service at the end of the war; they kept it until the 1960s. Since then it has passed from collector to collector before finding a well-deserved home in this small but fascinating museum.

SOURCE OF THE ACQUA SACRA

57 Via Passo del Furlo (Montesacro)
• Tel: 06 86898223
• www.acquasacra.it
• Monday to Saturday 8am-6pm; Sundays and public holidays 8am-1pm

Rome is a city of water and aqueducts. But you can also drink and buy water directly from the source. The Acqua Sacra rises at Via Nomentana, among the villas of the Montesacro district north of Rome.

The source is located in the courtyard of a small building that looks no different from the

> *Buy water from Rome's sacred spring*

others. Taps on one side distribute natural mineral water, on the other side carbonated water. You can just have a glass of water, or for a few centimes fill a bottle. The water is perfectly drinkable as it is regularly monitored by the Ministry of Health.

It is quite a sight to see the local residents in the street, empty bottles in hand, queuing up to buy their water from the spring.

GARDEN CITY OF MONTESACRO

Getting to the Acqua Sacra source is the perfect excuse for a walk among the villas of the garden city. This revolutionary urban project, devised in 1924 under the auspices of the Italian equivalent of council housing, was inspired by the experiments in England some years earlier.

The neighbourhood is laid out around a central square, Piazza Sempione, and consists of villas, gardens and green spaces. It managed to keep its character for some thirty years until the post-war housing crisis, when many of the houses were demolished and replaced by small apartment blocks.

Today, the garden city of Montesacro is a protected site; along with Garbatella and Pigneto, it is one of the few surviving examples of innovative pre-war urban projects.

OTHER SPRINGS IN ROME

Egeria (Appia): http://www.egeria.it
Acqua sorgente (Appia): http://www.appiasorgente.it
Capannelle (Appia): http://www.fontecapannelle.it